D1453084

THE CONSCIENCE

OF

A LAWYER

By

DAVID MELLINKOFF
Professor of Law, University of California, Los Angeles

ST. PAUL, MINN.

WEST PUBLISHING CO.

1973

Mellinkoff Conscience of Lawyer MTB

For Helen
and
the memory of Albert

*

PREFACE

Pause, friend, before it is too late . . .

Before you are hooked on the law.

Better to find out right now that not everyone likes lawyers. In fact . . . But find out for yourself. In the Introduction to this book you will get a quick rundown on the hate-the-lawyer cult, a taste of the venom it reserves for the ethics of lawyers. It's worth looking into; you may have to live with it; the venom and the ethics. You may even want to do something about it.

This book does not cover the whole vast spectrum of the sins of lawyers nor of their ethics. It does take on some of the basic strains on the conscience of the lawyer, direct incidents of his major role as one who speaks for someone else. These are not wispy, hypothetical concerns reserved for Sunday or the ivory tower, but part of the daily life of lawyers. So the examination here starts with a flesh and blood case. It is a celebrated Victorian whodunit, in which you have the details of murder, discovery, arrest, a man on trial for his life, examination and cross-examination, speeches to the jury; verdict. Enough so that you too can become a partisan in the heated controversy that pursued counsel for the defense to his grave and beyond.

The ethical problems of this lawyer and of others discussed here, problems for their consciences and ours, are persistent problems that don't evaporate in the heat of trial or afterwards. Yet resolution is a necessity. The on-the-spot decisions by lawyers in court, the second guessing, and attempts to resolve their ethical torment out of court are examined here in the light of the changes over the years in the moral and legal notions of the right to counsel. We come right down to now, and what to do about it. Not pat solutions for everything, but something that might help.

Except where otherwise noted, I am indebted for general historical facts, as distinct from inferences, to Pollock & Maitland's *The History of English Law Before the Time of Edward I,* Holdsworth's *A History of English Law,* and Stephen's *A History of the Criminal Law of England.* Though much has been

PREFACE

written about *Courvoisier's Case,* there is no verbatim account of the trial itself; the contemporary accounts are incomplete, inconsistent, and often contradictory; accordingly, the account here is a reconstruction based on comparison of varying reports and my own conclusions from "Minutes of Evidence . . ." in the *Central Criminal Court Sessions Papers,* stories in the press, manuscripts in the Public Record Office and the Library of Westminster Abbey, and the miscellaneous publications included in the Bibliography; where anything critical remains in controversy, a footnote documents the variants.

Much of the opinion in this book arises from personal encounters with colleagues and adversaries at the bar; some of it from absorbing the spoken and written complaints of non-lawyers; a little of it has been voiced before in a book review in the *UCLA Law Review;* some of it has been tried out on suspecting law students. On the basic issues discussed in this book I have found almost as much diversity of opinion among law students as among laymen; some have cheered the conclusions here; others have joined non-lawyers and some lawyers in intense irritation. This book won't end those irritations, but it may make the itching more endurable for understanding better why it itches, and where to scratch. Even lawyers ought to know better.

DAVID MELLINKOFF

Los Angeles
January, 1973

SUMMARY OF CONTENTS

*

TABLE OF CONTENTS

TABLE OF CONTENTS

✝

THE
CONSCIENCE
OF A LAWYER

LOVE ALL THE LAWYERS—AN INTRODUCTION

Forgive us our transgressions . . . And love
all the lawyers, for we know not what they do
. . .

Lord love a lawyer? He must, you know. Who else does?
Lord love a lawyer, indeed. How else explain the mystery of
survival, surrounded by so many natural enemies?

To hear the lawyers tell it, the fact that they are not universally loved can only be attributed to some innate human pervers-
ity possibly related to original sin. Lawyers like to recall that
they are members of an old elite, one of the three learned pro-
fessions—medicine, theology, the law. Alike they share an ancient dedication to learning. Each ministers to a common psy-
chic need for outside help. Taken together they encompass the
most basic concerns of men everywhere—life, death, justice.
It's a beautiful embroidery. And it is a constant sorrow if not a
surprise to lawyers that their own estimate of the profession's
worth is not shared by the rest of mankind.

Those who aren't lawyers agree with the lawyers only a little
bit. Sure, the law is the third oldest profession all right, in
close order after whoring and pimping. Even that is not the
worst. The heaped up abuse of the centuries identifies the lawyer with the evil qualities of the Bible's great *adversary* (*Satan*
in Hebrew), the father of lying, a fallen angel. As Stephen Vincent Benét has dramatized it in the great debate between *The
Devil and Daniel Webster,* it is Old Scratch himself who is the
King of Lawyers; [1] a lawyer trying to go straight will have to
turn on his master, and beat him. Lawyers are, in the name of
their volunteer corps dating from the threat of Napoleonic inva-
sion, *The Devil's Own.*[2]

1. 2 S. V. Benét, Selected Works 32,
39 (1942); see also S. Foote, *The
Devil Upon Two Sticks* (1768), 3
Works 18–20 (1830).

2. 3 Campbell, Lives of the Lord
Chancellors 298, note c (5th ed.
1868); 8 *id.* 367–368; 13 Holdsworth, A History of English Law

Whenever men have cried out against injustice, the lawyer has been the scapegoat (although as John Selden once remarked of another scapegoat, "When the Dog is beat out of the Roome where will they lay the stinke?").[3] In the English peasant's revolt of the 14th century, Wat Tyler demanded a royal commission "to behead all Lawyers" and anyone else connected with the law; [4] with a drop of literary license, Shakespeare adapted Tyler's demand to give the anti-legal flavor of Jack Cade's 15th century rebellion.[5] It remains with us as the most direct, most frequently quoted remedy for the profession, "The first thing we do, let's kill all the lawyers." [6]

The bitterness, the restrained fury of the assault is epitomized in the King James Version:

> And he said, Woe unto you also, ye lawyers! for ye lade men with burdens grievous to be borne, and ye yourselves touch not the burdens with one of your fingers.[7]

* * *

> Woe unto you, lawyers! for ye have taken away the key of knowledge: ye entered not in yourselves, and them that were entering in ye hindered.[8]

These denunciations of ancient scribes have been repeated too long for it now to make any difference that Jesus was speaking of men we would not call lawyers. Whether originally so intended or not, Jesus' "Woe unto you, lawyers   .   ." has expressed for ages, as it still does for 20th century detractors,[9] a popular loathing for the profession and all its works. Beware the lawyer and his law as well: "And if any man sue thee at the

587 (1952); W. Andrews, ed., The Lawyer 144–149 (1896).

3. Selden, Table Talk 18 (F. Pollock ed. 1927; 1st publ. 1689).

4. 1 Stow, Survey of London, Book I, page 86 (J. Stripe ed. 1720; 1st publ. 1588); Shakespeare's Holinshed 61 (R. Holsey ed. 1968); cf. 5 Froissart's Chronicles 339–350 (2d ed. T. Johnes 1806).

5. Shakespeare's Holinshed, *supra*, note 4, at 182, and see xiii.

6. Shakespeare, Henry VI, Part 2, act iv, scene ii, line 74 (Arden Ed., 3d ed. 1957).

7. Luke 11:46; B. Nicholson, The Lawyers Bane, title page (1647).

8. Luke 11:52.

9. F. Rodell, Woe unto You, Lawyers! (1939); N. Dacey, How to Avoid Probate 7 (1965).

law, and take away thy coat, let him have thy cloke also." [10]
From his grave, the poet calls out,

> A Lawyer art thou?—draw not nigh!
> Go, carry to some fitter place
> The keenness of that practised eye,
> The hardness of that sallow face.[11]

Complaints against the profession come in all sizes—sniveling complaints, petty complaints, medium petty, on up the line to the vomitous, revolting enormous complaints. They come variously packaged, and stacked to the sky. Even so it is not difficult to separate out from the mass the fundamental and lingering and brutal complaint, which is simply that lawyers are indifferent to the truth. Some make it even simpler: lawyers are liars; but that doesn't take in all the nuance of indifference. A lawyer and his truth are soon separated. He can take it or leave it alone. The truth bounces off him like dried peas thrown against the wall. It rolls off him like water off a duck's back. Here today; gone tomorrow. He couldn't care less. So pervasive is the complaint that the lawyer is indifferent to the truth that even some lawyers believe it, and it rests on paradox: The profession is living contradiction of the absolutism that all men insist upon (for others to live by) that there is one Truth, whole and indivisible.

Living with a thousand daily uncertainties each as capricious as a shy breeze, men have always found it comforting to believe that somewhere there is a truth. It is assumed that in all the pleasant and unpleasant affairs of men—in the intertwined frictions of flesh, paper, steel, nerves, chemicals, wills, words, ideas, longings, sighing—that in all of this there must be, and so there is a truth, and by God we'll find it.

It is assumed that that is what a system of justice is about. Search for the truth. Find it. The notion that it is there simply waiting to be discovered is too satisfying to let loose of, though very few men presume to know what God's truth is in the case of *Smith v. Jones*, and even though we come to the disheartening conclusion that God won't do the day-to-day work in an earthly system of justice, won't take the bench or enter the jury box. Way down here, where we do the work, most of us

---

10. Matt. 5:40.   11. Wordsworth, *A Poet's Epitaph*,
                        2 Works 172 (1919).

recognize a truth in justification of our own conduct and by its absence in the conduct of our neighbors. Perhaps because of that secret recognition of our own weakness, perhaps it is the innate modesty of the human race that makes it more important than ever that we believe that someone here knows, somebody else. So we say there can be truth on but one side, and assume there is some direct pathway to God's truth which a system of justice must surely follow, forgetting the lawyer's lament three centuries old: ". . . the truth lies many times in such a deepe well, that every Lawyer hath not a Bucket to draw." [12]

We assume or pretend that a system of justice is nothing more than a search for the truth despite abundant evidence around us and inside us that points in another direction.

No one approves of a system of justice that in its search for truth convicts him of wrongdoing, when he knows in his heart he is in the right, or—in any event—should not be punished. This is not a matter of what our Constitution calls "cruel and unusual punishments." [13] Even a usual punishment is cruel for me; it is you who needs protecting from unusual punishments.

No one approves of a system of justice that searching for truth arrives at a judgment that shocks his own personal sense of what is right. The greying, respected old family abortionist stays out of prison. The people's banker who does nothing but good—sharing embezzled deposits with every deserving cause and destitute in the community—is dealt with lightly. Police raids on the illegal church lottery or pinochle for charity in the temple basement are condemned by the pillars.

For centuries we have lived by a system of justice that finds innocent men "Guilty" and guilty men "Not guilty"—with no uniform sense of outrage.

The notion that it is the natural right of an outraged husband to kill (but not maim) the man he finds seducing his wife is so firmly established in American folk law that it is called the "unwritten law." [14] This is a softer way of saying that the killer is guilty but a jury will find him "Not guilty."

12. J. Cooke, Vindication of the Professors 8(1646).

13. U.S.C.A.Const. Amend. Art. VIII.

14. Webster's 2d (1934); and see Black's Law Dictionary (rev. 4th ed. 1968).

In 1735 Peter Zenger, a New York newspaper editor, published a seditious libel against the royal governor. No question of his guilt under the law. A jury, coaxed by an old Philadelphia lawyer, found Zenger "Not guilty," and the "Not guilty" guilty Zenger has become an American hero, along with his lawyer Andrew Hamilton who persuaded the jury to ignore the law.[15]

On November 24, 1963, Jack Ruby shot to death without trial Lee Harvey Oswald, who most people think murdered President John F. Kennedy. Ruby killed Oswald while millions of Americans watched the episode on television. Eventually a jury found Ruby guilty of murdering Oswald, but the trial had been a public circus, and the conviction was reversed on appeal.[16] Before he could be tried again, Jack Ruby died—presumed to be an innocent man.

In 1964, a jury acquitted a Mississippi under-sheriff Cecil Ray Price of helping to murder three civil rights workers—Michael Schwerner, James Earl Chaney, and Andrew Goodman. In 1968, another jury convicted Price of the lesser crime of denying the men their civil rights by helping to murder them.[17]

In 1969, a Federal judge in Oklahoma ruled that Paul Goodwin was innocent of the murder of a policeman. He thereupon freed Goodwin from the Oklahoma state penitentiary where he had been imprisoned for 30 years on conviction for the murder.[18]

Paul Goodwin's case is not as unusual as we would like to think. Professor Edwin M. Borchard of the Yale Law School in *Convicting the Innocent* (1932) and the late Judge Jerome Frank and his daughter Barbara Frank in *Not Guilty* (1957) have documented 100 cases of the innocent found guilty of crimes ranging from prostitution to murder. These are not tales of lynching nor the celebrated cases of public controversy—not the Mooney Case, Sacco-Vanzetti, Scotsboro. These are the daily "crimes" we wash down with a cup of morning coffee. Thir-

---

15. J. Alexander, A Brief Narrative of the Case and Trial of John Peter Zenger (S. Katz ed. 1963).

16. Rubenstein v. State, Tex.Cr. App., 407 S.W.2d 793 (1966; *reh. denied*, 1966); see generally, J. Kaplan and J. Waltz, The Trial of Jack Ruby (1965).

17. Posey v. United States, 416 F. 2d 545 (5th Cir. 1969, *reh. denied*, 1969); *cert. denied*, 397 U.S. 946, 90 S.Ct. 964, 25 L.Ed.2d 127 (1970); *reh. denied*, 397 U.S. 1031, 90 S.Ct. 1267, 25 L.Ed.2d 544 (1970).

18. Los Angeles Times, Mar. 9, 1969, section A, page 6, columns 6–8 (UPI).

ty-two men and women in the Frank account spent a combined
total of 178 years in prison for crimes they did not commit. In
the 100 cases, compensation by the state for the wrong done the
man falsely accused is the exception not the rule, substantial
compensation as rare as public outcry.

It is not certain on earth as it is in heaven that if you know
the truth, ".   .   .   the truth shall make you free." [19] It is
not even certain that the truth can be found, here and now. We
shy away from saying that usually. Too unsettling. Better to
cling to the belief that a system of justice is a search for the
truth and a finding of it.

If our daily conscious expressions about searching for truth
don't accurately describe our system of justice, we have nonetheless "established justice" of a rough sort—human, often humane,
sometimes harsh justice that is neither an abstract search for
truth nor omniscient. It is a system of continuous justice as
distinguished from "justice in my case," emphasizing continuity
of the system itself over this particular result. It is the common
law system of slip and slide and scramble, with a few things to
hold on to—something of principle, something of what people
have come to expect, something of respect for individuality, but
more than anything else the knowledge that there is some system to it, that cannot be overturned in a moment of corrupt or
ignorant impulse. It is not a precise system. There are rules,
but the rules bend sometimes to fit the contours of hard cases,
without overturning the whole system. It is a continuous system, that day in and day out operates on a general plan which in
a great mass of instances—if not in this one—satisfies us that
justice is being done.

Few of us really believe that a man is innocent until proved
guilty beyond a reasonable doubt. "I know him; he's a good
man; he couldn't have done anything like that." "I've know'd
her since she was that high; she was a bitch even then." Individually, we convict and acquit long before a jury ever does.
Yet we are satisfied that as a hedge of decency against human
fallibility—indigestion, liars, cheats, headaches, haters, poor vision, jealousy, disappointment—a system is fairer that acts as
though a man were innocent until he has been proved guilty beyond a reasonable doubt. Too many things can go wrong out-

19.   John 8:32.

side as well as inside a courtroom; too many pressures that can bend good men and crack impoverished and oppressed and weak men. A system of justice has got to respond to what happens right here on earth. Our system of *justice* is just that. It insists that men cannot be permitted to perjure themselves; but it searches not for truth but justice. And that is what we live by in comparative harmony. It is a compound of honest testimony, rules of law, and a not inflexible application of both to a particular controversy between human beings.

Despite the reality of the justice that we live by, we continue to talk in terms of law as a search for truth, the crown that will be awarded to one side—which is then called "right," the victor over "wrong." For this simple explanation of the legal process as an exercise in Sunday school morality the lawyers are in good part responsible. Ignoring an occasional reminder that something else is involved,[20] lawyers insist that the ". . . basic purpose of a trial is the determination of truth," [21] indulge themselves in easy talk of the "search for truth," [22] even "ultimate truth." [23] Few lawyers now have the hardihood to join Hoffman (a 19th century sage of American legal ethics) in asserting or "believing . . . that in most cases one of the disputants is *knowingly* in the wrong . . .." [24] Still, in many ways, lawyers who ought by bitter experience to know better encourage non-lawyers in their belief that law and truth are indivisible, and that the only trick the lawyers have is that they have learned in which part of the haystack to hunt for the needle. Against great odds, the lawyers have succeeded in convincing generations of laymen of that which they have never really convinced themselves—that the law is clear. Just look it up. It's right there. It can only be one way. That's what the judge is for. As the lay author puts it, "Judges, because they are paid to make decisions, are supposed to be sure." [25]

20. White, J., dissenting and concurring, in United States v. Wade, 388 U.S. 218, 256–258, 87 S.Ct. 1926, 1947–1948, 18 L.Ed.2d 1149, 1174–1175 (1967).

21. Tehan v. U. S. ex rel. Shott, 382 U.S. 406, 416, 86 S.Ct. 459, 465, 15 L.Ed.2d 453, 460 (1966), *reh. denied*, 383 U.S. 931, 86 S.Ct. 925, 15 L.Ed.2d 850.

22. M. Freedman, "The Professional Responsibility of the Prosecuting Attorney," 55 Geo.L.J. 1030 (1967).

23. R. Braun, "Ethics in Criminal Cases: A Response," 55 Geo.L.J. 1048, 1050 (1967).

24. 2 D. Hoffman, A Course of Legal Study 746 (2d ed. 1836).

25. M. Mayer, The Lawyers 529 (1967).

When a decision is announced, even in very complicated cases where batteries of lawyers have bombarded each other and the judges for weeks with careful argument and high megaton precedent, the opinion solemnly says that the losing argument was *without merit*, or *devoid of merit*, or had *no merit*.[26] Now to anyone but a lawyer who refuses to understand English, those are almost fighting words; *without merit* says pretty clearly that there just isn't anything to be said for such a position. So the lawyer who made the argument must be a fool or a crook. Yet within the profession, *without merit* is not so much an insult as a mild discouragement. He may never get to the point of actually liking it, but a lawyer knows that one day he may have to tell a client who has not yet paid his bill that the court said his argument was *without merit*. And that, even when the argument was good enough to get the judges snapping at each other,[27] and even though the United States Supreme Court has said that for its part it won't believe a lawyer who says an indigent's case is *without merit*.[28]

The lay public is less accustomed than lawyers to disbelieving the words it uses. It believes that the losing side really was *without merit*, translated variously as lying, crooked, no damn good, at the very least—in the wrong. It was inevitable. In every case someone is wrong and must lose; "the truth will out;" the legal process has been vindicated again; it is the means of discovering the truth that lay waiting to be discovered; an educated dummy could have found it if only he were honest. It is against this standard of truth, and of the certainty of the law that goes with it, that the lawyers are measured and found basically immoral.

Instead of stopping to explain that they are helping to administer a continuous system of justice rather than searching for

---

26. Diddlemeyer v. Mississippi, 234 So.2d 292, 297 (Miss.1970); *cert. denied*, 400 U.S. 917, 91 S.Ct. 177, 27 L.Ed.2d 157; Ledford v. State, 215 Ga. 799, 800, 801, 805–807, 113 S.E.2d 628, 629–631, 633–634 (1960). (1970); People v. Garner, 57 Cal. 2d 135, 141, 142, 149, 153, 154, 156, 18 Cal.Rptr. 40, 43, 44, 48, 50, 51, 52, 367 P.2d 680, 683, 684, 688, 690, 691, 692 (1961); *cert. denied*, 370 U.S. 929, 82 S.Ct. 1571, 8 L. Ed.2d 508.

27. Gillette v. United States, 401 U.S. 437, 463, 91 S.Ct. 828, 843, 28 L.Ed.2d 168, 188 (1971); Coleman v. Alabama, 399 U.S. 1, 6, 90 S.Ct. 1999, 2001, 26 L.Ed.2d 387, 394

28. Anders v. California, 386 U.S. 738, 744, 87 S.Ct. 1396, 1400, 18 L.Ed.2d 493, 498 (1967); *reh. denied*, 388 U.S. 924, 87 S.Ct. 2094, 18 L.Ed.2d 1377.

truth, lawyers do the very thing needed to bring down the moral judgment upon their heads. They fall over themselves rushing to line up on the side of the angels, insisting that their morality is the same as the common morality, that "There is no difference between personal and professional ethics." [29] If anything, lawyers lay claim to a morality a notch higher than the common, saying theirs is a profession "dedicated to a spirit of public service," [30] "that underneath, most lawyers are boy scouts," [31] that law is a "public profession." [32]

The law is of course a public profession but only in a very special sense. It is not that lawyers are some superior breed of dedicated men. Lawyers as a group are no more dedicated to justice or public service than a private public utility is dedicated to giving light. It just happens that for a variety of personal reasons lawyers, like the private public utility, have chosen to engage in an occupation that more than others is "affected with a public interest." Because the public interest is so great in seeing to it that the role is properly performed, lawyers are obliged to pursue their work according to certain standards of competence, dispassion, and faithfulness. Lawyers accept those standards because that is the only way they may be lawyers; they are not lawyers so that they may be competent, dispassionate, and faithful. The profession is a public profession because as a profession it exists to satisfy a public need. But individual lawyers are members of that public profession to satisfy private, personal needs—whether for money, security, power, excitement, respectability, recognition, immortality, or even public service. As human beings lawyers have trouble enough reconciling their private needs with the special moral requirements of a system of

29. H. Williams, Legal Ethics 203 (1906). Accord: G. Warvelle, Essays in Legal Ethics 34 (1902); C. Wolverton, "The Ethics of Advocacy," 8 The Am. Lawyer 62, 67 (1900); and see also Canons of Professional Ethics of the American Bar Association [hereafter cited as ABA Old Canons], Canon 32 (1908–1963).

30. M. Pirsig, Cases and Materials on Professional Responsibility 38 (1965; 2d ed., page 46, 1970); see Pound, The Lawyer from Antiquity to Modern Times xxvii, 5 (1953).

31. G. Hazard, *Reflections on Four Studies of the Legal Profession,* Law and Society 48 (1965).

32. R. Smith, *Survey of the Legal Profession Its Scope, Methods and Objectives,* in Pound, *supra* note 30, at vii (1953); R. Smith, Foreward, in A. Blaustein and C. Porter, The American Lawyer vi (1954).

continuous justice. They have multiplied their troubles by letting non-lawyers think that the system has no special moral requirements.

Unlike abstract principle, a system of justice calls for rules to make it work, rules that take a principle off the shelf and dirty it up with people. The rules need explaining to those who don't know them, and they have got to be explained in terms more earthy than truth and beauty and empyrean harmonies. It takes a bit of explaining, for example, to have it understood why under our system of justice a lawyer is not a scoundrel when he pleads the statute of limitations to defeat an honest debt. It is not self-evident even to a dishonest man. It is insufficient and misleading to lace fingers and gravely assure everyone that "We are searching for truth as much as you do if not more so."

These claims to a morality the same as or better than the announced (if not practiced) morals of ordinary citizens have gotten the lawyers very far out on a very dead limb. When the layman looks around him he can see with half an eye that the side that was against the truth, the side that was wrong, and so lost the lawsuit, also had a lawyer. So lawyers must be wrong or worse at least half the time. With right and wrong to choose from, lawyers too often speak for the wrong, often with apparent enthusiasm if not actual relish. In no other occupation or profession can a man be wrong or crooked so often and still go to work the next day. It must be a profession where the truth doesn't count for anything.

It is an old repeated story. In the 14th century *Vision of Piers the Ploughman*, for the planned marriage of Lady Fee (daughter of Falsehood) to Fraud Serpent's-tongue (a "cursed creature begotten of a devil"), "All the rich company who owe their places to Falsehood were invited to the wedding . . .." The "advocates" are of course included.[33] Three hundred years later Robin Conscience, alarmed on a visit to Westminster to hear it said " 'Twas no great matter . . . If Conscience quite were knocked in th' head,' " runs off in haste, concluding that lawyers cannot abide the one who chides them "for falsehood." [34]

---

33. W. Langland, Piers the Ploughman 39–40 (rev. ed. J. Goodridge transl. 1966; 1st publ. 1370).

34. *Robin Conscience*, 1 Harleian Miscellany 63, 64 (1808).

The basic complaint of the lawyer's indifference to truth is coupled with a charge of evil compounded: that the lawyer's siding with untruth (or evil or wrong), and even his occasional standing up for truth (or good or right), are not to be explained as accident, ignorance, or stupidity. The Devil is evil but not a fool. The choice is deliberate, and dictated solely by naked avarice rather than any moral consideration.

Of the lawyers *Piers Ploughman* saw silk robed pleading their cases, he thought "you could sooner measure the mist on the Malvern Hills than get a sound out of them without first producing some cash!"[35] In the next century, John Lydgate sharpened the attack, translating for English eyes the earlier French of Guillaume de Deguileville's *The Pilgrimage of the Life of Man.* When the old hag Avarice goes to the King's Court and turns Advocate (certainly one of the earliest female lawyers in English literature), she bluntly announces:

But first I swear without a doubt,
My tongue I shall not put it out,
For right nor wrong, nor for no thing,
But where I see right great winning . . .

For gold and silver, Avarice does not hesitate to make:

Right of wrong, and wrong of right;
Turn the matter upside down,
And prove it out with good reason."[36]

In the pejorative dissection of the anatomy of lawyers—"As cold as charity in the heart of a lawyer;"[37] "They say a witch will sail in a sieve, but I believe the devil would not venture aboard your conscience;"[38] etc.—the lawyer's tongue has been a well worked symbol of his debasement. It is the "tongue venal,"[39] the "prostituted tongue,"[40] a more precious member

35. W. Langland, *supra* note 33, at 31.

36. Transl. from Lydgate, The Pilgrimage of the Life of Man 487–488 (Furnivall ed. 1899–1904; 1st publ. 1426).

37. "Old Proverb," in E. O'Brien, The Lawyer 172 (1842).

38. Attributed to Congreve, in E. O'Brien, *id.*

39. Quoted in J. Yunck, "The Venal Tongue: Lawyers and the Medieval Satirists," 46 A.B.A.J. 267, 268 (1960).

40. Attributed to Blackstone, in G. Sharswood, A Compend of Lectures on the Aims and Duties of the Profession of Law 36 (1854).

and so worse than the whore's traffic.[41]   After that, D'Israeli's "loose-tongued lawyer" [42] is almost friendly.

Talent for sale at a price, without reference to morality, is a persistent theme of attack: "intellectual and moral prostitution," [43] "chicane in furs," [44] "advocates of falsehood for a guinea," [45] their "bought honour, is honour the whore, not honour the virgin." [46]   George Bernard Shaw at least gave lawyers more company. He put them along with playwrights, journalists, and some others in the "great prostitute classes of men   .   .   ." adding that "rich men without conviction are more dangerous in modern society than poor women without chastity." [47]

The full force of the complaint is not alone the denial of truth, even coupled with avarice, but that with a God given talent the lawyer stands in the way of every man's birthright, the right to justice. The lawyer, in John Stuart Mill's phrase, is ready to "frustrate justice with his tongue." [48]

Can anyone fall any lower? It can be managed. The lawyer reaches the utter depth of moral degradation as a natural consequence of his indifference to truth. For the avarice that brings the lawyer to speak for evil when paid to do it puts him on the side of those who can pay the most. Inevitably these are the wealthy, those who must settle for Heaven here because they'll never make it on the other side. What did the poor ever do for me?

The patron saint of lawyers St. Ives, a teetotaler who colored his water with a drop of wine when dining with his drinking

41. 1 Matheolus, Les Lamentations 283 (A.-G Van Hamel ed. 1892–1905); see, a transl. in J. Yunck, *supra* note 39, at 269.

42. J. Stammers, The Case of the Queen v. D'Israeli 4 (1838).

43. J. Dymond, Essays on the Principles of Morality 136 (1834; 1st ed. 1829).

44. Attributed to Alexander Pope, in W. Whewell, Two Introductory Lectures to Two Courses of Lectures on Moral Philosophy 6 (1841).

45. The Examiner (London), Aug. 17, 1854, quoted in 20 Law Magazine (New Series) 267, n. 1 (1854).

46. "Some Advertisements for the new Elections of Burgesses for the House of Commons," *verso* of unnumbered first page, in J. Cooke, Vindication of the Professors (1646).

47. B. Shaw, Preface, Ayot St. Lawrence ed., in *Selected Plays* xxvi (1948–1949).

48. 7 Bentham, *Works* 479 (J. Bowring ed. 1843).

bishop,[49] is hailed as a rare bird—"the poor man's advocate," [50] and was certainly not canonized by a bar association. An old doggerel praises the wonderful St. Ives in the same moment it damns the profession at large:

> *Santus Yvo erat Brito,*
> *Advocatus et non latro,*
> *Res miranda populo,"* [51]

in sense, though not in so many words, saying this saint from Brittany was:

> A lawyer and not a thief,
> A thing almost beyond belief.[52]

St. Ives is recorded as refusing to take fees for his services as a lawyer, working ably for the downtrodden, and canonized on the strength of several miracles—including one that must endear him to the profession—three times snatching a condemned man from the gallows.

Thus the classic epitome of the lawyer emerges and spreads through the western world: a consummate malevolence, callousness to truth the basic vice, hardened with the sin of avarice, and a consequent denial of God's favored—the downtrodden poor. Even the rich and the inbetween could agree in a classless damnation: the lawyer is the immoralist, denying truth for a fee. With that agreed, subsidiary evils fall quickly into place. It is to be anticipated:

> That the lawyer will be faithless to his client, not merely overcharging him, but playing the ambidexter,

---

49. 7 The Golden Legend 191–201 (F.S. Ellis ed. 1900).

50. 5 A. Butler, Lives of the Saints 242 (H. Thurston & N. Lesson rev. 1936); G.-A. Lobineau, Les Vies des Saints de Bretagne 245 (1725); and see Redelius, Annus coronatus hymnis sanctorum omnium, "19. Maii. S. Ivo." (1761 ; 1st publ. 1696?).

51. 2 P. Levot, Biographie Bretonne 980 (1852–1857); M. S. Ropartz, Histoire de Saint Yves 73, n. 1 (1856); R. Delachenal, Histoire des avocats au Parlement de Paris, 1300–1600, 45, n. 2 (1885); 6 Vies des Saints 34, n. 3 (Les Petits Bollandistes ed. 1878); 2 U. Chevalier, Reportorium Hymnologicum 552 (1892–1920); 5 S. Baring-Gould, The Lives of the Saints 301 (rev. ed. 1914); A. Masseron, Saint Yves 6 (ed. L'Art et Les Saints 1923?); M. Radin, "The Ancient Grudge," 32 Va.L.Rev. 734, 742, n. 19 (1946); 3 L. Réau, Iconographie de L'Art Chrétien 1353 (1959).

52. *See* Macmillan, Law & Other Things 17? (1937).

ready to take money from both sides; "five guineas make a criminal today, and 10 tomorrow wipe the stain away;"[53]

* * *

That he will discover holes in solid walls and wrinkles in smooth surfaces, creating complication where there need be none, promoting and prolonging litigation to get a fee; he is the *shyster*, the *ambulance chaser*, the *pettifogger*, the *Philadelphia lawyer*, the *mouthpiece*, the word *attorney* itself so pungent with opprobrium as to be abandoned in general British usage;[54] the Emperor Justinian's ancient warning repeated for the profession as early as 13th century England:

> Let all attorneys and judges refrain from taking money, and let them not regard the controversies of others as a source of plunder.[55]

* * *

That two lawyers—in apparent opposition—are really conniving with each other and with the judge, speaking and writing in words no one else can understand, covering up each other's mistakes, a continuing conspiracy to promote their own fraternal interests; and the public be damned.[56]

* * *

Finally, that the profession is organized to oppose any reform of the law that would promote justice, because reform would deny the lawyers opportunities to fatten on error and discontent.[57] Under this head, the 18th and 19th century thundering of Jeremy Bentham is now echoed in pointed suggestions that lawyer-legislators just won't pass laws to worsen the lot of lawyers.[58] And Bentham achieves his most terrible

53. Attributed to Dr. Garth, in 2 [A. Polson], Law & Lawyers 271 (1840).

54. D. Mellinkoff, The Language of the Law 198; and see generally 81, 98, 196–198, 202–203, 208–210, 225–231 (1963).

55. Bracton, De Legibus 53 (G. Woodbine & S. Thorne ed. 1968–).

56. D. Mellinkoff, *supra* note 54, at 4; 230–231; 261–262.

57. *Id.*

58. N. Dacey, How to Avoid Probate! 7–9 (1965); M. Bloom, The Trouble with Lawyers 336–342 (1868).

posthumous victory in the stark, quiet exaggeration of the lawyer-philosopher Felix Cohen:

> But the fact remains that legal ethics centers about the problem of how to secure a larger income for lawyers.[59]

* * *

With all that against them, true or not, the mystery is not that people hate lawyers, but that there are any left to hate. To essay a solution of that mystery, we proceed as lawyers have done with most of their legal problems—less with abstractions than with people. Take a case. *Courvoisier's Case,* more properly *Regina v. Courvoisier,*[60] the *Queen v. Courvoisier,* which like so much else in American law comes to us from England and continues to influence the law and lawyers a century and more after it was decided.

---

59. F. Cohen, The Legal Conscience 18 (L. Cohen ed. 1960).

60. 9 Car. & P. 362 [1841], 173 Eng. Rep. 869 (1840), 12 Central Criminal Court Sessions Papers 216 (1840).

Chapter I

THE MURDER

Under a blackface headline:

HORRIBLE MURDER OF LORD WILLIAM RUSSELL, UNCLE TO LORD JOHN RUSSELL, SECRETARY FOR THE COLONIES

The Times of London for May 7, 1840 described Lord Russell's Swiss valet Benjamin François Courvoisier as the stereotype of a Victorian man servant—faithful, prompt, efficient, impeccable. The story told how a maid had awakened the valet because of the disordered appearance of the home, and went on:

> "The valet instantly rose; and, on discovering that, from the appearance of the packages in the passage, there had been some thieves in the house, he instantly went up to the room where his late lamented master slept. Upon entering the apartment his suspicions were more strongly excited that there had been thieves in the house, and he proceeded towards the bed, where he was horror-struck upon finding the noble Lord lifeless, and his head deluged in blood. He observed likewise that there was a most dreadful gash across his throat. He hurried out of the room and acquainted his fellow-servant with the terrifying sight he had witnessed, and at once ran to the house of Mr. Elsgood, a medical gentleman residing in the neighborhood."

Four days later, with no glance backward, *The Times* announced "with perfect confidence" that the police, while still delving, "have to a considerable extent, succeeded in fixing the guilt of the murder upon the party to whom suspicion pointed from the first . . . We mean, of course, the Swiss valet."

Shocking as it may be to its present editors, *The Times* had nominated Courvoisier for the gallows before either indictment or trial. No one had seen Courvoisier kill his master, nor did any eye witness ever appear against him. No murder weapon had been found; indeed, as Courvoisier's trial started over a month later, the police were still dragging the waters of the Ser-

16

pentine in Hyde Park in a fruitless search for a weapon. Above all, the nominee steadfastly declined the honor, repeatedly asserting his innocence to the only people he was permitted to talk to—mostly the police.

What shocked Victorian London was the crime itself, for it was undoubted that a crime had been committed. As the bumbling surgeon Mr. Henry Elsgood told a hastily assembled coroner's jury, the wound could not have been self-inflicted, for after such a cut, the noble lord could not "have covered himself with the cloth" that was found over the dead man's face. Mr. Elsgood had observed a clean cut by a sharp instrument extending seven inches from left shoulder to trachea, four or five inches deep, apparently cutting the carotid artery and the jugular vein, though he later found the jugular intact. He insisted that he saw no thumb wound, though a juror reminded him that the ball of a thumb was nearly cut off. Mr. Nursey, an apothecary, confirmed that "the ball of the right thumb was cut off and hanging to it." The killing, Mr. Elsgood thought, had occurred between 3:30 and 4:30 on that very morning—Wednesday, May 6—apparently while Lord Russell slept. The coroner told Courvoisier he did not have to say anything, and although not sworn Courvoisier answered questions freely. The foreman said that a former employer had given Courvoisier "an excellent character." The verdict of the coroner's jury was "wilful murder by some person or persons unknown." As to the identity of the murderer ". . . there is no evidence."

Lord William Russell, a widower approaching age 73, enfeebled and hard-of-hearing, was an unlikely victim. Twenty-five years earlier he had been aide-de-camp to the Duke of Wellington at the Battle of Waterloo, and for a time had served in Parliament. But for years he had not been active in public life, if one excepts daily visits to Brookes'—his club in St. James Place. A respected if undistinguished member of a family noble since the 16th century and Dukes of Bedford since the 17th, Lord Russell was not really a lord. It was a courtesy title, primogeniture's nod to the younger sons of noblemen, carrying with it none of the vast estates or wealth of the Russell family. Though he lived in the fashionable Park Lane section of London, the house at No. 14 Norfolk (now Dunraven) Street was rented, described as "second rate," three stories plus basement and attic, a cramped red brick row house, decorated with several portraits of

Lord Russell's Swedish sheep dog and a number of inexpensive prints. His staff included a coachman and groom, but they did not live in. In the attic just above the master bedroom were a bedroom shared by the cook and maid, and another for the valet; in the relatively modest household, the valet doubled as butler.

The maid Sarah Mancer and the cook Mary Hannell had each been with Lord Russell for almost three years. Courvoisier was employed as valet five weeks before the murder. At 19, Courvoisier had left his father's farm in Switzerland to make his way in England where an uncle was butler to Sir George Beaumont. Ignorant of English, Courvoisier took a job as waiter in a London hotel catering to foreigners and operated by a Frenchman Louis Piolaine and his English wife Charlotte. This was the Hotel Dieppe in Leicester Square, where François Benjamin Courvoisier was called for convenience "Jean." After a month or so at the Dieppe, on the recommendation of his uncle, Courvoisier was employed as footman (i. e. waiting table, attending the carriage, etc.) in the home of Lady Julia Lockwood. That job lasted nine months, from which experience Lady Julia, testifying as a character witness at his trial, was to describe Courvoisier as "a quiet, harmless, and inoffensive man." For the next three years, he was footman for Mr. Fector, a Member of Parliament, leaving Mr. Fector's with an "excellent character" to become Lord William Russell's valet. It was now something over four years since his arrival in London; Courvoisier's English was good; the job with Lord Russell was an important step up.

Chapter II

THE CASE AGAINST COURVOISIER

1. THE MAID'S STORY

By the time of the trial it seemed to the maid she had repeated "almost 50 times" her account of what preceded and immediately followed the finding of the body. With few variations she told the same story—to the police, the coroner's jury, at the preliminary examination, and finally on direct examination at the trial. It was a story at marked variance with the original report in *The Times*, which could hardly have been improved upon if Courvoisier had written it himself.

As Sarah Mancer recalled it, the routine of the day before the murder was like every other day except that Courvoisier forgot to send the coach to Brookes' on time; Lord Russell had to come home in a hired cab. His annoyance was brief, and as usual he walked the dog before dinner, dressed for dinner, and ate in the ground floor dining room, waited upon by Courvoisier but otherwise alone. Dinner over, Lord Russell went to his library, one flight up at the rear of the house, where it was his practice to read and write till bedtime. In the later public outcry at police ineptitude in solving the mystery of the crime, someone wanted to know what the Swedish sheep dog had been doing while his master was being murdered, but the maid's story cleared the dog. At nine, as usual, the coachman took the dog to the stables for the night.

At about the same time, Miss Mancer and Courvoisier had dinner together in the basement kitchen adjacent to the butler's pantry; the cook had gone out. When the cook came in around 10, Courvoisier went to a nearby pub, returning in a few minutes with some ale which the three drank in the kitchen. By this time, all doors to the outside had been locked for the night. A short time later, Miss Mancer, feeling drowsy, left the kitchen, lit the fire in Lord Russell's bedroom (on the floor above the library), and went to bed. Mary Hannell followed a quarter of an hour later.

Nothing disturbed Sarah Mancer's sleep. She awoke next morning at her usual 6:30, the cook still asleep. Sarah Mancer dressed, and as she passed Courvoisier's bedroom gave her customary wake-up knock at his door, continuing downstairs to the next floor. Here was the first little out of the ordinariness. The warming-pan, to take the chill off Lord Russell's sheets even in May, was on the landing near his bedroom door instead of having been returned to the kitchen; not usual but not unique; Courvoisier had been remiss on this score once before. Miss Mancer got a broom from the back room on the same floor, and continued downstairs to Lord Russell's library. No one is neat to a cleaning woman, but the library was in somewhat more than usual disarray. The Davenport desk was turned round from its normal position, open, and jammed with scattered papers. Some of the papers as well as a bunch of keys were on the hearthrug. A screwdriver was lying on a chair; Miss Mancer recognized it as one she had seen in the pantry a few days before along with the former valet's toolbox.

Next stop was the front drawing room; there all seemed well. But one flight further down Miss Mancer "saw a number of things lying" on the hall floor near the front door. The heap included Lord Russell's blue cloak (usually in the dining room), his opera glass (usually in his bedroom), and—as she later observed—a number of small items of gold and silver "tied up in a napkin." Worse yet, the front door, with its double bolts and chain latch all usually fastened for the night, was closed but unlatched and unbolted. The maid next unshuttered the dining room; silver candlesticks were on the floor, sugar was scattered about. This was enough for Sarah Mancer. Alarmed, she ran upstairs and woke Mary Hannell, whose response was prompt and direct: "For God's sake go and tell Courvoisier!"

Thus, ten minutes after her first knock at Courvoisier's door, Sarah Mancer knocked again. Normally it would have been a half to three-quarters of an hour after the first knock that Courvoisier would come downstairs coat in hand, sometimes shoeless, to wash up in the pantry. Now he came to his door, shoes on, and fully dressed except for his coat. To the maid he appeared pale and agitated as she spoke to him:

"Courvoisier, do you know of anything the matter last night? I found all the silver lying about."

The valet said nothing, but immediately started downstairs, putting on his coat as he went, Miss Mancer at his heels. At the first landing Courvoisier picked up the warming-pan, left it downstairs in the dining room, still saying nothing, and led Miss Mancer into the basement pantry. The cupboard and drawers were all open. At this Courvoisier exclaimed, "My God, some-one has been robbing us!"

Mancer suggested they go upstairs, and in the entrance hall she blurted out, "For God's sake, let us go and see where his Lordship is!"

Courvoisier led the way upstairs to Lord Russell's bedroom with Miss Mancer close behind. A spring door, covered with green cloth, opened into the hall; Courvoisier entered, the door closing quietly after him; Miss Mancer followed in at once. The head of Lord Russell's bed, partially curtained, was against the right wall as you go in, and as Miss Mancer entered the room, Courvoisier had already passed the foot of the bed and was opening the shutters of the windows that faced out on Norfolk Street. Miss Mancer called out, "My Lord, my Lord!", at which Courvoisier said, "There he is." By then Miss Mancer was about half-way to the foot of the bed, saw blood on the pillow, and ran screaming from the room. She started upstairs, changed her mind, and ran downstairs, out the front door and across the street calling for help. Her cries brought Emanuel Young, the butler at No. 23 Norfolk Street; he went for the po-lice. That done, Mancer returned through the open front door just as the cook came downstairs. Outside help had not yet ar-rived when the busy Miss Mancer went back into the dining room to find Courvoisier writing a note.

"What the Devil do you sit there for?" Miss Mancer shouted at him, "Why don't you go out and see for some one or a doc-tor?"

"I must write to Mr. Russell," replied Courvoisier, referring to Lord Russell's son who lived about a mile away.

"Someone must go for Mr. Russell," said Miss Mancer, and maid and valet went out the front door. Courvoisier hailed a passing workman, but the maid objected that that wasn't the sort of man to take a message to Mr. Russell.

By this time, Lord Russell's coachman William York had come into No. 14 Norfolk, and Emanuel Young was back from calling the police. In a few minutes the police arrived.

In addition to her scheduling of events, the maid volunteered several items generally harmful to her fellow servant.

She recalled that at dinner the night before the murder Courvoisier complained that Lord Russell was too fidgety for him, adding that he didn't expect to stay too long at this job. Courvoisier, she said, talked about his employer's peevishness at the loss of a locket (with some hair of the dead Lady Russell) when Russell, attended by Courvoisier, had visited Richmond about two weeks earlier. He told her too that he had only about five or eight pounds in the bank, had less money than when he first came to England. On two distinct occasions that she remembered Courvoisier had said of Lord William Russell and in identical language, "Old Billy is a rum chap, and if I had his money I would not remain long in England." On one of these occasions, Miss Mancer had replied that Lord Russell was not a very rich man. Mancer also thought it worth mentioning that Courvoisier, unlike his predecessor Ellis (who had worked there for over two years) seemed always to be looking through Lord Russell's clothes.

On one other point Sarah Mancer cast serious doubt on part of Courvoisier's unsworn testimony at the inquest. He had told the coroner's jury that on the night of the murder he had lighted the rush light (an inexpensive slowburning candle used as a dim night light) which Miss Mancer had placed fresh in Lord Russell's bedroom. Also, he told them, he had brought to the bedroom a lighted candle and a book, after which he had gone to bed and heard nothing till awakened by the maid. Miss Mancer said that Lord Russell was afraid of fires, and it was not his habit to read in the bedroom, an observation later confirmed by Russell's former valet. Thus, if Miss Mancer's story would not convict a man of murder, it still was not calculated to comfort a man suspected of murder.

2.   THE EARLY POLICE INVESTIGATION

Two police officers, Constable John Baldwin and Constable William Rose, arrived at No. 14 Norfolk Street shortly after 7 in the morning, minutes after discovery of the body. Baldwin asked for the man-servant in the house, and the "female" who let him in pointed out Courvoisier.

"I saw a man sitting behind the door, with his hands up to his face; he had his face from me," Baldwin testified. "I asked why he did not get up and render us assistance; he did not get up or take his hands from his face; he made me no answer. I asked him after that, why in the world he did not get up and render some assistance, but he did not give any answer the second time. I turned round and said to Rose, 'Rose, he must know something about this.'"

Baldwin quickly examined the pantry door that let out of the basement into the backyard, concluding that no entry had been made from there. With Courvoisier still sitting, saying and doing nothing, Baldwin felt the mystery was over and told him so: "I think you have made a damned pretty mess of this, and you know all about it." Courvoisier said nothing.

With that, Baldwin and Rose walked out into the backyard, completely closed in by high walls—a party wall on one side, a building on the other, stables at the rear. The weather had been dry, and it appeared to both of the officers that dust on the walls and the adjacent roof (which they examined by using a ladder that was there in the Russell backyard) "was not in the least disturbed."

Less than half an hour after the two constables, Inspector John Tedman entered the house and the investigation. He noted bruises on the pantry door and door post which, as he expressed it, "appeared to have been made by some blunt instrument." Not all of the marks on post and door seemed to correspond, and at the moment he "could not exactly say whether the bruises were made from within or without." Some definitely seemed to have been made from inside the house. In the basement Inspector Tedman met Miss Mancer and Miss Hannell, and saw Courvoisier, still sitting, unresponsive to Miss Mancer's plaintive, "Oh dear, my Lord is murdered." Tedman asked to be shown the body, and the four went upstairs to Lord Russell's bedroom.

In short order, the inspector let more light into the room, took the cloth off Lord Russell's face and turned down the bedclothes, uncovering a large pool of blood. Blood was "running partly from a large gash in the throat extending from ear to ear," had soaked through the mattress, and was now dripping onto the floor. The eyes were closed as though in sleep, the tongue slightly protruding. At this sight, Courvoisier standing at the foot of the bed, fell back into a chair, ending his silence in the presence of the police with, "Oh dear, this is a shocking thing; I shall lose my place and character." Tedman sent for the surgeon Mr. Elsgood.

On the floor near the bed was a pair of eyeglasses and a book, *The Memoirs of Sir Samuel Romilly,* who, someone recalled, had committed suicide by slashing his throat with a razor. (Tedman found six of Lord Russell's razors in the room, none with any sign of such use.) Courvoisier told the inspector that he had left Lord Russell reading the book when he went to bed. Tedman noted that the candle was burned out, and that the silver candlestick stood on a nearby bookshelf where a candle would have given enough light to read by.

Near the head of the bed was the "night convenience," and on its flat top an empty watch stand. Inspector Tedman asked where the watch was. Courvoisier said that the watch was gone, a ten pound note and a five pound note he had seen yesterday were missing, and also five gold rings that Lord Russell had worn his last day alive. Five other rings were still in their accustomed box; two gold mounted walking sticks were in place. Tedman thought out loud that it was "a very curious thief to leave all this valuable property behind." Courvoisier agreed, "It is certainly very strange."

In the dining room where drawers of a sideboard were open, with silverware lying on the floor, Tedman again asked if anything was missing. Courvoisier said some forks and spoons were missing but he couldn't tell how many. At the sight of the cloak, opera glass, and assorted small gold and silver worked pieces piled up near the front door, Tedman told Courvoisier, "No thief would ever leave that property behind," and Courvoisier rejoined, "It is certainly very odd." As the party returned to the pantry door, Courvoisier suggested that Tedman examine it again, pointing out some marks the inspector had missed on his earlier examination. Tedman looked again, and then said to Courvoisier, "Some of you in the house have done this deed."

Courvoisier replied, "If they have I hope they will be found out."

"There is not much fear but they will," said Tedman, and walked out into the walled-in backyard. Here he confirmed the findings of his constables; he thought it "next to impossible" that anyone could have come that way without leaving some mark in the dust, and there were none.

Inspector Tedman and his men searched the bedroom of the maid and cook; nothing suspect. Joined by Police Commissioner Mayne and Inspector Beresford, Tedman searched Courvoisier's bedroom, Courvoisier personally, and all of his belongings kept in a wooden box and a black leather trunk. The valet accounted for a five pound note and some coins; the search turned up nothing of interest to the police. No tell-tale blood stains and no apparent murder weapon anywhere in the house.

From the moment the police arrived, Courvoisier and Mancer and Hannell were kept under constant surveillance. They had the run of the house; none of their private belongings were seized or locked up. But they were prevented from talking privately with one another, and though no formal arrest was made of anyone, they were "detained;" none of them left the house. Tedman noted that Courvoisier "kept running and drinking water;" he was certain that "the man seemed very much concerned" about the police investigation.

3.   THE PUBLIC, THE PRESS, AND THE POLICE

Thus matters stood on Wednesday morning: the one solid fact a brutal murder discovered. Close on the police, Londoners on foot and in carriages crowded into the narrow confines of Norfolk Street—about 250 feet long and wide enough for two coaches to pass. Without the aid of telephone, words spread quickly throughout London—Old Lord William Russell dead and murdered in his bed and his valet suspect—even reaching the Palace, where Victoria's husband Prince Albert sent out to get the latest news.

As word of the death spread, so speculation and rumor spread: that someone might have hidden in Lord Russell's house when the valet went out for ale; that the murderer was still hiding in a chimney of No. 14 Norfolk Street; that a next-door neighbor Mrs. Anstruther had heard groans from Lord Russell's house early that Wednesday morning, groans which strangely none of Lord Russell's servants said they had heard; that the murderer had hidden the murder weapon in Lord Russell's body; that the missing silverware had been found in the bedroom of a friend of Courvoisier's; that a bloody glove had been found among Miss Mancer's clothing. All of these were disposed of in the course of the continuing police investigation. One rumor survives today, that at about the time of the murder a gentleman across the street from No. 14 Norfolk had observed the silhouette of a nude man first in Lord Russell's bedroom and then descending into other parts of the house, but that the gentleman had not come forward with the "evidence" lest he compromise the honor of a lady at whose home he was a guest for the evening.[1]

An exceptional crop of rumors was to be expected, for the nature of the crime struck at the heart of the Victorian structure. As *The Times* reported in successive stories:

> "It was stated, that such was the panic produced by the news of the murder, that many families at the west-end, and more particularly aged persons living as the deceased had done in comparative retirement, enter-tained, perhaps for the first time, a feeling of insecuri-ty, and began almost to doubt those employed around them."

* * *

> "The excitement produced in high life by the dread-ful event is almost unprecedented, and the feeling of apprehension for personal safety increases every hour, particularly among those of the nobility and gentry who live in comparative seclusion."

Public excitement also excited certain commercial possibilities. An advertisement appeared for *The Biophulax*, "an ingenious contrivance for the protection of life and property from destruction by fire, thieves, or murderers." It was offered for public inspection on Picadilly as a machine that lets out "a peal that would not only awaken the soundest sleeper, but frighten the most determined depredator . . . The late assassination of a venerable nobleman, and the calamitous fire that took place a few nights back in Marylebone-street, seem to testify to the necessity of some means of safeguard being adopted by those who wish to sleep in security."

Inevitably, demand for allaying public unease and for a resolution of the mystery took the form of search for a scapegoat as

---

1. J. B. Atlay, Famous Trials 62 (1899); C. Biron, Without Preju-dice 147 (1936); Y. Bridges, Two Studies in Crime 121, and App. II (1959); A. Brock, A Casebook of Crime 23 (1948); M. Frewen, Mel-ton Mowbray 19–20 (1924); cf. H. M. Walbrook, Murders and Murder Trials viii, 79, 86 (1932).

well as a murderer. If not surely the valet, then at the very least the police. That force had been reorganized a decade earlier by Sir Robert Peel as paid, tax-supported professionals and only a year before the Russell murder had undergone further reorganization. (This was the body that has come to be known as the Metropolitan Police Force, popularly "Scotland Yard.") The press called attention to a similar murder-robbery a short time before, still unsolved. And *The Times* intoned:

> "Of the activity, zeal, and intelligence, of the new police as a body there can be no doubt; and as far as these qualities can be exerted, we are sure they will be in the present instance. It would be frightful, indeed, to suppose that from any defect in the system of police as at present constituted, however admirable it works in other respects, they should be found unequal to the duty of bringing offenders to justice stained with the most atrocious crime that can disgrace a civilized community. We hope and trust that constables the most experienced in the whole force may be selected on the present occasion, so that the cold-blooded murder of a kindhearted and unoffending nobleman may be brought to sure and speedy justice."

That was only two days after the murder. When the next day, *The Times* reported that the police had not yet completed a close examination of Lord Russell's house, it commented:

> ".   .   . we cannot but feel that such delay on the part of the police implies a want of tact and foresight of which experienced constables would never have been guilty in prosecuting an inquiry of this important description."

In the meantime, the government had taken the unprecedented step of offering a 200 pound reward for information leading to the conviction of Lord Russell's murderer, and the Russell family had added to the incentive another 200 pounds.[2] Later, a separate 50 pound reward was offered for recovery of the silverware ("the plate") missing from Lord Russell's dining room, now identified as ten silver spoons and four silver forks, each

2. The London Gazette, May 8, 1840, no. 19854, pages 1152–1153.

marked with the crest of the Russell family—a goat in a stand-ing position, and bearing the family motto *che sara, sara,* what will be, will be. This 450 pound total may be compared with Courvoisier's starting salary as Lord Russell's valet—45 pounds for a year's work, to be raised to 50 pounds (the rate at which his seasoned predecessor had been paid) if Courvoisier's services proved satisfactory after six months. (As of the date of Lord Russell's death, Courvoisier had been paid nothing.)

The police team—three inspectors and seven constables—on continuous duty at No. 14 Norfolk Street, working round the clock (and without benefit of fingerprint analysis), were soon reinforced by workmen of every description—carpenters, plumb-ers, chinmeysweeps. The rented house was torn apart in a des-perate search for the missing plate and other missing property of the dead man. Gutters on the roof, sewer pipes, water clos-ets, and cesspools were searched, their contents strained and probed. In the butler's pantry, the searchers hit their first pay dirt.

While workmen opened up the drains in the pantry, Inspector Nicholas Pearce removed a portion of the skirting-board near the sink. There, wedged in between the board and the sink, he found a purse containing five gold coins, five gold rings—one a wedding ring, and a bit of sealing wax. Removing a further piece of the skirting-board, he pulled at a bit of ribbon, eventual-ly drawing out a silver Waterloo medal attached to it, inscribed "The Hon. Captain Russell, Aide-de-Camp." In the same cranny was a folded ten pound Bank of England note. With Constable George Collier, Inspector Pearce immediately looked for Courvo-isier, and found him sitting in the dining room, another con-stable keeping him company. Displaying his treasure-trove, Pearce told the valet: "I have found these things concealed in your pantry behind the skirting. Can you now look me in the face?"

Alone with three policemen, Courvoisier's reply was prompt and emphatic: "I know nothing about them. I am innocent. My conscience is clear. I never saw the medal before."

Unconvinced, the inspector led Courvoisier down to the pantry showing him where the discovery had been made. Courvoisier repeated, "I am innocent. I know nothing about them."

About then, a workman removed a waterpipe, and behind it found another ring—a split one. Courvoisier told Constable Collier that Lord Russell had a split ring on which he kept his seals. Questioned by the constable, Courvoisier also said that the five gold rings found were ones Lord Russell had worn the day before his death, and at night were left on a table in the bedroom. Collier said the whole business was "a most shocking thing." Courvoisier agreed, adding: "I am innocent of it; but it would not look so bad against me had not the property been found in my pantry."

Collier replied that it looked "very suspicious," which Courvoisier topped with a further dollop of mystery: "I shall say nothing, at least until I hear that the whole truth is told."

Inspector Pearce and Sergeant Frederick Shaw now led Courvoisier up to his attic bedroom. There inspector and sergeant searched through all of Courvoisier's clothing in the box and in the trunk, finding—as had Inspector Tedman on the first search—nothing at all suspicious. For a second time also, Courvoisier was personally searched; this turned up five shillings in silver, a small bunch of keys with Lord Russell's name on one of the keyrings, and a small locket that Courvoisier said was his own. Sometime on this same Friday afternoon, Courvoisier was informed for the first time that he was to consider himself in custody.

By the next day (Saturday) the sink in the butler's pantry had been entirely removed and set down in the backyard where it was used as a rest bench for the weary workmen. Constable Collier and Sergeant Shaw continued in the work of dismantling the pantry. Collier helped take down a plate rack, exposing a lead water pipe behind which, jammed against the wall, he found a gold seal with coat of arms, and nearby a signet ring bent with the pressure of having been squeezed in between pipe and wall. Workmen took up the stone hearth in the pantry, and sifting the dust there close to a floor joist, Shaw discovered a gold locket.

As the search continued, each new discovery was leaked to the ever present crowds in Norfolk Street and to the press. Still critical of the police, for the mystery was not officially ended, the press did not hesitate to give the prospective jurors of anxious London a detailed view of what right-thinking people thought of the Swiss valet. Reporting the discovery of the rings and the ten pound note in the pantry (along with a five pound note, an error later corrected), *The Times* said:

> "The valet, it appeared, performed the duty of butler; and as such no other person but himself had a right to use the pantry, so that the general supposition is that the notes and rings were placed there by him—an inference which appears to be warranted by the great uneasiness which he manifested when told the workmen were about to examine the premises, and further by the change which was manifested in his appearance and manner when informed of the discovery which had been made. His face was described by one of the workmen to be 'as white as his shirt', and it was further stated, that he was taken suddenly ill when the intelligence was conveyed to him . . .
>
> We understand that as soon as the banknotes and other property were found the valet was told he was to consider himself from that time in custody. His agitation was extreme, although he persisted in declaring his innocence."

The same edition noted that the surgeon Mr. Elsgood and other "professional gentlemen" had performed an autopsy the previous night, checking for the presence of narcotics in Lord Russell's stomach, as an explanation of why he had slept so soundly that he was murdered without an outcry. None was found. (Privately Mr. Elsgood told friends he had no doubt that Courvoisier was the murderer.)

Saturday (the fourth day after the murder) crowds of "respectably-dressed" people made the sidewalk outside No. 14 Norfolk Street impassable, and some stood in the muddy street itself so as to miss nothing. Nobility continued to visit inside the house. In the afternoon, England's hero of Waterloo the Duke of Wellington sent a messenger to the house to learn the latest on the murder of his war-time companion. A rumor circulated that Courvoisier had confessed, yet as of the evening it was reported that "Up to this time, he has made no confession of his having been the perpetrator of the diabolical act, or of his having any knowledge of the guilty party, but, on the contrary, when speaking on the subject of the murder, he protests his innocence of any guilty knowledge of or participation therein." The *Observ-*

er nonetheless thought it worth mentioning that Courvoisier had not slept at all the previous night.

Their daily remarks to the valet at No. 14 Norfolk made it clear that the police shared, as indeed they had stimulated, the general suspicion of Courvoisier. The circumstantial inferences from the finding of missing property in the butler's pantry were reinforced by more careful examination of the bruises on the pantry door. Many of them were not only quite definitely made from the inside, but a number of the indentations could be matched with a bent poker, a screwdriver, and a chisel, all from the pantry. The cheering effect of such confirmations was somewhat diminished by two worrisome gaps in the case. The plate was still missing and so was the weapon. Though the house was full of potentially murderous weapons—the six razors; a full assortment of carving knives; hammers, chisel, screwdriver, poker—it could not be established that any of them had been used on Lord William Russell.

If not Courvoisier, who? At one stage of the investigation attention had focussed on an unemployed friend Henry Carr, who had visited Courvoisier at Lord Russell's house the day before the murder. The owner of a pub reported to the police "that a woman of loose character, who was drinking in his bar, had stated that on the day previous to the murder a man named Carr, who was a servant out of place, had invited her to drink his health, stating that he was about to quit this country for Australia." On such bubbles Henry Carr was arrested, but after some harassment in the press, he established an alibi, and was released. For the police, Courvoisier was their best, their only remaining suspect. Still troubled by their inability to locate the plate or the weapon, and needled daily by the press, the police determined to charge Courvoisier with the murder.

To avoid the crowds outside the Russell home, dispersed only by rain and only thinning at night, the police decided on a midnight delivery. Inspector Pearce woke Courvoisier at 11:30 Sunday night to tell him they were taking him to jail; Courvoisier said nothing "beyond a fervant declaration of his innocence." At midnight, arm in arm, with Courvoisier between them, Inspector Pearce and a constable, unnoticed by late hangers on, walked their prisoner out of the front door of No. 14 Norfolk Street, and hurried him into a waiting coach that took off at a gallop for Bow-street station house. Inspector Pearce signed the booking: "François Benjamin Courvoisier, charged with the wilful murder of Lord William Russell, on the 6th instant, at No. 14

Norfolk-street, Park-lane." He was jailed for the night, making a favorable impression on police Sergeant Driscoll who would stay with him in the cell until Courvoisier was taken to court in the morning. "Courvoisier remained very firm and free from all symptoms of agitation. He frequently expressed his confidence that he should be eventually honourably acquitted of the dreadful charge alleged against him, and told Sergeant Driscoll that when again at liberty he should not forget him for the civility he had shown him." *The Times* sleepwatcher, a puzzled Victorian believer in the relationship between a clear conscience and a good night's sleep, conscientiously reported that Courvoisier "sleeps soundly whatever may be his feelings with respect to the serious nature of the charge preferred against him."

4.   THE PRELIMINARY EXAMINATION

The news that Courvoisier had at last been charged with murder went through London faster than newspapers could be printed. Crowds, "the simple and the gentle," wedged into Norfolk Street; others packed the magistrate's court at Bow-street for a first look at the murderous valet. They saw a heavy-set man of middle height, dark brown hair, prominent cheekbones, a somewhat aquiline nose, looking on the whole considerably older than his 23 some years, brought into court by Inspector Pearce and three constables. Correctly attired in a butler's brown frock coat, slate colored figured waistcoat, with black pants and shoes, "there was not much of a foreigner in his general appearance." Someone thought his "face and lips . . . deadly pale." A spectator, resembling Courvoisier, rushed towards the prisoner as though to talk with him. Police took the man into custody thinking he might be involved in the crime; they later reported he was an unemployed servant, with an alibi for the night of the murder; he wanted "to touch the prisoner from curiosity only, as he might not have an opportunity of getting so near to him again."

The "preliminary examination" that was about to begin, like the comparable preliminary examinations or preliminary hearings in the United States, was not to establish guilt or innocence of the accused. Chief Magistrate Hall would decide only that there was or was not enough of a case to warrant holding Courvoisier for action of the grand jury and a trial by jury.

The case against Courvoisier would be presented for the Commissioners of the Metropolitan Police by a solicitor retained by them, Mr. Hobler. And now for the first time, Courvoisier too had a lawyer. A solicitor well known in London, Mr. Flower, rose to inform the court he had been "instructed" (i. e. employed) to attend on behalf of the prisoner. Who had instructed Mr. Flower? One rumor had it that the servants of London, sensing a class issue, had pooled together to hire a lawyer. A more persistent and likelier report is that money for lawyers came from Sir George Beaumont, for 18 years the employer of Courvoisier's uncle and said to believe that Courvoisier was in "unjust peril." Much later, Sir George denied as "totally devoid of truth" a published report that he had subscribed 50 pounds to Courvoisier's defense fund, but that in the language of the law was a negative pregnant with the admission that he had subscribed less, or more, than exactly 50 pounds. (After Beaumont's death, his solicitor confirmed that Sir George had paid for the defense.) Under the division of the profession of law in England, solicitor Flower would represent Courvoisier in the magistrate's court; if the case went to trial, Mr. Flower would "brief" (i. e. employ) a barrister to continue the defense.

Mr. Flower's first move was to complain that he had not been permitted to see his client at the station house before this session of court. The Chief Magistrate replied that such consultation in serious cases required a court order; he now made one, at once stopping proceedings to permit brief and private consultation between lawyer and client. Very shortly Courvoisier returned to the dock; just time enough (here one must speculate) to tell his lawyer he was innocent, and for his lawyer to tell him to stop talking about the case, beyond acknowledging that he was indeed François Benjamin Courvoisier. That is all Courvoisier had to say in the numerous sessions in the magistrate's court, though the argot—perhaps harking back to an earlier, inquisitorial function of the magistrate—refers to the preliminary examination as the "examination of Courvoisier."

The police witness of the day was Inspector Nicholas Pearce to give the bare outlines of the crime—the finding of Lord Russell's body with the throat cut, the verdict of the coroner's jury, the discovery of missing property in the butler's pantry, Courvoisier's denial of guilt. Mr. Hobler felt that was enough for the moment, enough to warrant holding Courvoisier for another hearing later in the week. The Chief Magistrate disagreed; he wanted something more before ordering any further detention. Questioned by Mr. Hobler the witness added details of the suspicious character of the bruises on the pantry door. (At a later hearing Inspector Beresford was to give a succinct cop's eye view of this evidence. "I am quite satisfied," he said, "that the marks on the door were not made by a regular housebreaker, or with the instruments usually employed by them.") On this, the magistrate continued the hearing till Thursday, in the meantime Courvoisier to be held in Westminster Bridewell, the Tothillfields prison, and to be permitted visits by his solicitor. Mr. Flower conferred with him twice before the next session. Others came simply to have a look at the latest London curiosity. To one Courvoisier's "manner was calm though dejected; " for another he was "not .   .   . in the slightest degree depressed in spirits."

Even as the first hearing was in progress, back on Norfolk Street Inspector Tedman and his men continued the search for something that would tie the case down. Sergeant Shaw, with Constables Humphreys and Collier in the room, went through Courvoisier's clothing a third time, examining piece by piece the articles in the box and the trunk. Again a zero.

The next day, Constable Cronin, working in the scullery next to the pantry, found imbedded in the flooring the key of Lord Russell's watch, a stem-winder with bells, the watch itself still at large. But the following day (Wednesday, a week after the murder) in the backyard the inquisitive Cronin re-inspected the sink that had long since been removed from the pantry. It seemed to him that a part of the lead edge of the sink had been turned up and then down. With a chisel he pried the lead up, and there was the missing watch, its crystal broken, otherwise undamaged. Workmen had been sitting on the evidence. The same day a plumber working in the pantry, where the floor had now been torn up, found a single sovereign, which he turned over to the police.

This same day too, the day before the second session of the preliminary examination, Courvoisier's uncle came to the door of Lord Russell's house. He said Courvoisier wanted a clean shirt and stockings. Tedman's orders were to give Courvoisier any clothes he wanted, but since (the inspector later said) he himself was going to Bow-street the next morning, the uncle was sent away empty-handed. Next day (Thursday), the request in mind, Inspector Tedman with Sergeant Lovett went up once more to Courvoisier's attic bedroom. It was the second time that Inspector Tedman, and the fourth separate occasion that any policeman, had examined the clothes in Courvoisier's trunk.

He took a white shirt out of Courvoisier's trunk, unfolded it on Courvoisier's bed, picked it up and shook it over the trunk. Out fell a pair of servant's white cotton gloves that neither the Inspector nor any other of the police reported having seen there before. Moreover, the gloves were slightly stained with blood.

On the trail of more blood, Constables Collier and Cronin had another go at Courvoisier's trunk; this was the second time that Collier had been present at an inspection of Courvoisier's belongings, the third police search since Courvoisier had been jailed, and the fifth time that any policeman had gone through the trunk. Near the top of the pile of clothing in Courvoisier's trunk Collier uncovered two handkerchiefs, one cotton, the other silk, each marked "B.C.", each spotted with blood. A moment later, Collier pulled out of this Pandora's box a white shirt-front, not blood stained, but missing both shirtsleeves and the body of the shirt. Neither the handkerchiefs nor the shirt-front had been noted in the four previous searches of Courvoisier's clothing, which had now been inspected by nine different policemen, including a Police Commissioner and three Inspectors, three of the police having been in on the search in the attic twice each.

London fully expected some such discovery. The police needed it, and it was leaked to the press. Two days after the bloody gloves had been found, *The Times*, continuing to marvel that "Courvoisier . . . we understand, still persists in protesting his entire innocence of the horrid crime imputed to him," indicated that hope was in sight. The paper reported "a discovery of a most important character, the exact nature of which we have not been able accurately to obtain, owing to the great secrecy maintained by the police and every person connected with the inquiry. It is, however, very currently stated in the neighbourhood that some article of attire belonging to Courvoisier has been found, which is spotted with blood, which, if a fact, will tend greatly to strengthen the suspicions against him."

Having been told by *The Times* before the first preliminary examination started that the police had fixed the guilt on Courvoisier, readers could only wonder why Courvoisier had not already confessed and why the police had not tied the knot still tighter. Public excitement was not abating in the slightest with the jailing of Courvoisier; it tended "rather to increase as the probability of the discovery of the perpetrator of the horrid deed becomes more certain."

When the magistrate's preliminary examination resumed on Thursday, a Russell family solicitor Mr. Thomas Wing was there to observe for the family. London society turned out for the show, competing for place on the bench with the judges. Side by side with Chief Magistrate Hall were His Highness the Duke of Brunswick and his Equerry, Baron Audlam, the Earls of Clarendon, Mansfield, and Essex. Each day Mayfair sent a full complement of spectators, four earls, six assorted lords. The Minister of Wurtenberg was there, and Count Stregonoff of the Russian Embassy. There were Lady Alice Peel and Lady Emily Wortley, the courtroom becoming so filled that "several persons of distinction   .   .   .   were compelled to mingle with the crowd, an inconvenience which they willingly put up with so long as they could obtain a view of the prisoner, and hear the evidence brought against him." Courvoisier was the silent star, his every movement, the lows and highs of his emotional flux closely watched: "listened attentively   .   .   .   occasionally   .   .   .   restless and uneasy;" " .   .   .   occasionally exchanged a few words with his solicitor;" " .   .   .   the greatest coolness and self-possession, except when the watch, ring, and other articles were produced, when his countenance changed, and he appeared giddy, laying hold of the bar behind which he was standing   .   .   ." "   .   .   .   more alive to his situation   .   .   .   communications with his solicitor   .   .   .   more frequent; " and on the day of the final session —"   .   .   .   he entered the dock with a light step and a cheerful countenance, and it might be added that his appearance indicated increased confidence as the protracted inquiry drew towards a close."

The testimony itself extending through six long sessions over a period of two weeks could not have given Courvoisier much cause for cheer, except the negative consolation that little was presented not already described in the press. Sarah Mancer's story received some embittered embellishment. When she and Mary Hannell were picked up in a coach to give their testimony, they had already been cooped up in the gloomy house at No. 14 Norfolk Street for more than eight days, at first with Courvoisier, the police, and the corpse. Even now the blood soaked pillow and the disorder of the upstairs furniture left undisturbed, the house still swarming with workmen and surrounded by inquisitive gawkers, maid and cook continued under police surveillance though Courvoisier was in jail and Lord Russell buried. His remains had been taken from the house in a purple covered casket, and buried with medieval pomp after a funeral procession of carriages the 22 miles from London to Buckinghamshire to the Russell family chapel built in 1556 by Elizabeth, Countess of Bedford, wife of the first Earl. Queen Victoria and Prince Albert had requested that their carriage join "the mournful cortege" but the family had declined the honor, in favor of a private funeral. It was now reported that Mancer and Hannell had "both been much affected by the dreadful circumstances, and the housemaid is much depressed in spirits respecting her character, fearing that she will be unable to procure a fresh situation, alleging that no respectable person will engage her when they ascertain she had formed one of his Lordship's establishment."

In her testimony, Miss Mancer gave her impressions of Courvoiser on the day of the discovery of the murder.

"It struck me," she said, "that there was something singular in his manner that morning."

Asked by the magistrate to explain, she continued:

"I noticed that his manner was very strange on the Wednesday, and the next day; when he saw me crying, his hand shook very much, and he gave me an evil look, as if he thought I suspected him. I saw him use a pocket handkerchief which I knew belonged to his Lordship, and when I asked him to give it to me, as I was making an inventory of the things in the house, I thought he looked very strange at me."

The cook recalled that when the body was discovered, Courvoisier cried out, 'My God, they'll think it's me, and I shan't get another place."

The neighborhood servants were called, the police, the surgeon, identification of the secreted property, Courvoisier's responses, the bruises on the pantry door, the bloody gloves, witnesses to each detail and scrap of circumstantiality, enough so that Mr. Flower readily conceded (at the fourth session) there was "a case of strong suspicion" requiring a trial. That being clear to Courvoisier's lawyer, he was if anything more anxious than Mr. Hobler that all of the evidence the prosecution had against Courvoisier should be spread upon the record for future study. He told the court "that the prisoner was extremely anxious that the fullest possible inquiry should take place." Mr. Flower was sparing with his cross-examination.

Usually, he contented himself with the occasional plums that fell unplucked: neither maid or cook had missed any silverware before the murder; although a coachman at the home of the M. P. where Courvoisier once worked as footman said that Courvoisier did "wear white cotton gloves when he went out with the carriage," Sarah Mancer had never seen him with any gloves but "a dark kid pair." Cross-examining Inspector Tedman, Mr. Flower made it very clear to everyone, especially the prosecution, that when the bloodstained gloves were finally found, Courvoisier's clothing was in the possession of the police, the discovery having been made eight days after Courvoisier "was first searched and four days after he was locked up."

During the course of the hearings two letters addressed to Courvoisier were opened under the eye of the magistrate. One was in French from Courvoisier's sister who lived in France. She expressed "her conviction of his innocence of such a crime, and her hope that he would put his entire trust in God." The other was "from some religious enthusiast, who earnestly implored the prisoner to make his peace with God, on the supposition, of course, that he was guilty of the crime laid to his charge."

With all the evidence in, on a Friday three weeks after the murder, Chief Magistrate Hall did the expected. The press reported the scene as he addressed Courvoisier:

"You will now, therefore, be conveyed from this court to Newgate to await your trial, and in the mean time any further evidence which may be procured will be brought against you, and you will have on your trial the same opportunity of producing evidence in your defence. If you now wish to make any statement or observations I am ready to hear you, but it is my duty to caution you, that whatever you do say will be taken down in writing, and may be produced in evidence either for or against you.

"Mr. Flower looked at the prisoner apparently with a view to ascertain if he wished to say anything. The prisoner, however, shook his head to signify that he had nothing to say, and

"Mr. Flower said—He has nothing to say, Sir, at present, but that he is entirely innocent of the murder.

"Mr. Hall 'Then he stands committed to Newgate for trial.' "

Even before the hearings had concluded, the irreverent, perceptive Charles Greville, clerk of the Privy Council, whose Queen was horrified when his candid *Memoirs* were later published,[3] wrote in his journal:

"Just after I got back to Newmarket, the intelligence arrived of the extraordinary murder of Lord William Russell, which has excited a prodigious interest, and frightened all London out of its wits. Visionary servants and air-drawn razors or carving knives dance before every body's imaginations, and half the world go to sleep expecting to have their throats cut before morning. The circumstances of the case are certainly most extraordinary, and though every day produces some fresh cause for suspecting the man Courvoisier, both the fact and the motives are still enveloped in great mystery. People are always ready to jump to a conclusion, and having made up their minds, as most have, that he must have done the deed, they would willingly hang him up at once." [4]

3. L.   Strachey,   Queen   Victoria   396–397 (1921).

4. 1 C. Greville, Memoirs (Second Part) 246 (Henry Reeve ed. 1885).

Chapter III

OF COUNSEL

The ending of the preliminary examination placed Courvoisier in a stronger prison—the celebrated Newgate, but it left the case with its "yet impenetrable mystery in which the murderous transaction is enveloped." Courvoisier was no longer making offhand remarks to the police, yet inexplicably—for all the evidence against him—he was still asserting his innocence. For the London public Courvoisier had been thrice tried—at the coroner's inquest, in the magistrate's court, and in the newspapers—and already twice convicted. What remained to gall the police, and worry the prosecution, was the lack of a weapon, the missing silverware, and a haunting dread that even a press-conditioned jury would not hang a man on circumstance.

The same diarist who believed the public ready to hang Courvoisier had personal thoughts of a somewhat different nature. Greville wrote again in his journal after public intimations of blood found on the valet's clothing. He had been to have a look at the scene of the crime, and came away finding it "impossible not to be morally convinced" that Lord Russell's home had not been broken into, that the marks on the pantry door were "fabricated," that Courvoisier had hidden the recovered items, and so was the murderer.

> "[B]ut," Greville confided to himself, "there is as yet no evidence to convict him of the actual commission of the deed, and though I believe him to be guilty, I could not, on such a case as there is as yet, find him so if placed on a jury. I am very skeptical about evidence, and know how strangely circumstances sometimes combine to produce appearances of guilt where there may be none. There is a curious case of this mentioned in Romilly's *Memoirs* [the book found in Lord Russell's bedroom], of a man hanged for mutiny upon the evidence of a witness who swore to his person, and upon his own confession after conviction, and yet it was satisfactorily proved afterward that he had been mistaken for another man, and was really innocent. He had been induced to confess at the instigation of a fellow-

40

prisoner, who told him it was his best chance of escaping." [1]

Even before the result of the preliminary examination was confirmed by a grand jury indictment (with some of the grand jurors reportedly in favor of throwing the case out), it was anticipated that Courvoisier would be brought to trial at the Old Bailey on June 18, less than three weeks after his commitment to Newgate. In the interval, the policy while continuing the search for weapon and silver were constantly distracted in running down a miscellany of rumor. Nothing ever came of the rumor that someone had been seen leaving the house on the morning of the murder. Another was the false report of the finding of a bloody shirt in Hyde Park, an easy walk from Lord Russell's home. This turned out to be a twisted version of the finding by the police of "a pair of bloody stockings, which are supposed to have belonged to one of the numerous miserable females who infest the Park at nights, but to have no connection with the murder." In the interval, too, counsel had to be selected for the impending trial.

1. JOHN ADOLPHUS, PRIVATE PROSECUTOR

Three barristers joined in the prosecution of Courvoisier, the choice of "leading counsel" (chief prosecutor) left to the exercise of an ancient prerogative: the bereaved family might name and pay a private prosecutor.

Time was when the killing of Lord Russell would have started a vendetta or blood feud between the Russells and the Courvoisiers. If it turned out that the vengeful Russells got the wrong man, that started another feud. The laws of the Anglo-Saxon kings in England attempted to end the blood feud by payment of money, but a secret killing, such as that of Lord Russell, was bootless, too heinous to be bought off, and ".   .   .   the murderer shall be given up to the kinsmen." [2] (A politician in this country has recently suggested that this system be revived.) [3]

1. 1 C. Greville, Memoirs (Second Part) 247 (H. Reeve ed. 1885).

2. II Canute 56, in The Laws of the Kings of England from Edmund to Henry I, 203 (A. J. Robertson ed. and transl. 1925).

3. Los Angeles Times, May 11, 1970, pt. 1, page 4.

The system of the regulated feud gave way to another device of personalized justice, the "appeal." This was not an appeal to a higher court to correct the decision of a lower court. The old "appeal" was an ordinary lawsuit, appealing not a decision but the man who had wronged you. You appealed him, sued him, called him to justice. You appealed people not only for murder, but for all manner of wrongs, those we now call "crimes" as well as those we consider occasions for private ("civil") lawsuits. The distinction was not drawn between crime and civil wrong. Our notion that a "crime" is a wrong against the state (even though it is my throat that was cut, my jaw punched, my horse stolen) is a complicated notion, at once mystical, self-deceptive, and abstract. It is a Chaplinesque sort of dream world in which we pretend that when you club my head, the "state" feels the pain. In an earlier day it was my head, my lump, my right to vengeance, and later, my right to appeal you for the wrong. The old appeal was an individual's personal action, whether it ended with a death sentence or money paid to the survivors. It served a purpose that law courts still serve, giving an injured man enough of satisfaction that he won't take the law into his own hands.

The common law gradually weaned Englishmen away from personal to substituted satisfaction, discouraging the appeal as a malicious form of legal procedure. By the end of the 13th century indictment became the usual method of starting a "criminal" case; statute and decision ate away at the appeal; but side by side with the possibility of public prosecution by indictment the appeal of felony as a private right continued for centuries. The appeal of murder was still alive in 1818: Thornton had been indicted and acquitted of the murder of William Ashford's sister. Unhappy over this result, Ashford appealed Thornton of the murder. As had happened twice in the 18th century, this appeal could have resulted in a death sentence, despite an earlier acquittal under indictment for the same offense. That was not the result this time, for the defense countered one archaism with another: if the appeal of murder still existed, the right of the appellee (defendant) to trial by battle existed, and Thornton threw down his glove in a 19th century court challenging Ashford to combat. The court upheld the procedure; the parties thought better of the old appeal; and it was ended without combat.[4] The next year parliament abolished the appeal of felony as well as trial by battle;[5] that was in 1819, only 21 years before *Courvoisier's Case.*

Despite the recourse to indictments for "crime," English (as well as American[6]) law continued to recognize the intense personal interest of the dead man's family in the outcome of the prosecution. And so, about 10 days before the trial, the Russell family picked John Adolphus to lead the prosecution of the valet charged with murdering their kinsman.

Adolphus was a logical, almost inevitable choice of counsel for the Russell family. A man of intelligence and scholarship, he had already made his mark as an historian before being called to the bar at the relatively late age of 39. His published historical works covered France, the French Revolution, the British Empire, and a many volumed work on the reign of George III. The early volumes had been praised by the King, and one of the King's sons, the Duke of Sussex, was his friend.[7]

Adolphus' success at the criminal bar quickly made him a much sought after counsel, appearing in many important trials, most impressively for the defense in the Cato Street Conspiracy. He combined an easy-to-understand and persuasive rhetoric with a fire that won juries. The fire, in other circumstances becoming temper, also was his chief failing. Many years before Courvoisier's case, he fell to quarreling with another barrister Peter Alley over something said in court, and finally sent an insulting letter to Alley at his home. Mrs. Alley is said to have intercept-

---

4. Ashford v. Thornton, 1 B. & Ald. 421, 106 Eng.Rep. 149 (1818).

5. 59 George III. c. 46 (1819).

6. 2 E. Thornton, Treatise on Attorneys at Law 1106–1110, 1122–1123 (1914); 42 Am.Jur. "Prosecuting Attorneys," s. 10, 241–243, 1971 Cum.Supp. 40; Goldsby v. State, 240 Miss. 647, 669–671, 123 So.2d 429, 437–438 (1960); *cert. denied,* 365 U.S. 861, 81 S.Ct. 829, 5 L.Ed. 2d 824 (1961); see "Parole Board to Review Case of Sheriff's Killer," Los Angeles Times, July 26, 1971, pt. 1, pages 14–15; cf.

Pound, "The Causes of Popular Dissatisfaction with the Administration of Justice," 29 A.B.A.Rep. 395, 403 (1906).

7. On Adolphus generally, E. Henderson, Recollections of the Public Career and Private Life of the Late John Adolphus (1871) [hereafter cited as Henderson]; W. Ballantine, Some Experiences of a Barrister's Life 53, 56–58, 61, 273, 391 (8th ed. 1883; 1st ed. 1882) [hereafter cited as Ballantine]; Robinson, Bench and Bar 37–38, 66–67 (2d ed. 1889) [hereafter cited as Robinson].

ed the letter, and, enraged, told her husband, "Peter, much as I love you, I would sooner see you brought home on a stretcher than submit to such an insult." [8] The result was a pistol duel on the sands of Calais, ended when Adolphus shot off a piece of Alley's ear. Honor satisfied, the duelists continued as half-way friends.

Though urged to leave criminal work to others, the practice was lucrative, Adolphus became the acknowledged leader of the criminal bar, and stayed on—perhaps too long. When retained to prosecute Courvoisier, he was an active and dignified 72—as old as the dead Lord William Russell, weakened in health but not in mind, "somewhat sour and crabbed in his manner," [9] and bitter over the loss of clients to newer stars at the bar, in particular the handsome Irishman Charles Phillips. In the robing room of the Old Bailey one day, he told Phillips, "You remind me of three B's—Blarney, Bully, and Bluster." And Phillips replied to the irritable old man, "You never complained of my B's until they began to suck your honey." [10] To an aged colleague, Adolphus confided bluntly, "There was a time when you and I, Curwood, made a decent income out of this court until that Irish blackguard, with his plausible brogue and slimy manner, deluded people into trusting him." [11]

2. CHARLES PHILLIPS FOR THE DEFENSE

It was thus Charles Phillips who was selected to oppose Adolphus. Now the leader of the criminal bar, having wrested the eminence from Adolphus, at 53 Phillips was at the peak of his career.[12]

Despite the age gap of almost two decades, Phillips was called to the Irish bar but five years after Adolphus commenced practice in London. Irish advocacy of the day called for passion, wit, and bold invective, of which Phillips took careful note in a collection of *Specimens of Irish Eloquence* he edited at 32. A

---

8. W. Ballantine, *supra* note 7, at 57.

9. Robinson, *supra* note 7, at 66.

10. W. Ballantine, *supra* note 7, at 58.

11. Robinson, *supra* note 7, at 67.

12. On Phillips generally, 15 Dictionary of National Biography 1082–1083 (L. Stephen & S. Lee ed. 1917) [hereafter cited as D.N. B.]; W. Ballantine, *supra* note 7 at 31, 35, 56, 58–59, 60–64, 125–126; Robinson, *supra* note 7 at 37–38, 53–55, 57–65.

model for Phillips' later style is recorded there in John Philpot Curran's denunciation of O'Brien, the informer:

> Have you any doubt [Curran asked his jury] that it is the object of O'Brien to take down the prisoner for the reward that follows? Have you not seen with what more than instinctive keenness this blood-hound has pursued his victim? how he has kept him in view from place to place until he hunts him through the avenues of the court to where the unhappy man stands now, hopeless of all succour but that which your verdict shall afford? I have heard of assassination by sword, by pistol, and by dagger, but here is a wretch who would dip the evangelists in blood . . .[13]

Only five years after entering practice, Phillips had published a selection of his own speeches, displaying an especial gift for the vivid epithet—"human hyenas! ";[14] "a base, abandoned, profligate ruffian;"[15] "amid drunken pandars and corrupted slaves, debauching the innocence of village life . . ."[16]

He could also change pace, as in *Blake v. Wilkins*, defending "a wealthy dotard," the 65 year old widow Wilkins sued for £5,000 for breach of promise to marry young Lt. Blake of the royal navy, who

> could not resist his affection for a female he had never [seen]. Almighty love eclipsed the glories of ambition —Trafalgar and St. Vincent flitted from his memory— he gave up all for the woman, as Mark Antony did before him . . .. Like the maniac in the farce, he fell in love with the picture of his grandmother . . .. Does he claim on the ground of sacrificed affection? Oh, gentlemen, only fancy what he has lost—if it were but the blessed rapture of the bridal night! Do not suppose I am going to describe it . . . I shall not exhibit the venerable trembler—at once a relic and a relict; with a grace for every year and a Cupid in every wrinkle—affecting to

13. C. Phillips, Specimens of Irish Eloquence 125–126 (1819).

14. C. Phillips, Speeches 117 (1817).

15. *Id.* 150.

16. *Id.* 151.

shrink from the flame of his impatience, and fanning it with the ambrosial sigh of sixty-five! [17]

For a taste of more typical early Phillips, read aloud Phillips *on chastity:*

> Let foreign envy decry us as it will, CHASTITY IS THE INSTINCT OF THE IRISH FEMALE: the pride of her talents, the power of her beauty, the splendour of her accomplishments, are but so many handmaids of this vestal virtue; it adorns her in the court, it ennobles her in the cottage; whether she basks in prosperity or pines in sorrow, it clings about her like the diamond of the morning on the mountain floret, trembling even in the ray that at once exhibits and inhales it! [18]

Or Phillips *on adultery,* as counsel for the cuckolded husband in *Guthrie v. Sterne:*

> With the serpent's wile, and the serpent's wickedness, he stole into the Eden of domestic life poisoning all that was pure, polluting all that loverly, defying God, destroying man; a demon in the disguise of virtue, a herald of hell in the paradise of innocence. His name, gentlemen, is WILLIAM PETER BAKER DUNSTAN-VILLE STERNE: one would think he had epithets enough, without adding to them the title of *Adulterer.*[19]

There was a final note in *Guthrie v. Sterne,* a stereotype Phillips had developed for troubling the jury, leaving them uneasy about what they might decide:

> Gentlemen, my part is done; yours is about to commence . . . Oh, how awful is your responsibility! . . . I do conjure you, not as fathers, but as husbands;—not as husbands, but as citizens;—not as citizens, but as men;—not as men, but as Christians;— by all your obligations, public, private, moral, and religious; by the hearth profaned; by the home desolated; by the canons of the living God foully spurned;—save, oh! save your firesides from the contagion, your coun-

17. *Id.* 179–197.

18. *Id.* 153–154.

19. *Id.* 95–96.

try from the crime, and perhaps thousands, yet unborn, from the shame, and sin, and sorrow of this example! [20]

Detractors dubbed Phillips "Counselor O'Garnish," guilty of the ultimate in the English lexicon of forensic depravity—overstatement, "extravagant," even "horticultural," [21] winning verdicts by "fascination." [22]   One English barrister, in dubious compliment, professed to believe the speech of Dickens' Serjeant Buzfuz in *Bardell v. Pickwick* [23] "was largely indebted to the eloquence of Charles Phillips" in *Guthrie v. Sterne*. [24]   Friends conceded that his style "may be a novelty," [25] yet they were pridefully aware that Phillips combined in one charming package attributes certain to offend the Victorian establishment; he was Irish, Catholic, and successful.

Nine years after his debut in the Irish courts, Charles Phillips was called to the English bar, a barrister of 34, already famous. At the Old Bailey (the Central Criminal Court of London) he was soon crowding his seniors at the bar, among them Adolphus, despite a continued carping at Phillips' oratorical style.

3.   THE COURT AS COUNSEL FOR THE PRISONER

A few years earlier none of Charles Phillips rhetoric could have been available for the defense of Courvoisier, and Phillips himself had been among those trying to keep it unavailable. He had testified in futile protest against passage of the Prisoner's Counsel Bill, which after centuries of denial finally in 1836 gave an Englishman indicted for felony the right to a full defense by counsel, including the right to have his lawyer address the jury. Phillips had opposed the measure on the ground it would encourage passions and destroy the calm, judicious determination of guilt or innocence. He told a Select Committee considering the

---

20. *Id.* 114–116.

21. 15 D.N.B., *supra* note 12, at 1082; J. Hutchinson, Catalogue of notable Middle Templars 191 (1902); cf. "Eloquence of the Irish Bar," 3 The L. Magazine 303, 305–307 (1830).

22. C. Phillips, Speeches xii (1817).

23. 2 Dickens, Pickwick Papers, c. 6 page 90 (D. Lothrop ed. [188?]

24. 2 J. B. Atlay, The Victorian Chancellors 163, n. 3 (1906–1908); Holdsworth, Charles Dickens as a Legal Historian 68, n. (1928).

25. C. Phillips, Speeches xii (1817).

Bill that it would have a profound effect for the worse on the nature of a trial by jury:

> It will [he said] be a contest depending entirely on the Superior Talents of the Advocates employed. Your Lordships know that there is a great Variety of Talent at the Bar, and that there are Men who will be quite certain of so misleading a Jury, at least in comparison with others, as to get a Verdict, not by the Merits, but by their own Ingenuity.[26]

There would also be, he thought, a preliminary contest to obtain the best legal talent, and in that race he feared the Crown would have the advantage over the accused.

If the argument seemed in the slightest peculiar coming from Charles Phillips, it had as much to it as the rationalizations of the great Elizabethan lawyer and Lord Chief Justice Sir Edward Coke that had become the standard for almost 200 years. Coke had written that when a man's life was at stake (treason or felony), he ought not to be convicted without proof "so clear and manifest, as there can be no defence of it," [27] and that "the court ought to be in stead councell for the prisoner, to see that nothing is urged against him contrary to law and right." [28] Springing to the defense of "our common law" against what he took to be Jesuit slander, Coke said "the Judge ought to be for the King, and also for the party indifferent; and it is far better for the prisoner to have a Judges opinion for him, than many counsellors at the Bar; the Judges to have a special care . . . that justice be done to the party." [29]

These expressions of solicitude for the prisoner could not be squared with the policy in practice. The accused stood alone, a king-appointed counsel arguing his life away, with only a king-appointed judge to restrain excess. Coke knew the practice better than most. As Attorney General he had denounced a coun-

---

26. "Prisoners Defence Bill—Report from the Select Committee," 68 H.L.Jour., Appendix No. 4, pages 50, 51 (1836); see also "The Prisoners' Counsel Bill," 15 The L. Magazine 394, 402 (1836).

27. 3 Coke Inst. c. 2, page *29 (1797; 1st publ. 1644); accord, *id.* c. 63, page *137.

28. *Id.* c. 63, page *137.

29. Rex v. Thomas, 2 Buls. 147, 80 Eng.Rep. 1022 (1614).

selless Sir Walter Raleigh as "monster," [30] "viper," [31] "a spider of Hell," [32] prosecuted him to conviction of treason and sentence of death. Fourteen years later, the same Coke, as judge, faced down the still counsel-less Raleigh's complaint about the unfairness of his trial, and ordered the death sentence executed.[33]

Coke's dictum that *the court is counsel for the prisoner* left unexplained the enormity of a rule that denied counsel when a man's life was in jeopardy yet permitted him counsel in trials for the less serious crimes, the misdemeanors. It also left unexplained the apparent contradiction between a rule that denied counsel to the man *indicted* for felony, while permitting counsel when his life was equally in jeopardy in an old-style *appeal of felony.*

This last difficulty had been plausibly written off in the 16th century by the barrister Christopher St. Germain. He said that when the trial was by the old appeal of felony, prosecuted by the injured party or his family, it was "common presumption the appellant hath great malice against the appellee." "But when a man is indicted at the king's suit, the king intendeth nothing but justice .   ." [34]

St. Germain's stress on the difference between trial on indictment and by the older appeal of felony also gives us some clue as to why the accused was entitled to counsel in trials for misdemeanor. Misdemeanors had come into being as an indirect descendant of the old appeals, via the intermediate form of action *trespass.* Like the old appeal, trespass had always been thought of as a private lawsuit, whether it resulted in damages or punishment; both sides had lawyers. Accordingly, when trespass later gave rise to strictly civil lawsuits and to misdemeanors, the traditional right to counsel was preserved intact.

With the more serious offenses, trial after indictment gradually superseded the old appeal of felony, and here in the earliest days there was a serious impediment to having counsel for the prisoner. It was no longer a private legal battle, but a struggle

30. Rex v. Raleigh [1603], 2 How. St.Tr. 1, 7 (1816–1826).

31. *Id.* 10.

32. *Id.* 19.

33. *Id.* [1618] 34–35.

34. C. St. Germain, Doctor and Student, Dialogue II, c. 48, pages 258–259 (W. Muchall ed. 1874; 1st publ. 1523–1532) [hereafter cited as St. Germain].

between an individual and the king, a creature still not shorn of wisps of divinity, a powerful human overlord as well as an institutional embodiment of power. Who shall oppose him? There had been a time when an oath alone could settle a controversy, and then (*circa* 695) the laws of King Wihtred of Kent said "A bishop's or a king's word, [even] though unsupported by an oath, shall be incontrovertible." [35] The flavor lingered, and from the earliest days of trial for felony brought on by an indictment, a prosecution in the name of the king, the accused had no counsel. As prosecution of felony by way of indictment came to be the usual criminal proceeding, and the appeal of felony a rarity, one incidental practical result was that in most trials involving life and death the defendant could have no counsel, though for lesser offenses and for civil cases he could. For stealing 12 pence—no felony—you were entitled to counsel; for stealing 13 pence—felony—you could have no counsel and might be hanged. These anomalous results of forgotten or misunderstood history shocked even Blackstone. He thought the denial of counsel was "not all of a piece with the rest of the humane treatment of prisoners by the English law," adding that the rule was not "strictly speaking, a part of our ancient law." [36]

Apart from the rationalizations and accidents of history, there was a further, seldom articulated reason for the denial of counsel, i. e. fear. From the end of the 13th century on when prosecution under indictment was firmly established, it was felt more clearly than ever that the serious crimes—the treasons and the felonies—represented a threat to the state, which must be defeated at all cost, and that defense counsel was an obstacle. It is now a thing of pride to the Anglo-American legal system that as early as the 15th century a once Chief Justice of the King's Bench could write:

> I should, indeed, prefer twenty guilty men to escape death through mercy, than one innocent be condemned unjustly.[37]

---

35. Wihtred c. 16, in The Laws of the Earliest English Kings 27 (F. L. Attenborough ed. and transl. 1922).

36. 4 Blackstone, Commentaries *355–*356.

37. Fortescue, De Laudibus c. 28, page 65 (S. B. Chrimes ed. and transl. 1942; written c. 1460).

But in the warring, unsettled condition of the English state for centuries, the real fear is not Fortescue's that an innocent might hang, but that an evil person might just possibly escape. On trial under an indictment, the weight of the crown was in the balance against the accused, and, expressed or not, the presumption is not of innocence but of some sort of guilt. Counsel could be tolerated in trials for misdemeanors, since history supported it and the nature of the offense posed a less serious threat, though there were doubtless those in authority to whom defense counsel in any case was an unnecessary burden. Thus, the notorious Sir George Jeffreys, if the report may be trusted, addressed himself to counsel for Richard Baxter, a theologian on trial in 1685 for the misdemeanor seditious libel:

> Mr. Wallop, (says the lord chief justice) I observe you are in all these dirty causes; and were it not for you gentlemen of the long robe, who should have more wit and honesty than to support and hold up these factious knaves by the chin, we should not be at the pass we are at.[38]

In any event, when it came to treason and felony, too much was at stake to think of changing a rule, convenient to the state, that it alone should have counsel.

The role of the prosecutor and of many judges was not to see justice done to an accused without counsel, but to serve a master. At his treason trial, when Sir Walter Raleigh looked to the court to rescue him from Attorney General Coke's abuse, the Chief Justice told him, "Mr. Attorney speaketh out of zeal of his duty for the service of the king . . ." [39] And when Lord Cecil tried to cool the prosecutor's venom, Coke replied:

> If I may not be patiently heard, you will encourage Traitors, and discourage us. I am the king's sworn servant, and must speak! If he be guilty, he is a Traitor; if not deliver him.

---

38. Rex v. Baxter [1685], 11 How. St.Tr. 493, 498–499 (1816–1826). But see 2 J. F. Stephen, History of the Criminal Law of England 314 (1883).

39. Rex v. Raleigh [1603], 2 How. St.Tr. 1, 10 (1816–1826).

At which point, the reporter noted:

> Here Mr. Attorney sat down in a chafe, and would speak no
> more, until the Commissioners urged and entreated him.
> After much ado, he went on . . . .[40]

Officialdom took the position, not unheard of today, that a
man indicted was undoubtedly guilty; respectable people aren't
indicted. The King's Attorney-General for Ireland, writing in
1615, made it explicit in a rare statement, a personal opinion as
candid as it is careless of fact:

> And as our Judges do discountenance bad Counsellours, so
> doth our Law abhor the defence and maintenance of bad
> Causes, more than any other Law in the world besides . .
> And this is one cause, among others, why our Law doth
> not allow Counsel unto such as are indicted of Treason,
> Murther, Rape, or other capital crimes. So as never any
> Professour of the Law [i. e. lawyer] of *England* hath been
> known to defend (for the matter of fact) any Traitour,
> Murtherer, Ravisher, or Thief, being indicted and prose-
> cuted at the Suit of the King . . . And therefore it is
> an honour unto our Law, that it doth not suffer the Profes-
> sors thereof to dishonor themselves (as Advocates and Ora-
> tors in other Countries do) by defending such Offendours.[41]

There were always those who sensed a flaw in this reasoning,
believing that justice for a man accused meant something more
than "Give him a fair trial and hang him!" As early as the
13th century, the *Mirror of Justices,* reflecting not fact (as
Blackstone seemed to think) [42] but criticism of the law, pointed
out that counsel were necessary in civil cases "and more necessary are they for defense upon indictments and appeals of
felony." [43] In the 17th century, an anonymous "barrester, who
partly through sickness, and partly for conscience, deserted the
profession of our laws, as epidemically evil . . ." suggested as
a cure for one of the "notorious errors and abuses" of the law,

---

40. *Id.* 26.

41. "A Preface Dedicatory" 19, in
J. Davies, A Report of Cases and
Matters (1762; 1st publ. 1615).

42. 4 Blackstone, Commentaries
*355.

43. Mirror of Justices, c. 3, § 1
[13th c. ?], as quoted and cited in
4 Blackstone, Commentaries *355;
cf. Mirror of Justices, Book III, c.
I, in 7 Selden Society 80 (W. J.
Whittaker ed. 1895).

"That persons, accused for life, be permitted council, in regard their fears render them often speechless and unadvised; bare accusations are not sufficient condemnations, as to deprive any (though innocent) of council in such extremity." [44]   Any defendant soon became painfully aware that *the court is counsel for the prisoner* was a catchphrase that could not be depended on. As one accused observed to a judge questioning a witness in a way that was pointing to guilt, "Alas, my lord, if you were my counsel, you would not ask that question." [45]

The unfairness of denial of counsel was most sharply revealed during times of domestic upheaval, and especially in the spate of treason trials that accompanied the successive "revolutions" in England.   No "counsel" meant no trial lawyer, but an Englishman was still entitled to his law, and as Coke himself had said ".   .   . any learned man that is present may inform the court for the benefit of the prisoner, of any thing that may make the proceedings erroneous." [46]   A court might, if it were so minded, permit a prisoner to have a lawyer advise him in advance on how to conduct his own defense.   This was a day, however, when an accused was not given a copy of his indictment, nor told who would be witnesses against him, so it was a matter of some difficulty to get real help from a lawyer before the trial. Stephen Colledge had special difficulties placed in his way.   He had been given leave to have help from lawyers before trial, but on the way to court, his jailers seized his notes; these were made available to counsel for the crown, who tailored their case accordingly.[47]

A court might also permit a lawyer to argue a point of law for the prisoner, but there was a catch to it.   A prisoner, ignorant of the law, must first identify the point of law he wanted argued.   If the prisoner overcame that obstacle, a court less than dispassionate might decide the point wasn't worth arguing after all.   That was what happened to Colonel Algernon Sidney who pleaded with the Lord Chief Justice (history's "Bloody" Jeffreys) that he needed counsel because he was too ignorant "to

44. *The Law's Discovery* [1653], in 6   Harleian   Miscellany   322–324 (1810).

45. Rex   v.   Don   Pantaleon   Sa [1654], 5 How.St.Tr. 462, 466 n. (1816–1826).

46. 3 Coke Inst. c. 2, page *29; *accord, id.* c. 63, page *137.

47. Rex v. Colledge [1681], 8 How. St.Tr. 549 (1816–1826).

raise a point of law." Denied counsel, he argued on his own, each point rejected by Jeffreys, one a "point of fact" not law, another not even "a question. You had as good ask me, whether the first chapter in Littleton be law." In long harangues, first the prosecutor, then the judge belabored Sidney for his ignorance, Jeffreys telling the jury that "Mr. Sidney is mightily mistaken in the law . . ." [48] Still no counsel.

For Jeffreys this was more than temperate. One accused he addressed as "an old rogue, a schismatic knave, a hypocritical villain;" [49] a witness he denounced as an "impudent rascal," a "blockhead;" [50] and to poor Lady Alice Lisle, accused of treason, who said she did not suspect that the man she took into her home was in the army, "being a Presbyterian minister, that need to preach, and not to fight," Jeffreys replied, "But I will tell you, there is not one of those lying, sniveling, canting Presbyterian rascals, but one way or other had a hand in the late horrid conspiracy and rebellion . . ." [51] That much Colonel Sidney was spared; he was convicted of treason and beheaded on December 7, 1683. With a change of administration, Sidney was given posthumous vindication. [52]

From the grave, Algernon Sidney's protest against the unfairness of his trial, written just before his execution, charged his prosecutor with having had "so much confidence and so little charity, as openly to avow, that I should not have counsel, lest they should furnish or teach me the points of law that I might insist upon." He had been victimized, he shouted to posterity, "merely from my own ignorance in the law, and want of counsel, which if I had had, the court could not have imposed so notorious a fraud upon me . . ." [53] Others added their voices to the growing demand for change; even Sidney's nemesis the irrepressible Jeffreys commented:

> I think it is a hard case, that a man should have counsel to
> defend himself for a two-penny trespass, and his witnesses

---

48. Rex v. Sidney [1683], 9 *Id.* 813, 834–836, 862, 867, 877, 879, 880, 892.

49. 2 Campbell, Lives of the Chief Justices 327 (6 vol. ed. with J. Arnould 1881), citing "10 St.Tr. 1315, Life of Baxter, ch. iv;" cf. Rex v. Baxter [1685], 11 How.St.Tr. 494, 497 n. (1816–1826).

50. Rex v. Lisle (Lady) [1685], 11 How.St.Tr. 297, 336–337 (1816–1826).

51. *Id.* 359.

52. Rex v. Sidney [1683], 9 *Id.* 817, 996.

53. *Id.* 916, 921.

examined upon oath; but if he steal, commit murder or felony, nay, high-treason, when life, estate, honour and all are concerned, he shall neither have counsel nor his witnesses examined upon oath: But yet . . . the practice of the law is so; and the practice is the law.[54]

As the lawyer, judge, historian Sir James Fitzjames Stephen was to write years later:

What the political trials of the 17th century really did was to expose men of high rank and conspicuous position to the calamities which must have been felt by thousands of obscure criminals without attracting even a passing notice.[55]

4.   CHANGE: COUNSEL   IN   TREASON   TRIALS

Twelve years after Algernon Sidney was beheaded the law was changed (1695, effective the next year).[56]   The conscience of the men of parliament had been moved: they gave the accused a right to a full defense by counsel, to have counsel assigned if that was requested, to have a copy of the indictment five days before trial, and to have witnesses for the defense give their testimony under oath.   But the limits of the reform of 1695 are remarkable.   The new grant of rights applied only to those indicted for high treason, and not to all high treason at that.   This was just possibly the give away: the Treason Act of 1695 did not apply to counterfeiting, high treason at the time but like stealing and throatcutting hardly a crime for a gentleman.   Old fashioned treason on the other hand was an aristocratic crime. After all, an earlier Lord William Russell (of the same family as the man Courvoisier was accused of killing) had himself been convicted of treason and executed, though with a change of government, he like Algernon Sidney had been posthumously rehabilitated.[57]   In the rapid changes taking place in England, today's solid citizen was tomorrow's traitor, and the wheel might turn again;   those who were losing their heads were not raga-

---

54. Rex v. Rosewell [1684], 10 *Id.* 147, 267; see also B. Shower, *Reasons for a new Bill of Rights,* in 10 Somers, A Collection of Scarce And Valuable Tracts 568, 570 (2d ed. Walter Scott rev. 1809–1815; 1st ed. 1748–1751).

55. 1 J. F. Stephen, History of the Criminal Law of England 402 (1883).

56. 7 William III, c. 3., § 1.

57. Rex v. Russell (Lord) [1683], 9 How.St.Tr. 577 (1816–1826).

muffins. It could happen to me. That far only the conscience of parliament was moved. In the course of the next century other treason acts gave an accused the right to lists of prosecution witnesses and prospective jurors, to have a copy of the indictment 10 days before trial,[58] and to have counsel in trials by impeachment.[59]

When Francis Bacon wrote, he, with Coke, could at least find pattern in the law: "In felony, no counsel is to be allowed to the party, no more than in treason." [60] With counsel now allowed in treason cases (and in the rare appeals of felony) was it still possible to justify denial of counsel to those indicted for felony? William Hawkins tried it in his celebrated *Pleas of the Crown,* published in the first quarter of the 18th century. Himself a lawyer, Hawkins modestly professed to believe it was not an advantage to an indicted defendant to have a lawyer. "[I]t requires no manner of skill," he wrote, "to make a plain and honest defence, which in cases of this kind is always the best; the simplicity and innocence, artless and ingenuous behavior of one whose conscience acquits him, having something in it more moving and convincing than the highest eloquence of persons speaking in a cause not their own." Since the judge would be impartial, "the innocent, for whose safety alone the law is concerned, have rather an advantage than prejudice in having the court their only counsel." For the guilty, it was just as well that their manner "may often help to disclose the truth, which probably would not so well be discovered from the artificial defence of others speaking for them." [61] Despite these benefits to defendant and to the cause of justice of the system of no counsel, Hawkins concluded that the law had reason to allow counsel where the law allowed counsel. Since appeals of felony were motivated by "a desire for private revenge," the accused should have the same unspecified "advantage in them as in common actions." [62] In high treason, "generally managed for the crown with greater skill and zeal than ordinary prosecutions," it had

58. 7 Anne c. 21, § 11 (1708).

59. 20 George II. c. 30. (1746).

60. F. Bacon, *A Preparation toward the Union of the Laws of England and Scotland,* in 5 Works 83, 97 (B. Montagu ed. 1825–1834).

61. 2 W. Hawkins, Pleas of the Crown c. 39, §§ 1, 2, page 564 (6th ed. T. Leach ed. 1787; 1st publ. 1716–1721).

62. *Id.* c. 39, § 3, page 565.

been found that the prisoner experienced great unspecified "disadvantages from want of counsel." [63] He preferred not to dwell on the details. Whatever the rationalizations, the split system persisted for another 150 years. It could not help but be observed that one consequence was that a wealthy man's crime meant a lawyer and a poor man's crime meant none. "Gentlemen are rarely hung. If they were so, there would be petitions without end for counsel." [64]

5. CHANGE: THE PRISONERS' COUNSEL BILL

In the course of the 18th century political life in England became more stable, the judges independent, the courts liberal in permitting counsel to assist the man accused of felony. Counsel were questioning witnesses, were even writing speeches for the defendant to read to the jury; they might not fit all the turns of evidence, but it was often better than stumbling by yourself. The crown still clung to its advantage; the prosecutor spoke to the jury; prisoner's counsel could not.

Early in the next century efforts increased to change the rule. Repeatedly bills were introduced and hotly debated in parliament.[65] In the independent United States, even in the British West Indies, lawyers addressed the jury. Climax came in July, 1836, with debate impending in the House of Lords on a Prisoners' Counsel Bill already approved by the Commons. *The Times'* leading article was confident of passage:

> Most men, of whatever party, are agreed that prisoners should be allowed counsel, and that the shocking anomalies

63. *Id.* c. 39, § 10, page 566.

64. S. Smith, *Counsel for Prisoners* [1826], in 2 Works 200, 232 (2d ed. 1840); see also, speech of Sir James Mackintosh, 11 Parl.Deb., H.C. (New Series) 199 (April 6, 1824), and 1 J. F. Stephen, A History of the Criminal Law of England 226 (1883).

65. 11 Parl.Deb., H.C. (New Series) 180–220 (April 6, 1824); 15 *id.* 589–633 (April 25, 1826); 28 *id.* (3d ser.) 628–633 (June 10, 1835); *id.* 865–873 (June 17, 1835); 29 *id.* 355–365 (July 9, 1835); 31 *id.* 225–226 (Feb. 9, 1836); *id.* 497–501 (Feb. 17, 1836); 91 H.C.Jour. 55 (Feb. 18, 1836); 31 Parl.Deb.H.C. (3d ser.) 1142–1161, and especially 1150–1152 (Mar. 2, 1836); 34 Parl. Deb.H.L. (3d ser.) 760–778 (June 23, 1836); *id.* 1061 (June 30, 1836); 35 *id.* 171–186 (July 14, 1836); *id.* 228–232 (July 15, 1836); *id.* 249–250 (July 18, 1836); 34 Parl.Deb. H.C. (3d ser.) 599–603 (July 27, 1836); *id.* 612–613 (July 28, 1836); *id.* 1210–1211 (Aug. 12, 1836); 34 Parl.Deb.H.L. (3d ser.) 1247–1249 (Aug. 16, 1836); 34 Parl.Deb.H.C. (3d ser.) 1323–1325 (Aug. 19, 1836).

that now exist . . . should be removed . . . . [W]e must be allowed to believe that successful opposition to the bill is impossible, because it cannot be other than discreditable to the House.[66]

Three days later Lord Wharncliffe led the debate against the bill. As *The Times* faithfully reported:

[H]e trusted, although out of doors it had been stated it would be most discreditable to that house if they refused to pass this bill at the present moment, their lordships would not be intimidated from rejecting a measure which would, in his opinion, prove detrimental to those institutions of the country in which the lives and liberties of their fellow subjects were most intimately involved.

The bill was, he said, "entirely uncalled for." The ". . . effect likely to be produced by the skill and eloquence of counsel directed to influence the jury in favour of the prisoner . . ." would not be ". . . that the criminal would with more certainty be found guilty," but ". . . would have the effect of increasing that uncertainty upon which professed rogues were accustomed to calculate . . . Judging from the practice already in force with respect to misdemeanours where counsel were allowed," he thought that "if it were extended to felonies, the chances of wrong verdicts would by no means be lessened." With treason, on the other hand, ". . . to any one at all acquainted with the history of the country and the usual course of procedure," it ". . . must be at once apparent . . ." that there was good reason to allow counsel, copy of the indictment, and the names of prosecution witnesses. "[B]ecause charges of treason could so easily be converted into oppression from political motives . . . the policy had been wisely to surround the accused with every possible facility for making out a complete defense." Finally, he warned, if counsel were to have a last word for the prisoner, ". . . the judge, in summing up would most painfully be called upon in many instances to answer the speech of his advocate, and direct the jury to send the prisoner from the bar to the scaffold." [67]

Wharncliffe was immediately answered by Lord Lyndhurst (born in Boston, Massachusetts) a former solicitor general and

---

66. The Times (London), July 11, 1836, page 4, col. 4.

67. 35 Parl.Deb.H.L. (3d ser.) 171–174 (July 14, 1836).

attorney general, twice Lord Chancellor of England. Ten years earlier he had opposed a similar bill,[68] had since been persuaded into eloquent support. Of Wharncliffe's fears that a lawyer's speech to the jury would pervert the even course of criminal justice, Lyndhurst thought it "a most extraordinary proposition to maintain that the only cases in which zeal, in which eloquence, in which powerful reasoning should not be made use of were those where the liberties and lives of our fellow-creatures were at stake." This brought from the lords the first of a series of "Hear, hear's" that punctuated his argument for the bill.

If, Lyndhurst continued, the rule was as Coke had stated it, that no one was to be convicted of felony unless the case was so clear as to be unanswerable,

> . . he for one should not feel apprehensive of any effects that could be produced by the eloquence or impassioned zeal of counsel in the due administration of justice. But if another rule were to be adopted which he had sometimes seen attempted to be enforced, that parties on trial for their lives were to be found guilty on a bare balance of evidence, on plausible subtleties, on slight presumptions as to facts, or minute details of evidence, depending on the character of those who gave it, he did hope the eloquence and arguments of counsel in cases of that description would prevail, because in such cases every man must feel they ought to prevail. (Hear, hear.)

As Lord Lyndhurst saw it, "the evils of the present system could not well be exaggerated." He asked the lords to picture the aged and infirm (as was Lord Lovat when convicted of treason), the foreigner ignorant of language and procedure, even the deaf and dumb, all alike denied counsel to speak for them. "Could anything," he asked, "be more monstrous and cruel? (Hear, hear). This case might appear extravagant and absurd in terms, but he had seen instances substantially to bear out the description. (Hear, hear.) Yet such was the system which his noble friend eulogized, and which must revolt every man of plain and ordinary understanding who for a moment contemplated it." If counsel could write out a hypothetical speech for the accused to read, ". . . why not allow a defence to be addressed to

---

68. See 34 *id.* 770–771 (June 23, 1836).

the jury, founded on the actual facts placed before the jury?
(Hear, hear.)"

> What [he asked the lords] was the first principle of
> justice? That no man should be condemned without
> being heard in his own defence. How were we to inter-
> pret that? Narrowly, according to the letter, or
> largely and liberally, as every proposition in morals
> ought to be expounded? Did it mean that after a trial
> of ten hours, an ignorant man should be allowed to
> stand up and submit his comments to the attention of
> the jury? Would that be hearing him in his defence?
> No, that would not satisfy the rule of justice. The rule
> of justice meant this—that for everything which could
> fairly and properly be urged in the prisoner's defence
> there should be the opportunity of urging it on the at-
> tention of the jury before he was pronounced guilty of
> the crime laid to his charge. (Hear, hear.)

He called upon "their lordships, as the hereditary judges of
the land," upon "the right rev. prelates . . . whose minds
must be deeply imbued with the principles of justice, to wipe out
this stain—the relict of a barbarous age . . ." [69]

The fine speech left the Earl of Devon unconvinced. "[H]e
thought that the new system would enable counsel to instil so
many doubts into the minds of a jury as would induce them to
give the prisoner the benefits of those doubts and so acquit him,
where a verdict of a directly opposite nature would best satisfy
the justice of the case." [70]

Those very doubts that troubled the Earl of Devon convinced
the Duke of Richmond. Echoing Fortescue, he replied "he
thought it better that a guilty person should escape than that an
innocent person should be convicted." [71]

In a house generally favorable, some damning support to convince waverers came from the great advocate James Scarlett,
become the Chief Baron of the Court of Exchequer, Lord Abinger. His doubts had been resolved in favor of the bill by something said in the House of Commons debate two years before.

---

69. 35 *id.* 174–179, and see 180–181,
182, 185 (July 14, 1836).

70. *Id.* 184.

71. *Id.* 184–185.

It was then stated [he recalled] that allowing prisoners to defend themselves by counsel would not tend
to facilitate convictions. To that statement it was replied that, when it was considered that the counsel who
defended prisoners were generally young men not of
much experience, the tendency of the bill would, in all
probability, be to facilitate convictions. It was likewise
stated that the object of the bill was not that the prisoner should be acquitted, but that the truth should be
investigated. That argument had produced a powerful
effect on his mind; for he thought that truth would be
better investigated, and that justice would be done
more efficiently between the prisoner and the country,
if a free discussion of the charge were had on both
sides. . . . from no inconsiderable experience [he]
considered the practical effect of the present system to
be . . . that it was favourable to the acquittal of
the prisoner. . . . He did not expect that if this bill
passed it would greatly lengthen the time of our assizes
and sessions. Many prisoners would still remain without counsel to defend them, for they would not have
funds to procure such assistance; and in cases where
the prisoner's guilt was clearly proved, no counsel of
the least discretion would think of addressing the jury
to assert his innocence. . . . He had no hesitation
in declaring it to be his opinion that in a majority of
cases, in which counsel were employed for the prisoner,
they would be of the greatest utility to the judge and
the jury.[72]

The last substantial speech of the debate was less embarrassing to the bill's supporters. The Lord Chancellor gave it his
"cordial support:"

He was glad that in the course of this debate they had
at last got rid of the fiction so contrary to fact, 'that
the judge was counsel for the prisoner'—counsel for
the prisoner, without having any communication with
his client, and without having the slightest previous
knowledge of what it was for the interest of his
client to prove. (Hear, hear.) He would not enter

<hr>

72. *Id.* 182–184.

into any details to prove the propriety of their lordships assenting to this bill.　He would merely remind
them of the fact which struck even the most unobser-
vant with surprise.　In cases which involved a man's
property the courts of law heard both sides; but in
cases which involved a man's life, they heard only one
side.[73]

Final passage of the Prisoners' Counsel Bill came on July 18,
1836.[74]　Four years later, it could have been no surprise to anyone, least of all to Charles Phillips, that he was briefed to defend
Courvoisier.　The English "brief" prepared by the solicitor in-
cludes, in a bundle of papers bound with a red ribbon, all of the
known evidence, the expected testimony of witnesses, the defen-
ses the barrister is "instructed" to rely upon—in this case that
Courvoisier was innocent.

Phillips was later to say that he believed from the beginning
that Courvoisier was innocent.[75]　Just why is not completely
clear.　So far as we know, he never saw his client before the day
of trial.　Phillips knew what all of London knew, that while
crying Courvoisier's guilt the press continued to report his own
insistence that he was innocent.　If the public was pretty certain
that Courvoisier did it, there was still not the public rage
against the accused that accompanied some other British trials
of the century.　Not the excited prejudice stirred up against the
Mannings accused of the Bermondsey murder,[76] nor the hostility
that dogged Mr. Palmer, the Rugely poisoner—so thoroughly
convicted before trial that a special act was rushed through parliament to permit the trial to be transferred to London.[77]　In
Courvoisier's case, the papers still expressed concern that the
police work was not complete—no silverware, no weapon.　Two
weeks before the trial, "A Frequent Reader" wrote *The Times*
suggesting that all of the feather beds, mattresses, and pillows
be opened, that the tops and backs of bedsteads, and all hearths

73.　*Id.* 185–186.

74.　6 & 7 William IV, c. 114, § 1.
But see *supra* note 65.

75.　Correspondence Between Samuel Warren, Esq., Barrister-at-Law
and Charles Phillips, Esq., Relative
to the Trial of Courvoisier 11

(1849) [hereafter cited as Warren-
Phillips].

76.　The Times (London), Oct. 27,
1849, page 5.

77.　The Queen v. Palmer 307 and
174 (1856).

in the house be taken up to find the murder weapon. The letter suggested that the "villain" might have used one of Lord Russell's own razors and hid it on the premises, "unless there was an accomplice."

Above all—no eyewitnesses. It was precisely the sort of case Lord Lyndhurst had mentioned in one of the debates on the Prisoners' Counsel Bill where counsel was of "utmost importance," "murder depending upon circumstantial evidence," where anyone, even a judge, might omit some important detail, where counsel with his detailed study of the case could point the way through what ". . . was very often a labyrinth to a person who had not known anything of the case before."

From an advocate's viewpoint, the case was not hopeless. Suspicion of murder, but murder meant hanging, and suspicion wasn't conviction. Stronger suspicion of thievery, but that (in 19th century England) could mean not hanging, but "transportation" to Norfolk Island, a dismal isolated dot in the South Pacific off the coast of New South Wales; besides, for the present at least the charge was not theft but murder.

Whether or not Charles Phillips knew it at the time, we now know how his adversary John Adolphus felt about the case against Courvoisier only 10 days before trial. He wrote in his diary:

> "I have not the slightest doubt of the wretch's guilt, but many are of opinion that a jury will not convict on circumstantial evidence, and I am far from being sure they are mistaken." [78]

78. Henderson, *supra* note 7, at 204.

Chapter IV

TRIAL: OPENING DAY

Thursday, June 18, 1840 was not a good day to be brought to trial for the murder of Lord William Russell. A week before, the young Queen Victoria, four months a bride, had been fired on while driving through Hyde Park with Prince Albert. The same grand jury that indicted Courvoisier for murder indicted Edward Oxford for treason "in attempting the life of Her Majesty." [1] Ultimately Oxford was found insane, fitter for Bedlam than the gallows, but as Courvoisier's trial began, Oxford was yet to be tried, and London was jittery. On the morning of Courvoisier's trial, a false rumor spread of another attempted assassination of the Queen. Inevitably, the theme of innocent nobility under murderous attack would pervade the courtroom, bringing comparison between the crimes charged to Oxford and to Courvoisier. In addition, as Mr. Adolphus was to remind the jury in discussing the theft of Lord Russell's Waterloo medal, June 18th was the anniversary of the Battle of Waterloo. The auguries were poor for a foreigner bearing the name François Courvoisier.

A trial, "the play at the Old Bailey" Charles Dickens called it,[2] was good Victorian theatre. Courvoisier's trial competed for attention with a bill of over 200 others charged with every variety of criminal performance. It outdrew standard music hall entertainment, such as the favorite *Jack Sheppard,* the singing-talking stage adaptation of the life of the criminal folk hero, who in the previous century had twice escaped from Newgate prison, where Courvoisier was spending his days and nights.[3] The impending trial, being for murder, was most titillating; for a guilty prisoner only one sentence was possible, death by hanging, in 1840 a public hanging just outside the walls of Newgate. For this trial, the facts were already so notorious, the associations of the murdered man so high in a stratified society, everyone who could came—to witness the last moments of the chase, to see if there might be any other final scene than death.

1. See The Times (London), June 16, 1840.

2. Dickens, A Tale of Two Cities, bk. 2, ch. 2, page 67 (188?).

3. On Jack Sheppard generally, see H. W. Bleackley, Jack Sheppard (1933).

Anticipating the demands for admission, the Sheriff closed off the main door of the Old Bailey to make more seating space in the courtroom, on benches covered with green baize. Extra chairs for nobility and gentlefolk were placed alongside the judges' seats; extra chairs even on the raised and railed area opposite the bench, a feature of the British criminal court, the *dock*, usually reserved exclusively for the prisoner and his guards. By 8 o'clock in the morning "privileged persons" were already being admitted by ticket, the streets crowded with hopefuls beyond the capacity of the courtroom. As a young lawyer would recall it years later:

> "The occasion might, from the appearance the Old Bailey presented have been thought one of the most festive character. The court was crowded with ladies dressed to the eyes, and furnished with lorgnettes, fans and bouquets; the sheriffs and under-sheriffs, excited and perspiring, were rushing here and there, offering them what they deemed to be delicate attentions. A royal duke honoured the exhibition with his presence, and, upon the occasion of a witness giving a particular answer to a question from counsel, showed his approval by an ejaculation of 'Hear, hear!'." [4]

The "royal duke" was Adolphus' friend, the Duke of Sussex; he was given the seat of honor, the center chair on the bench. There were other lords and ladies in pairs and squads, the Dutch and Portuguese ambassadors, Lady Julia Lockwood, the former employer of Courvoisier.

Two hours later, with the courtroom filled, Courvoisier was led up into the dock, appearing to one observer "sullen and indifferent," to another attentive and without "the slightest fear as to the result of the trial . . ." Counsel present, Courvoisier was formally arraigned for the murder of "William Russell, Esquire, commonly called Lord William Russell." The reporter who saw a "sullen" Courvoisier now heard a "feeble" voice deny the charge; the reporter who saw Courvoisier without "fear" heard a "firm" plea of "Not guilty!" Offered the right to be tried by a jury of Englishmen or one half of foreigners (an option established by William the Conqueror to insure survival of

4. Ballantine, *supra* ch. III, note 7, at 60.

a Norman minority), Courvoisier chose a jury of Englishmen. The jury having been sworn without objection, the setting needed only the judges. There would be two, the Lord Chief Justice Nicholas Tindal presiding, actively assisted by Sir James Parke, Baron of the Court of Exchequer, referred to as Mr. Baron Parke. The judges now entered the courtroom and squeezed between elegantly billowing skirts to their cramped seats on the bench. The young lawyer noted that "Sir Nicholas Tindal, the presiding judge, was so hemmed in by the extensive draperies of the surrounding ladies that he had scarcely room to move, and looked   disgusted   at   the   indecency   of   the   spectacle . . . ." [5]

The Lord Chief Justice turned his eyes to the courtroom. The room became quiet. John Adolphus rose and began his prosecutor's opening speech to the jury:

> "If I had never read anything during the last five weeks concerning the very extraordinary transaction which is now the subject of inquiry," he told the 12 men, "the state of the court at the moment, crowded as it is by illustrious, noble, and dignified persons, would make me understand that a trial of the utmost public interest and importance is about to be entered on. In adverting to what has been so much discussed in public, I do so for the purpose of giving that caution which is usual on such occasions, that whatever you might have read—and, living and moving in this great world, you must have read a great deal—upon the subject of this most extraordinary murder, you should dismiss from your minds, whether it bears one way or another, attending only to the evidence which might be adduced, and to the directions of the learned judge in summing up. By this alone can you elicit the truth in a calm and dispassionate manner, as becomes a British jury.
>
> "That the present is an extraordinary case no one can doubt, both on account of the dignity and position in life of the unfortunate victim of some one, and from the important place his family occupies in the annals of this country. Without going back to remote periods of

5. *Id.* 61.

history with which the name of Russell is connected, I
will only mention that it is most extraordinary, with
respect to a family so distinguished by rank, renown,
and riches, that in the course of two generations there
have occurred two dreadful instances of a sudden de-
parture from this world in a manner most awful. The
Marquis of Tavistock, the father of Lord William Russell, who has experienced so melancholy a death, and
Francis Duke of Bedford, successor to John Duke of
Bedford, who led a life which entitled him to the splendid eulogy of Fox after his decease—these two noblemen died, not by the murderer's hand, but in a sudden
and awful manner, whilst in the honest pursuit of liberal occupations [Ed.—the Marquis fell from a horse
while hunting; the Duke died on the tennis court].
But the unfortunate nobleman whose death you have
now to inquire into, having gone to bed in his usual
state of health and spirits, was found the next morning
a lifeless corpse, his head being nearly severed from his
body, and it is for you to determine who the murderer
might be."

"Extraordinary," "most extraordinary," "remarkable," "curious," a refrain of the bizarre, the prosecutor offered up each
anticipated morsel of testimony with a full range of mellifluent
Victorian rhetoric. To the macabre tautology of his "lifeless
corpse," he soberly added: "Into that room his Lordship then
retired for the last time, and placed his cheek upon the pillow—
never to raise it again a living man. The morning's sun beheld
his Lordship, mangled and a corpse." By turn Mr. Adolphus
could be delicately vivid—burglars could not have entered over
the backyard walls of the Russell home, where the undisturbed
dust lay so thick "Even a cat's foot would have left a mark; " or
euphemistically vague—the death of Romilly "who terminated
his existence by an act of suicide." Meticulously, he added each
"damning fact" of the case made of circumstance that continued
to trouble him, aware, as he confessed to the jury, that " 'If any
one link be defective, the strength of the whole chain fails
. . .' " He also reminded them, over Mr. Phillips' objection, that Chief Baron Macdonald once told a murder jury that
unlike a case of direct evidence from a few witnesses the very
number of links to a circumstantial case made it ". . .

impossible for a variety of witnesses, speaking to a variety of
circumstances, so to concert a story as to impose upon the jury
by fabrication   .   .   . ; " if a witness' story was consistent
with itself and with the testimony of others, it might be that
circumstantial evidence would "bring conviction to your minds"
"more satisfactory than direct evidence."

Adolphus thought it "most extraordinary" that valuable articles had been left behind; no "common thief" would have been
so remiss. It was, ".   .   .   in my mind, a proof that the
burglary was not real but simulated." The valuables that had
been recovered came from the pantry, "the prisoner's own peculiar room." The marks of "this simulated burglary," the whole
scheme, "If I am correct in attributing the guilt of this murder
to the prisoner, it would of course be his plan to create an impression that a robbery had been committed by some person not
in the house."

Lord Russell's night light had burned only an hour and a half;
the "wax candle was burnt down to the socket. What then was
the inference? That the rushlight had been put out either before or after the perpetration of the murder, and that the wax
candle was lighted to enable the prisioner to go over the house
and place things in such a position as to favour the opinion that
his Lordship had been reading in bed," though it was not his
habit to do so and the light too distant for reading. "This," said
Mr. Adolphus, "is one of those circumstances by which over-cun-
ning deceives itself, and which betrays those who only seek to
deceive others."

From circumstance, he passed to shoring up other weakness in
the prosecution case and to anticipated attack by the defense.

Adolphus assured the jury he believed the character of his
witnesses Sarah Mancer and Mary Hannell to be "unexception-
able," coupling this with a measured commendation of Courvoisier:

> "Perhaps I might save my learned friends some trouble
> by stating (what it is only justice to the prisoner to
> state, and God forbid that I should withhold that jus-
> tice from the prisoner), that Courvoisier came to his
> Lordship's service not only with an unexceptionable,
> but with an honourable character, from persons of

wealth and distinction, who would not have given it unless he had deserved it　.　.　. I only state the
fact, that up to the time of the crime with which the
prisoner now stands charged I have never heard of any
blemish on his character."

From reading the newspapers, Adolphus said, he could foresee
the charge being made that Miss Mancer "is unworthy of credit."
(He was referring to a reported discharge of Mancer from an
earlier employment with imputations against her honesty, a report *The Times* had taken pains to deny three days before the
trial.)　He answered in advance, ".　.　. I will say this,
that her character is unblemished in every particular."

Phillips objected to these remarks; no witness' character had
been attacked, ".　.　. and, I hope," he added, "newspaper
announcements will not be taken to prejudice the prisoner in
any way."

Permitted by the Chief Justice to discuss the point "hypothet-
ically," Adolphus went on to say that if Miss Mancer's character were questioned, he hoped the jury would not be influenced
".　.　. by any mere declamation or the use of hard terms
and bad names. I challenge, I dare, I defy my learned friends,
to impeach her testimony on the ground of character."

All of this was by way of prelude to his saying something
about an embarrassment—the police. Adolphus anticipated that
"[a] similar attack might perhaps be made on" them. "It may
be said their exertions have been stimulated by a very large reward." It was unthinkable that the lure of £400.0.0 split many
ways could produce "a conspiracy to take away the character
and life of an unoffending man whom they never saw," any
more than it was possible that the cook and maid would falisfy
"to convict of murder a fellow-servant with whom they had never quarreled."

It was the best he could say for the police. He confided to the
jury his professional distaste for the way they had done their
work. "[H]ad I been present, I think I should have advised
them" to take Courvoisier into custody at once. Adolphus still
had to say something about the police search of Courvoisier's
trunk and box; the papers had been full of it, bloody gloves and
all. At best, it had been bungled; it had to be faced; Adolphus
did it boldly; it would be no part of the prosecution case. He

told how in the early search of Courvoisier's room, the police
"found nothing in it material to this inquiry."

> "I see," he said to the jurors, "that this observation
> has made some impression on you, and I will only ob-
> serve, that if the prisoner were guilty, and possessed
> even a moderate cunning, he would hardly put any of
> the stolen articles into his box, which he must have
> been sure would be subjected to investigation. His box
> was searched, and I do not rely upon anything found in
> the box on any occasion. I feel that I am speaking to
> men who hear and read what is published to the world.
> Something might have transpired with respect to linen
> found in the prisoner's box, marked in a particular
> way; but I attribute no weight to it, and I repeat that
> nothing arises in the present case from anything dis-
> covered in the prisoner's box."

One part of Adolphus' speech was more extraordinary than
the rest. Anticipating a defense that Courvoisier had no motive
to murder Lord William Russell, Adolphus lectured the jury on
motive in the criminal law, coupling it with allusion to the shots
fired at Queen Victoria.

> "The absence of apparent motive," he said, "is a very
> erroneous test by which to judge of a man's innocence.
> We are not able to know the motives and impulses
> which lead men to commit crime, and some offenses of
> the greatest importance to society occur, though no
> definite or rational motive can be discovered. A recent
> event has occurred which has filled the public mind
> with astonishment and horror, and which might have
> created confusion and desolation through the land, yet
> neither man, nor prophet, nor even angel, can tell the
> motive which induced it, and still it was done. Such is
> the state of the human mind, that motives cannot be
> discovered."

"Nevertheless," he continued, "it does not appear that there
was such a complete absence of motive for the commission of
this crime on the part of the prisoner as might be imagined at
the first blush." Adolphus proceeded to develop his own theory
of the crime: Courvoisier was a foreigner, with "no connextions

to attach him to the place," believing "what foreigners frequently believe, that English noblemen go about with a mass of gold
with them; " he had been heard to say that if he had some of
"old Billy's" money he "should no longer be in this country."
Courvoisier's thefts not having produced enough money to enable him to leave England, he had hidden Lord Russell's valuables for later removal, with the burglary simulated as a coverup.
Murder was incidental to the plan.

"Englishmen," said Adolphus, "are not in the habit
of considering murder as a prelude to plunder. With
foreigners it is different, for they imagine that if they
destroy the life of the person they rob there will then
exist no direct testimony against them. It therefore is
a natural supposition that the murder was committed
by the prisoner under the expectation that a considerable plunder would fall into his hands   .   .   .
That is the supposition I make, and it is for the jury to
consider whether the view I take is a proper one.
Somebody must have murdered Lord William Russell,
and if the prisoner had no motive, who could have?
It is impossible to say that his Lordship committed the
deed, and the conclusion to which I have come is that
the prisoner at the bar is the guilty person."

There was also the peroration, to remove the sting of vengeance from the fact of private prosecution, and with a low keyed
but hard pitch to the jury to strike a blow for the security of
the Englishman's home.

"I have only to add," said Adolphus, "that if in any
thing I have said I seemed to exceed the bounds of
moderation, you must attribute it to the warmth of my
mind, not the zeal and earnestness of an advocate, but
of an anxious inquirer after truth. The illustrious family for whom I appear have no desire to hunt a helpless
foreigner into the jaws of death, as if actuated by feelings of personal revenge. No such feeling could ac-
tuate them. The Bedford family prosecutes here as the
mere petitioners for public justice, not to gratify any
feeling of private revenge.

"I am aware that in cases of this kind appeals are
sometimes made to the merciful consideration of the

Court. I would guard the jury against all such appeals.
Mercy is the mitigation of justice, not the deprivation
of it. The weight of testimony must have its due effect
on your minds; and your verdict must be pronounced
as the result of that evidence, without regard to any
other consideration whatever.

"I can feel, as every other man must, for the case of
a foreigner, distant from his own country, and charged
under the most solemn circumstances with the commission of a capital crime. But there is a circumstance of
even paramount consideration—the safety of the vast
family of the British community; for on your unbiassed
verdict in such a case must depend whether the old
man retiring to rest, and the defenceless female and the
helpless child, having addressed their prayers to Almighty God, should be subjected with impunity to the
assassin's knife.

"The case is one requiring firm and upright hearts,
as well as cool and intelligent heads. I believe the jury
has both, and I fervently pray that God will so fortify
your hearts and enlighten your minds that you come to
a right conclusion. Should your verdict be one of acquittal, the Bedford family will have nothing to regret;
if, on the contrary, the testimony is such as to require
a verdict of guilty, your duty to your country demands
that you pronounce it fearlessly, whatever might be the
consequences."

The old lawyer sat down. The speech had taken two hours to
deliver, and had been "listened to with profound attention."

Bodkin, one of Adolphus' "juniors" (in British usage not necessarily a younger man but any barrister assisting the chief
counsel), now began the direct examination of Sarah Mancer.
In a court session lasting till after seven in the evening with
only one "refreshment" break, the prosecution presented eight
witnesses—the Russell servants, the neighbors' servants, the
doctors, and finally the first of the numerous police witnesses.
But the reluctant star of opening day was Sarah Mancer, painfully retelling with most of the old familiar detail the story she
had told so many times before. Miss Mancer was a worried witness, harassed enough with constant questionings since the

murder, the unaccustomed public attention, today apparently more worried than even at the preliminary examination, if over nothing else that even an innocent connection with the taint of the Russell murder would end her days of employability.

As she now stood in the witness box facing cross-examination by Charles Phillips, Miss Mancer appeared to one observer ".   .   . pale, breathless, and trembling in every fibre of her frame   .   .   ." Phillips had discovered in her story a curious, tenuous, yet a possible thread of what might perhaps be prescience, and he set out to test the possibility as well as her impartiality and reliability.

In her signed statement of testimony given at the coroner's inquest, in telling of the discovery of the body, Miss Mancer had said:

"I saw his Lordship ~~dead~~ murdered in bed." The word "dead" had been crossed out.

Mr. Phillips brought the uneasy Miss Mancer back to the horror of the 6th of May.

"I think you said, when you first went into Lord William Russell's room, you saw some blood on the pillow, and you ran away screaming?"

"I said, 'My Lord! My Lord!' ".

"Upon your oath, have you ever represented that you saw his Lordship murdered in bed?"

"Not to my recollection."

"Stop! stop! Did you not say you saw my Lord murdered in bed?"

"Not to my recollection."

"But did you not say so many hours after the occurrence?"

"No, I did not say so."

"If you have ever said so, is it untrue?"

"I do not know."

"Now recollect. I do not wish to hurry you. Did you ever represent to any one you saw my Lord murdered in bed when you first went in?"

"I could not say so. I did not see him."

"I do not know what you could do. Did you ever do it?"

Chief Justice Tindal attempted to rescue the confused witness from a linguistic tangle: "In giving an account of this afterwards to some other person, was the expression you used that you had seen my Lord murdered in bed, meaning lying in bed murdered, is that what you said?"

Miss Mancer would not be saved. "No. I recollect now. I said someone had murdered his Lordship. I said it in the street to Young."

Again Mr. Phillips: "Did you never say you saw him murdered in bed. You were examined before the Coroner; now I give you warning."

Here Mr. Baron Parke intervened to say that if what happened at the inquest were to be inquired into, the written statement of Miss Mancer's testimony would have to be produced.

Mr. Phillips: "Well, you say you always gave the same account of the transaction that you do now?"

"Yes. It is a thing which impresses itself on my mind. I was that frightened, I do not remember what I saw."

That was a good point on which to pass to another subject.

Phillips now went to the nature of Miss Mancer's reactions to the condition of the house.

"On the morning of the 6th day of May, when you went up to the cook, after having seen the things tossed about downstairs, what did you say to the cook?"

"I asked her if she knew if any thing had been the matter last night."

"And when you went to Courvoisier's room, what did you say to him?"

"I said, 'Courvoisier, do you know if anything has been the matter last night?'"

"The same words as you used to the cook?"

"She told me to call him. Those were the words I used to the cook."

"Pray, had you the least doubt that a great deal was the matter?"

"No, I had no doubt at all."

"That something was the matter?"

"I did not think there was any thing the matter."

"Nothing at all?"

"Not so much the matter as there was. Because I had frequently seen his Lordship's papers strewed about, much the same as they were that morning."

"Had you ever before found the passage strewed with things?"

"No."

"Had you any doubt then of any thing being the matter?"

"I did not know what to think. I thought there might be something the matter."

"Did you think the cook could give you any information?"

"I did not know."

"How much later was the cook up than you?"

"By a quarter of an hour."

"Did you think she could know about all this in a quarter of an hour?"

"No."

"Why ask her?"

"Because I had nobody else to go to."

"What did you think when you saw the things in the passage?"

"I did not know what to think."

"Were you surprised?"

"It surprised me very much."

"And did you go immediately to the cook?"

"Yes, I went immediately to the cook, and told her what I had seen."

"But you went into the dining-room first?"

"Yes."

"Why not instantly go up when you saw the things in the library and in the passage?"

"I did not know what the things were laid there for. I knew nothing about it."

.   .   .

"Were you not surprised to find the front door unchained and unbolted?"

"I sometimes have found it unfastened before."

"How long before?"

"I cannot say exactly; it might be before his Lordship went to Richmond. Once Courvoisier had forgotten to fasten it."

"Did that surprise you?"

"It did."

"Did you mention that to the cook?"

"I do not know."

"How often before had you seen the door unfastened?"

"It was only once."

"And were you not alarmed at seeing the things strewed about the passage?"

"I was surprised, but I was not so much alarmed till I went into the dining-room. I then became alarmed."

"What did you do in the dining-room?"

"I just opened the shutter."

"And had you gone into the front drawing-room to see if property was there?"

"No; I went there to open the shutter."

"When you went into the front drawing-room did you not suspect something?"

"No."

"Although you had seen the desk twisted round, the drawers open, and the papers sticking out, you never suspected any thing wrong?"

"No, I did not."

A little later, Phillips inquired as to what exactly it was Miss Mancer had said to Courvoisier just before the body was discovered.

"When I went down with Courvoisier, and saw the things tossed about, I said, 'Let us go and see where his Lordship is.' "

"Did you think any thing was the matter with his Lordship then?"

"I did not know what to think."

"Did you think he had been harmed?"

"He was unprotected, and nobody went to see."

"Your fellow-servants were safe?"

"Yes."

"Why did you not use the expression, 'Let us go and tell his Lordship the house is robbed,' instead of saying 'Let us go and see where his Lordship is'?"

"Those were the words I used."

"Where did you expect to find him?"

"In his bed-room."

"You had been in every other room except the kitchen?"

"Yes. I had not been in his Lordship's bed-room then."

"Did you know where he was?"

"No."

"At that time did you expect any mischief was done to him?"

"No. I was anxious to see where he was."

"Yet you had no doubt where he was?"

"No."

From Miss Mancer's reactions that morning, Phillips went on to Courvoisier's reactions.

"Now it has been opened to us to-day that Courvoisier never took the least trouble to give any assistance. If I remember right, you told me that the prisoner appeared to be writing, and said he was writing to Mr. William Russell?"

"He said he must write to Mr. Russell. I said somebody must be sent for him."

"And after that, he was about to send the first man he saw at the door?"

"Not that I know of; he had beckoned to the man. He had sat about five minutes after I told him Mr. Russell must be sent for."

"When he beckoned to the man, what did you do?"

"I gave him a push, and said, 'Don't call such a man as that.'"

"Did you know what he was calling him for?"

"No."

"What did you mean by saying, 'Do not send such a man as that'?"

"Because he did not look like a man to send anywhere."

"Did you think the prisoner was going to send him for Mr. Russell?"

"No. He was not a man I should send anywhere."

"If you found a house robbed, and a murder committed, should you not send the first person you could find?"

"I do not know whether I should or not."

. . .

"And before that, you had said to the prisoner, 'What the devil are you doing there?' "

"I was dreadfully frightened after I found his Lordship was murdered. It was after that I said that."

"Are you in the habit of speaking so?"

"No, I am not, but I did not know what I was about."

"Yet you observed what he was about?"

"I should not have said that had he got up and assisted me."

"Do you not think it was quite right to apprize Mr. William Russell immediately of the horrid event that had happened?"

"Yes."

"And he lived nearby in Belgrave-square?"

"It is not very far for a man to ride on horseback."

"Was there anyone else to go?"

"The coachman might have gone. Courvoisier might have gone for the coachman."

"And might he not have taken the opportunity of escaping, if he was conscious of any crime?"

"He might have escaped."

There was yet a little more to be drawn from the star witness for the prosecution.

All London knew that Courvoisier had brought in some ale the night before the murder, and that after drinking some of it, the maid and cook had become drowsy and had gone to bed. In his opening speech, Mr. Adolphus had placed beer and drowsiness in chronological sequence, without elaboration. Why hadn't Miss Mancer spoken of this on direct examination? Simply because no one had asked. It was true she had felt drowsy but it might have been as long as half or three-quarters of an hour after having some ale. Courvoisier too had some of the ale that night, and she had never meant to insinuate in earlier statements that the ale had been drugged, nor even that it was the ale that made her sleepy. So much for that.

The untold ladder story was even better. In that long opener, Mr. Adolphus had stressed the lack of access to the premises over the rear walls, but had not mentioned a ladder, nor had Miss Mancer, on direct examination. Yet when the police arrived at No. 14 Norfolk Street to investigate the murder, they had found a ladder conveniently against a wall in the back yard. How did the ladder get there?

Questioned by Mr. Phillips, Miss Mancer said the ladder had been at the house when she first went to work for Lord Russell. She had heard Inspector Tedman inquire about the ladder. She herself had not mentioned it in earlier investigation though she had "heard many inquiries as to how any body could have got over the walls."

"Is not the ladder exactly the height of the wall which separates the yard of the premises from another?"

"I never noticed it."

"Was the ladder always kept in the yard?"

"Not always; when it was not there it was kept in the bathroom, which goes off from the house."

"How high is the wall?"

"I cannot say."

"You have been in the yard often?"

"Hundreds of times."

"And you cannot say how high the wall is?"

"I have no idea how high the wall is."

"And you have seen the ladder often?"

"Hundreds of times."

"Have you used it?"

"I have gone up that ladder, but not in the yard. I have had it in the house."

"How high is the ladder?"

"I do not know the height of it; it is the height of other ladders."

"Could not a person on that ladder get over the sidewall?"

"I do not know?"

"Was the ladder standing there against the wall before the morning of the murder?"

"I never saw it standing there before that morning; I did not see it till the police saw it."

"Where had you last seen it?"

"It was standing in the passage on the Tuesday, the morning before the murder, and I asked Courvoisier to take it away, and he took it and placed it there himself; I remember that now; it stood inside when I asked him to take it; it was in the passage just below three stairs. I was cleaning the passage, and said to Courvoisier, 'Will you take this away?' and he took it out there."

Here a question from the bench: "It was standing in the house?"

"Yes; it had been left there on Monday; the late valet had been there hanging some pictures for his Lordship, and left it there. I asked Courvoisier to take it away, and he took it away, took it out of the house, on Tuesday. He set it where it was found by the police, on the side of the wall of No. 15, the left-hand side."

Mr. Phillips: "Did you desire Courvoisier to put it there?"

"No, I desired him to take it away."

"But you saw where he took it to?"

"Yes."

"So it did not surpise you in the least to see it there next morning?"

"No."

Again from the bench: "Did it reach the top of the wall?"

"Not exactly that I know; I never noticed it. It stood quite upright."

Mr. Phillips: "Was it leaning against the wall?"

"It must be leaning against the wall; I did not see it for a long time after; I saw it in the course of the day leaning against the wall."

"How far was it from the top of the wall?"

"I do not know."

"But anybody on the top of that could easily have got over the wall?"

"Yes."

By the end of Mr. Phillips' cross-examination the tidy package of Miss Mancer's story was somewhat crumpled. Whether she knew more than she had yet told was far from clear. Certainly cross-examination had raised questions not raised on direct. At the very least her actions on the day of the discovery of the murder were confused and subject to unfavorable inference.

After a miscellany of odds and ends on re-direct examination, Mr. Bodkin for the prosecution decided to end it all on a note of rehabilitation of the disinterested witness. He got from Miss Mancer: "I never in my life had any quarrel or cause of quarrel with the prisoner," and she left the box.

The cook Mary Hannell followed Sarah Mancer, generally corroborating the maid's story. She too had heard Courvoisier say something about "Old Billy" being "a rum old chap and if he had his money he would not be long in England", but on cross-examination by Mr. Clarkson (Phillips' junior) she explained that Courvoisier was joking when he said it. On the morning the murder was discovered she heard Courvoisier say "Oh dear, they will think it is me, and I shall never get a place again." Yes, she had thought that a strange thing for him to say, "but he was alarmed, and I thought at the time he did not know what he was saying. He seemed as confused and agitated as the rest of us."

Other servants added a miscellany of quotes from Courvoisier of that same day: "O my God, what shall I do!", "What shall we do? What shall we do?", "I have lived with his Lordship only five weeks, and what shall I do for my character?"; and —at the backdoor in the butler's pantry, "Here is where they came in."

The butler from across the way, Emanuel Young, who had gone for the police at Sarah Mancer's request, told how he had

assisted the surgeon as the body was examined, and how Courvoisier had fallen back into a chair at the sight of the wound.
Courvoisier's reaction was equivocal. Was it normal revulsion
or the prick of conscience? Mr. Phillips' cross-examination
tried to resolve the uncertainty.

"Was it not a spectacle to utterly shock and horrify any body
who saw it?"

"It was very horrifying."

"So much so as to affect the nerves of the stoutest, strongest
man?"

"It certainly affected me."

"Were you unnerved?"

"No. My nerves were shaken, but I was not unnerved."

The apothecary John Nursey, Lord Russell's "medical attend-
ant" of many years, gave a somewhat different version of Courvoisier's responses. He had found him helpful, assisting Nursey
and the police in putting things in the bedroom just as they
were when the body was first discovered.

A servant from next door, Thomas Selway, was the first witness to point out that the dust on the neighboring roof and the
whitewashed walls showed no sign of anyone having left or entered the Russell backyard via that route. His testimony was
reinforced by Constable John Baldwin, who had given Courvoisier some bad moments for not being more helpful. Baldwin
and his companion constable Rose had climbed onto the adjacent
roofs, using the Russell ladder that was already in the yard.
The tiles were unbroken, the heavy dust without footprints or
finger marks though the officers found that they themselves left
both. On cross-examination Constable Baldwin refused to con-
cede that he could have been mistaken in any of his testimony.
Mr. Phillips took a new line of inquiry:

"Have you heard of any reward being offered in this case?"

"No, never."

"How long have you been a policeman?"

"Several years."

"From the time the new force was first organized?"

"I joined it the first day."

"Now on the oath you have taken, do not you know that a placard with a reward was sent to every stationhouse in London?"

"I never saw it."

"Have you heard of it?"

"Never to this day."

"Do you not know there is a reward?"

"I do not know what it is to this day."

"Did you never hear what the reward was?"

"Never."

"Did you never hear of a reward of £400.0.0 for the conviction of the murderer of Lord William Russell?"

"I never heard of it, or of any reward."

"How often have you been in Lord William Russell's house?"

"Three or four times."

"Have you not talked to your brother policeman about this dreadful transaction?"

"No."

"Have you not seen him and talked to him?"

"I have seen him several times, but had nothing to say to him."

"Have you not talked to different policemen about the murder?"

"No; it has been mentioned."

"Have you not heard your brother policemen conversing about it?"

"No, not with any parties belonging to the house."

"I am not asking about parties to the house, but about your own brother policemen. Do you mean to tell the jury that you have not over and over again conversed with policemen about the murder?"

"I have certainly spoken to one or two, but never conversed with any body, not with the parties belonging to the house. I have spoken to people I know."

"To policemen?"

"Of course I have."

"How many have you spoken to on the subject of the murder?"

"I cannot say how many."

"Will you swear you have not spoken to twenty?"

"No I will not swear that."

"Will you swear you have spoken to twenty?"

"No I will not swear that."

"You might have spoken to 20, 30, 40, or a 100?"

"I might have."

"Why, then, did you fix upon one or two?"

"I fix upon nothing. I spoke to nobody in no particular manner about it."

"Did you not ask some one some question about it?"

"I asked nobody no question."

"Not of policemen belonging to the house?"

"No."

"Do you mean to persist in saying you never heard of a reward being offered?"

"I do."

"Were you never told of any reward?"

"Never."

"Can you write?"

"I can write my name."

"Can you read?"

"I cannot read much. I am not a very good scholar."

"Can you read print in very large letters on placards?"

"Yes."

"What station-house do you belong to?"

"Vine-street, Piccadilly."

"That is the station you have belonged to since the 5th of May?"

"Yes."

"How often are you there?"

"I am there every day."

"How many policemen frequent that station-house?"

"I cannot say."

"Approximately how many?"

"About 184."

"How far is it from Lord William Russell's house?"

"About three-quarters of a mile."

"Now, 184 policemen frequenting the same station-house with you, do you still mean, on your oath, to tell the jury that you never heard of a reward being offered?"

"I never was told of it."

"Did you not hear of it?"

"I never heard of the reward."

"But you know what the reward is?"

"No."

"Did you ever hear of any reward?"

"Never."

"Did you not hear of some reward being offered?"

"I was never offered anything, nor ever heard of any reward."

"Did you suppose I asked whether any reward was offered to you?"

"No. I say I know nothing about any reward."

"Were you ever employed in searching for the missing spoons or forks?"

"Never."

"Did you ever read of a £50.0.0 reward being offered for them?"

"I myself, no; I am a very bad scholar. There was something read out in orders about it, in the general orders."

"What was read out about it in general orders?"

"There was some reward, but I do not recollect it."

"What was the reward for?"

"I cannot tell."

"What sum of money was mentioned?"

"I do not recollect."

"Is that a thing you take no notice of, sums of money?"

"No, I do not."

"But you were present when it was read out?"

"Yes, I was."

"And you do not know what sum of money was named?"

"No."

"How long is it since it was read out to you?"

"I cannot tell."

"So long as two months ago?"

"It cannot be that long."

"Can you tell whether it was one month ago, or a week ago?"

"I cannot."

"Can you tell whether it was four days ago, or two days ago?"

"No."

"It might be one day ago for anything you know?"

"Yes."

"Was it yesterday?"

"I cannot tell."

"Can you tell us any thing at all about it?"

"No."

Whether Constable Baldwin had perjured himself throughout his testimony, or only on the subject of the reward, by the time he left the witness box he was a thoroughly discredited witness. It was a bad note for the prosecution to close the day on, but it was after seven, and the court adjourned.

For one young barrister, among the many in court, watching Courvoisier's case as the first murder trial he had ever seen, the impression of that first day remained strong a half century later:

> " . . . at the end of it, bets were freely made in the robing-room of three to one that the prisoner would be acquitted. I must say that this was the only time I have witnessed the unseemly course of men betting on the life of an accused fellow-creature. It was perhaps thought that the evidence was so weak that the prison-

er was in very little danger. There was a material link wanted in the chain of proof, for there was little to connect Courvoisier with the crime, except that he was in the house when it was committed, but then he was not there alone. Whoever the criminal was, he had made away with a large quantity of silver plate belonging to the deceased, and every effort to trace it had entirely failed." [6]

6. Robinson, *supra* ch. III, note 7, at 58.

Chapter V

TRIAL: SECOND DAY—THE SURPRISE WITNESS

News of the missing silver first reached the prosecution an hour before adjournment on the first day of the trial, the news brought by a solicitor until then not connected with the case— Mr. Richard Cumming. His story was to introduce a startling new witness into the case, Mrs. Charlotte Piolaine—Courvoisier's first employer in England. By the time the defense was notified of the development, shortly before the start of the second day of the trial, Mrs. Piolaine had been taken to Newgate prison early that Friday morning, where she picked out Courvoisier among the prisoners as the man who had left with her a bundle containing the missing silver. Even as the courtroom filled again to overflowing, the roster of distinguished visitors led again by His Royal Highness the Duke of Sussex, whispers reported the missing silver found. When Courvoisier was placed in the dock, "he appeared more anxious and depressed than on the previous day," and in the robing room a barrister observed Charles Phillips "evidently much agitated." [1]

As the session opened, Mr. Adolphus told the court that "yesterday afternoon a very important piece of evidence came to the knowledge of the prosecution," and since that had not been included in his opening statement, he offered now to outline to the jury what the new evidence would be. Phillips was outraged, said that "in justice to the prisoner a communication of the fact should have been made to him immediately it came to the knowledge of the prosecutor," and that in any event he certainly didn't want Mr. Adolphus at this late date to have another go at the jury. Adolphus said he had given word "as soon as possible," Phillips retorting that neither he nor Clarkson had heard anything "till within the last quarter of an hour;" no one had told solicitor Flower anything. Chief Justice Tindal ended the wrangle, saying an additional statement was "quite unnecessary." To Phillips he said, "Let us have no more inquiry about it," and to Adolphus, "Call the next witness."

1. See Ballantine, *supra* ch. III, note 7, at 61.

In the course of the day, Mr. Adolphus called 27 new witnesses, and recalled for brief appearances Mary Hannell and Sarah Mancer. Many of the witnesses were there to identify as Lord Russell's the items secreted in the butler's pantry, including the folded £10.0.0 note, traced by its serial number; a bank clerk had kept a record. Most of all this had long been public knowledge; the former Russell valet James Ellis had something of interest. He testified, and Sarah Mancer later confirmed, that it was the custom of the house for the silver to be kept for security in the valet's own bedroom. He had checked his own list against what was still on hand; missing were four table-spoons, four dessert-spoons, two tea-spoons, and four large forks. As Ellis stood in the box, solicitor Cumming exhibited to him a bundle of spoons and forks; Ellis examined them; the quantity was right; the sizes were right; the goat was right; *che sara, sara.* "I firmly believe," he said, that this was the missing Russell silverware. From that moment, the unfolding mystery of the silver was awaited as the piece de resistance of the day, and of the case.

Before he was ready to have that story told, Mr. Adolphus sent to the witness box seven policemen to reinforce the shaken Constable Baldwin's opinion that access to the Russell backyard was not possible absent broken tiles or marks in the dust, and to detail the nature of the bruises on the pantry door. They made it overwhelmingly clear that what had at first seemed to be a break-in was a calculated job of deception, the bruises made with tools at hand in the pantry—poker, hammer, screw-driver, and not consistent with the violence that would have been required to force the bolted door from the outside. This was also the opinion of John Christie, carpenter and builder, who had examined the socket of the upper bolt of the door "by applying my magnifying glass to it," thus qualifying him as one of the "scientific persons" Adolphus had promised as part of the prosecution case.

Inevitably too, the story had to be told of the finding of bloody gloves, bloody handkerchiefs, and detached shirt-front. In his opener, Adolphus chose to believe that these discoveries had no bearing on the case; doubtless he would have preferred to forget the whole episode, with its peculiar if not suspect chronology of unsuccessful and successful police searches, yet suppression would be even more suspect. He felt compelled to air in full trial what had already become a part of Courvoisier's case in the press and at the preliminary examination. This aspect of the prosecution, calling into question the conduct of the police throughout, was meat for the defense.

The cross-examination had an unstated theme: a circumstantial case of frame-up to match a circumstantial case of murder. With the gloves, handkerchiefs, and shirt-front, there was a pattern: meticulous search turning up nothing against Courvoisier; a reward offered; a new search, and guilty evidence.

All three inspectors—Beresford, Pearce, and Tedman—had searched and found nothing suspicious in either Courvoisier's box or trunk. Tedman told Phillips his first search was made "as carefully as I possibly could;" "there was no speck of blood on any thing that I saw in the trunk . ." Sergeant Shaw, who assisted Inspector Pearce, described their search as "a minute one." "We do not make a careless search when our object is to find anything suspicious." This is how they went about it:

> "We took all of the things out of the box one by one. We took each article in our hands, and placed it on the bed. We left nothing behind that we considered suspicious. We took every thing out, and put it on the bed, so as to see the box was empty and contained nothing more."

The only difference Inspector Tedman could think of between his first and second searches was that the first time he had unfolded everything, the second time he unfolded and shook—and the bloodstained gloves dropped out. But by that time a £ 400.0.0 reward had been offered; Courvoisier's room, his trunk, his box had been left open to policemen in the house and to Sarah Mancer and Mary Hannell; and Courvoisier himself was already in jail.

So it was too with the post-reward discovery of the bloodstained handkerchiefs, and the shirt-front. Constable Collier who had made both finds told Phillips:

> "The handkerchiefs were lying very near the top. No one could search the portmanteau without seeing them, if they had any eyes. I found the shirt-front after I

found the handkerchiefs—near the middle, a little below, under the handkerchiefs. I should consider a torn
shirt-front was a thing that would attract attention. It
attracted my attention. I do not see how any one could
miss seeing it. I could not, I know. If a person took
each article one by one, out of the trunk, I do not think
he could have missed seeing it, or the handkerchiefs
either, if they had been there."

Sergeant Shaw, who followed Collier to the witness box did
now recall, on excessive re-cross-examination by Mr. Phillips,
that he had seen the shirt-front or one very similar, but if this
testimony was truthful he had not previously thought it anything
worth mentioning. His recollection on handkerchiefs was even
less satisfactory; he vacillated about seeing them; in any event
he had not seen the bloody ones in his "minute search." And he
definitely rejected the notion put forward by Constable Collier
that the light in Courvoisier's attic bedroom was poor. "The
room was perfectly light enough to see any thing."

Whether all of this was corrupt or merely inept a jury would
have to decide. In the meantime, there was something more
about the role of the police that might help a jury in assessing
the fairness of the prosecution.

On Mr. Bodkin's direct examination, Inspector Pearce spoke of
confronting Courvoisier with the first of the Russell property
found hidden in the pantry. He testified:

"I said, 'I have found these things concealed in your pantry,
behind the skirting board.' "

"He said, 'I know nothing about them, I am innocent, my conscience is clear, I never saw the medal before.' "

Mr. Clarkson cross-examined the inspector:

"Now will you have the kindness to repeat what you say passed between you and the prisoner when you say his answer to you
was, 'I am innocent. I know nothing about them. My conscience is clear'?"

"I said, 'I found this property concealed in your pantry.' "

Pearce's testimony was less than candid, and Clarkson prepared to make the most of it. Repeatedly he suggested that the
inspector was trying improperly to squeeze a confession out of a

helpless man, and as often the witness doggedly denied this; it was simply "his duty to make him acquainted" with the discovery.

"Now attend to this," said Clarkson. "Did you not state this to the prisoner. Be careful how you answer. 'I have found these things concealed in your pantry; *can you now look me in the face?*' Did you make that observation?"

"Yes, I made that observation with others. Those were the words."

"On your solemn oath, why did you suppress those words when my friend [Mr. Bodkin] asked you the question, having as you say, no hope or expectation of obtaining a confession from the prisoner?"

"Why I should not mention to the Counsel that I found them concealed?"

"No. You say you went to the prisoner, and in the discharge of your duty presented the things to him, and said, 'I have found this property concealed in your pantry.' Why suppress the remaining part of the sentence, 'Can you now look me in the face?' "

"I had no motive or reason for suppressing it."

"Will you now swear you did not expect to obtain a confession from him, when you said, 'Can you now look me in the face?' "

"It is impossible for me to say what he might say."

As often as Clarkson branded the questioning "intimidation," Inspector Pearce denied it, finally conceding it might "very likely" intimidate "a guilty man." "I do not think the question I put was an intimidation," said Pearce. "It might be taken in that light by the Court, but I do not think so. If I had thought so I should not have put the question."

Clarkson plunged ahead to have the inspector admit knowing about the £400.0.0 and £50.0.0 rewards.

"Do you belong to the same station as Baldwin?"

"No."

"Do you expect to get any of the reward, if the prisoner is convicted?"

"Very likely I may. I do expect it, in the course of my duty. If I should say, 'No,' I should say false."

"Have you had some of it already?"

"I have had nothing at all yet, not a farthing from any body."

"How long after the reward was offered did you make the discovery in the skirting-board?"

"The property was found before I was aware there was a reward offered. I found the property on the Friday, and on that evening late, I think twelve o'clock, I called at the station-house, and found there was a reward offered. That was after all the property was found by me."

"What share will you get if there is a conviction?"

"I have not the least notion."

"And what will you get if there is no conviction?"

"I am not aware that I shall get any if there is not a conviction. The reward is upon conviction."

"If the prisoner is not convicted there will be no reward?"

"No."

"Did you not think of a reward at the time you said to the prisoner, 'Can you now look me in the face?' "

"Never."

Around noon, Mr. Adolphus called as his next witness Mrs. Charlotte Piolaine. Someone glancing at the man in the dock thought he "turned deadly pale" at the sound of that name.[2]

Charlotte Piolaine recalled that "about four years ago," at their French-speaking Hotel Dieppe, she and her husband had employed a waiter they knew only as *Jean*. He worked for them "a month or five weeks, it was not long," and she had not seen him again until "about six weeks ago," when he dropped in unannounced, staying only a few minutes. At first she did not recognize him, but he reminded her that he was "*Jean*, that used to live with you some time, over in the Square;" then she remembered. Jean told her he was working for a gentleman. On a Sunday evening a week or so later (this was before the murder of Lord Russell), Jean had stopped by again, carrying a parcel wrapped in brown paper, and asked if he might leave it with her until the following Tuesday. She agreed, with "no notion at

2. Robinson, *supra* ch. III, note 7, at 59.

that time what the parcel contained," put it in her closet, and
locked it up. Jean never returned.

Yesterday morning, Mrs. Piolaine's cousin Joseph Vincent,
who is her husband's partner, showed her something in a French
newspaper that made her curious about the parcel in the closet.
(On the last day of the trial a London newspaper said it was a
story saying the murderer was thought to be a foreigner and
that it was probable the Russell silver had been left at the home
of a foreigner.) She sent for Richard Cumming a solicitor
friend. With Charlotte Piolaine, Joseph Vincent, and Louis Gardie as witnesses, Cumming opened the package. Inside, padded
with clothing and something "like ravelled rope," so that "it did
not make the least noise" were "spoons and forks, silver I suppose," and "two instruments for the ear." The items were in-
ventoried, all present signed, the package was rewrapped and
turned over to the solicitor. She had not seen *Jean* again "until
today." Courvoisier was *Jean*. "An electric shock seemed to
pass through everyone in court   .   .   .   Charles Phillips
seemed to manifest nearly as much emotion as did the prisoner
in the dock." [3]

Thus, with only 15 minutes warning of testimony from a witness he knew nothing about, whose words if believed by the jury
could destroy the strongest suggestion of circumstance favoring
the defense, Charles Phillips began the cross-examination of
Mrs. Charlotte Piolaine of Leicester Place, Leicester Square.

He fixed the time of the opening of the brown paper parcel as
four o'clock the previous afternoon, and then set about having
the jury wonder with him whether this was a witness who could
be believed under any circumstances, and whether in this instance it was not beyond belief that truth should have rested
quietly in a hotel closet while a storm over the killing raged
throughout London.

Mr. Phillips' questioning commenced with a test of the general
moral tone of the Hotel Dieppe and incidentally of the conformi-
ty of its proprietress with Victorian standards of public decency.

"Is a billiard table kept at your hotel?"

"There is, but it is not much frequented, merely by the gentlemen who board and lodge in the house."

3. *Id.* 59–60.

"Do some come in to play?"

"A few."

"Then it is not kept exclusively for guests of the house?"

"No."

"Any body can go and play that likes? "

"Yes."

"Any stranger may come in and play? "

"Yes."

"Are there other games played in the house? "

"None."

"Not backgammon? "

"No. The house is conducted peaceably and respectably."

"Have not the police been there? "

"Not at all."

"Has no one ever been taken out of it?"

"No. I never heard of it."

"Was there not a gang of suspected persons taken out of the house lately by the police? "

"I think I can swear that never happened; neither a gang nor any person."

"What did you mean by saying you think you could swear it? "

"Because I am never down in the billiard-room myself, but I never heard any noise."

"Is there any gambling-house in Leicester-place but yours? "

"I do not think so, and ours is not a gambling house."

"Are there not a great many gambling-houses in Leicester-place? "

"Not that I am aware of."

"How long have you lived there? "

"We have lived there two years next September."

"Did you never inquire whether there were gambling-houses there? "

"Not much."

"Your house is, I believe, very much frequented by foreigners? "

"It is.　There are generally a good many there."

"By what name did the prisoner go in your service? "

"*Jean.*"

"Who gave him that name? "

"I did."

"Was that his name? "

"I do not know."

"Then why call him so? "

"For convenience sake.　Because it would be easy for us all in the house."

"Did you ever know him by any other name? "

"No."

"Do you take in the English papers at your house? "

"No."

"But you read the English papers? "

"Very seldom; I have no time."

"Do Englishmen never come to your house? "

"A few English gentlemen occasionally."

"And you do not take in any but French newspapers? "

"Never."

"Have you not for the last five weeks heard continual conversations about this dreadful event, the murder of Lord William Russell? "

"No.　I am never among the gentlemen downstairs, who have conversations."

"You have a husband? "

"Yes, but he is in France."

"For how long? "

"He has only been gone a fortnight."

"Does not your husband run the hotel? "

"He is the master of the hotel; that is all."

"Have you not heard your husband speak of the murder? "

"Not to my knowledge. If he has I have forgotten it, but I do not think he has mentioned the subject to me."

"Do you not walk in the streets on Sundays? "

"I am not in the habit of going out on Sundays."

"Do you not go to church? "

"I go to church sometimes."

"Have you not observed the placards of the Sunday newspapers? "

"No."

"Have you never seen posted up in large letters, 'The Murder of Lord William Russell,' nor heard the murder cried about the streets? "

"No."

"Do you mean to say you never heard of the murder? "

"I think I heard of the murder the day after it was committed."

"And were you not shocked? "

"Certainly, very much."

"And did you not say some thing to your husband about it? "

"I do not know that I did."

"Not even mention it? "

"It might have been named. I cannot recollect whether we did or did not speak of it. I have no time to talk of such things. I am so occupied."

"You and your husband dine together? "

"Very seldom."

"You breakfast together?"

"Sometimes."

"Was it your occupations that prevented you mentioning it to your husband? "

"I do not know."

"Do you now recollect whether you said any thing about it to your husband? "

"No."

"Did you say anything about it to his partner? "

"Not to my knowledge."

"Did you speak of it to any body."

"No; I am so occupied."

"Too occupied to speak to your husband or his partner? "

"Mr. Vincent is always occupied down stairs, and sometimes I do not see them the whole of the day, from morning to evening."

"You sleep with your husband? "

"Generally, yes, but sometimes I have gone to bed a long time before him."

"Was that the case the whole three weeks he was in town after the murder? "

"No."

"Were you not frequently awake when he came to bed? "

"I cannot say."

"During the three weeks were you too much occupied to hold any conversation with your husband? "

"I cannot say."

"Think, cannot you answer that question?"

"No."

Now it was Mr. Adolphus' turn for outrage. In rapid order he smoothed the rumpled feathers and repute of his witness:

"You have been asked about the reputation of your house. Is there any pretence on earth, to your knowledge, for calling it a gaming house? "

"No."

"Have the police ever to your knowledge broken in and taken any one out?"

"Never. It has never happened while we have lived there."

"Respecting your conversation with your husband, do you, like other women, converse with your husband on things that pass, and think no more of it after it is over? "

"Yes."

"Whether you heard of the murder of Lord William Russell or not, could you have any idea that *Jean* was the same person as François Benjamin Courvoisier who was accused of the murder? "

"No."

"Was there anything unusual about a parcel being left with you? "

"Parcels are sometimes left in our care, at the counter down stairs."

"What did you do with the parcel in question? "

"I put it in my closet, and locked it up."

"Did you ever move it out before yesterday? "

"No; it was put at the bottom."

"On what floor is the closet? "

"The first."

"Does the billiard-room have any connection or communication with that floor? "

"No; the billiard-room is on the parlour floor."

"Does any one coming to play at billiards have any business up stairs? "

"No."

"Is there a backgammon table in your house? "

"No."

There were other witnesses with some support for Mrs. Piolaine. Mr. Moltino identified the parcel's brown paper wrapping; it had been used by his shop to wrap prints for delivery to Lord Russell. Mr. Gardie, who witnessed the opening of the parcel, thought that he was present when the parcel had been delivered to Mrs. Piolaine, but he wasn't sure, and wasn't sure either that it was Courvoisier who had delivered it. Mr. Vincent testified through an interpreter. He witnessed the opening of the parcel, as did the solicitor Mr. Cumming, who, before he brought the news to the prosecution, had stopped off at a bookshop to verify the Russell family crest in the Peerage-book; it was their goat and their silver. For him Mr. Phillips, still smarting at the surprise of the Piolaine testimony, annoyed that he had not been given adequate notice, had a brief and scornful cross-examining:

"It was about six o'clock you came here yesterday evening? "

"About six o'clock."

"What did you do? "

"I came into Court, and proceeded to the seat of the solicitors."

"Did you see me here? "

"Yes."

"Do you know Mr. Flower? "

"No."

"Did you know that I was one of counsel for the prisoner? "

"Yes."

"You say you knew I was counsel for the prisoner—that is
enough, Sir, I shall ask you no more questions."

Some testimony was offered to connect the clothing in the
parcel with Courvoisier. A jacket was "similar" to one he had,
but the witnesses were not positive. The expert washerwoman,
who sometimes washed Courvoisier's clothes, said the dirty stockings had his mark on them, though she had never washed them.
These were "marked in the heel;" the only ones she had ever
seen were "marked at the top." She had washed some "marked
'C.B.',", but did not know whether any were marked without the
"B" as here.

It was around 7:30 in the evening when Mr. Adolphus announced, "That is the case for the prosecution." Phillips quickly responded that it was "quite impossible to finish tonight;" he
requested that court be adjourned till the morning (Saturday).
The request was granted, Courvoisier was taken back to Newgate prison, and Phillips went off to ponder his speech to the
jury. By law (not changed in England till 1898,[4] nor in Georgia
till 1962 [5]), Courvoisier could not be sworn as a witness in his
own defense. Except for witnesses to the good character of his
client, Phillips had no evidence to offer. The rest was with him.
The odds at the end of the second day are not reported, but they
had been drastically and dramatically reversed.

---

4. 61 & 62 Victoria, ch. 36 (1898).

5. Code of Georgia, §§ 38–415 and
38–416, as amended (1962); see

Ferguson v. Georgia, 365 U.S. 570,
81 S.Ct. 756, 5 L.Ed.2d 783 (1961).

Chapter VI

TRIAL: THIRD DAY—MR. PHILLIPS TO THE JURY

On Saturday morning, June 20, the day Courvoisier's case was to go to the jury, *The Court Journal*, which called itself "Gazette of the Fashionable World," published a delayed report of the inaccurate rumor that circulated through London even before Charlotte Piolaine testified. The central point of her testimony it had right: the Russell silver had been recovered from the hands of the person to whom Courvoisier had delivered it. "This" concluded the story, "is decisive of the case."

The jury had been locked up during the trial at the London Coffee-house, reportedly well fed at the expense of the under-sheriffs, and it is possible they did not see *The Court Journal's* view of their duty. But it was undoubtedly the view of most of those who crowded the Old Bailey courtroom that morning to hear from the defense. Before Phillips could begin, Mr. Adolphus reopened for a few minutes to have the sculptor who made the court-room model of No. 14 Norfolk Street give the precise measurements of the walls surrounding the backyard, and to recall once more for some final detail Sarah Mancer and Inspector Tedman. The prosecution was done.

In a hushed courtroom, Charles Phillips rose to say what could be said for Courvoisier.

"May it please you, my lords and gentlemen of the jury:

"I suppose I need scarcely say that, after 20 years of no inconsiderable experience in the criminal courts of this country, I have seldom risen to address a jury under more painful feelings, or with greater anxiety, than upon the present occasion. There are circumstances in this case, even as they were developed before the magistrates [at the preliminary examination], to cause me much anxiety. And, if such be the fact, I leave you to conjecture how much more must that anxiety be increased by the production before you, and that too without any notice whatever, of additional evidence by which the life of the unhappy man at the bar may be placed in the greatest peril and the most fearful jeopardy.

"I say 'may,' because I do not for one moment admit that such can fairly be the result of the production of such evidence on the part of the prosecution, for reasons which I shall state to you. Considering, however, all these circumstances, I cannot but be consoled by the thought that in the situation in which I stand I shall have your kindest sympathies and the sympathy of my associates.

"Of this I am assured, for we are embarked together in a common cause. We incur together a common responsibility. The life of a fellow-creature is entrusted to our keeping. And as surely as we deal with that life unjustly, as surely will we have to answer for it to the God who made us.

'Gentlemen, I have not merely to deal with the facts of this case as they appear in evidence, but I have to contend against the odious prejudices which have been engendered by the peculiar circumstances by which this case is surrounded. These things, therefore, fill me with apprehension—the horrid nature of the crime itself of which the prisoner stands accused, the rank of the deceased, the numerous connections mourning their bereavement, the opinions promulgated before the prisoner could be heard, the fact that this case has not been dealt with in the ordinary way in which justice is usually administered in this country, but that inquiries on the subject have been stimulated by the offer of a Government reward. As if the grave knew any aristocracy! These things fill me with the greatest apprehension.

"And when I look around me, on this crowded court, and see the intensity of the public gaze, I think I feel and almost hear the throb of popular indignation at the horrible crime that has been committed. And then, when I turn to the dock where the wretched object of this outburst stands, charged with this heinous offense, I see a stranger, alone amid this multitude, far from his native land, far from the friends that love, and the associates that in his hour of danger would have crowded round him. A poor, solitary, isolated, helpless foreigner. I own that I should feel my spirits fainting fast within me, were it not that I still have one anchor of hope to cling to, an anchor that is centered in the breasts of this jury.

"I can rely on the independence of a British jury. I can rely on your strict integrity. I can rely on your sense of justice. I can rely on your generous feelings—upon those feelings which, no doubt, induced the prisoner at the bar to decline all foreign interference in the jury box, and to trust his life to the watchful care of a jury of Englishmen. I think the prisoner was right. I have no fear in appealing to such a tribunal. I know that with such a tribunal, the whole case, whatever it is, will be fairly, fully, impartially heard and justly decided.

"Having made these observations, I shall proceed, then, to consider the most extraordinary and unparalleled circumstances of this painful case. And, having done so, I shall submit that in such a case, wrapped up in clouds, in mystery, and darkness, there is not only nothing upon which you can safely convict the prisoner, but that here and there probabilities start up which might make you suspect that he has been made the victim of an unjust and depraved conspiracy.

"Gentlemen, I have much to complain of the opening address of my friend, Mr. Adolphus. Not personally, indeed, for, in a case like this, I should be unworthy of the gown I wear if I did not throw aside all personal considerations. But, gentlemen, I have much to complain of on the part of the accused. I confess there is nothing here which I had not expected, nothing which I had not long ago anticipated. It is no new notion of mine, as the learned Judges know, that the consequence of an act of Parliament now in operation would be to make a court of criminal jurisdiction the arena of angry passions, and to place the life of a fellow creature in peril or in safety, just in proportion to the skill and talent of his advocate. I should be glad to know from the learned Judges who preside here, whether it is not startling to them, after the experience of their early life, when such a thought never entered into the head of any advocate, to find the defence of a prisoner anticipated—to find that defence answered by anticipation—to find appeals to passion and prejudice where anything should be decided by the coolest reason. I appeal to you to think for one instant in what a situation this places the advocate of the accused. Consider how this case has been met.

" 'This man is a foreigner,' said Mr. Adolphus, 'and foreigners always murder when they rob.' That expression filled me with horror. In the name of the human race, I protest against it. All men who do not belong to this country are foreigners, and it is a libel upon the human race to utter such a sentiment. I de-

clare most solemnly that when I heard it uttered my countenance
sank. I was ashamed to look up for fear I should meet the
glances of some of those representatives of foreign countries
who have filled the court. I was ashamed to see what their sen-
sations must have been, when they heard an English advocate
utter such a slander on their nations. But it is not true. Let us
maintain the character of England, high and noble as it stands,
but let us not seek to erect a character upon the ruined reputations of other countries. It is a bad compliment to us. We need
not detraction   .   .   .   And yet a man who ought to have
addressed you cooly and calmly set out by endeavouring to in-
still in your minds [the] poison that because the man at the bar
is a foreigner, he is also a murder   .   .   .

"But, gentlemen, let us pass from this monstrous assertion to
another, which is equally unfair, but, fortunately for my client,
even more absurd. Mr. Adolphus told us, forsooth, that it is not
necessary for a man to have a motive for committing a crime.
Mr. Adolphus knows, gentlemen, that if he were to ransack the
annals of his 30 or 40 years' experience, he could find no instance in which a man committed a crime of this nature without
a motive. And he knows equally well, that if he were to torture
his ingenuity to the quick, he could attribute no motive to Courvoisier for committing the murder for which he is now arraigned. And then he told you that it was not necessary to
have a motive.

"Why, my friend forgot that he was addressing a jury of adult
men, men of the world, men of reasoning minds, men who well
know that the most trifling action of the human life has its
spring from some motive or other. But my friend knew that no
motive for such a crime could be attributed to Courvoisier, and
therefore he broached the monstrous doctrine that crime, ay,
even the blackest crime, that of murder, might be committed
without a motive!

" 'What motive,' he said, 'had the man who fired the other
day at the Queen? ' Gentlemen, I do not know. How should I
or you know what motive that man had? For aught I know,
and I hope and trust it will appear so, that unhappy man is a
maniac. My belief is that the man is [mad]. For I cannot con-
ceive that any man in his senses, not actuated by a morbid crav-
ing after notoriety, would have attempted to commit such a

crime. Why, to lift the hand against youth, beauty, innocence, virtue, and talent, all centered in the person of her who sits enthroned, not merely in artificial state, but in the hearts of all her loyal people, how could such a crime be committed by an reasoning man, by any man who was not, if not actually mad, at least upon the very verge of madness? Gentlemen, in this circumstance Mr. Adolphus has found a very bad illustration.

"I know that there must be motives for the commission of crime. I could not have practiced so long before the criminal tribunals without being convinced of it. There are motives of hatred that might prompt to crime. There are motives of jealousy that might inflame men to madness. There are motives of revenge that might tempt men to murder. There are motives of avarice and plunder that might instigate the perpetration of wickedness. But try by any of these tests the conduct of Courvoisier.

"What motives had he of hatred? None whatever. We find him in attendance on a master who loved him, and whom he loved. He was that master's confidential servant, who accompanied him on his journeys, saw him to his repose at night, and was trusted with his keys. Was there in such a case any cause for hatred that could instigate such a person to murder?

"Of motives of jealousy there is not the slightest whisper. Were there motives of revenge? For what? For kindness always received?

"Motives of plunder? Good God! Why should Courvoisier commit this most dreadful crime from motives of avarice? I could fancy, gentlemen, a midnight depredator, alarmed in his progress, terrified at his discovery, driven to madness from fear for his own safety, and committing the last dreadful crime to screen himself from detection. But was it necessary or expedient for Courvoisier to break into the house [in which he lived], to rob where he had daily and hourly opportunity of plunder—the suspicion not cast upon him at all, but if cast upon him, shared with others? . . . Nay, more if Courvoisier were the man who committed this offence, do you think he was in his senses? Do you think that he could be in his senses, and remain in that house after the commission of the deed, with the certainty of being detected? . . . When a man commits the most trifling crime in the street—setting aside the crime of murder—what does the instinct of self-preservation prompt him, nay, imperatively command him to do? Why, to fly—to fly while there is a chance for him. He may outstrip his pursuers, and possibly, he may not be pursued at all. He may not even be suspected. But here is a man, committing, according to those who are conducting the prosecution, a most dreadful crime, affecting his life, and yet he remains in the house after having committed it, as if to be detected. Committing the crime without a motive, with the chance, nay, almost the certainty of escape—you are told he had horses at his command—and not seeking to avail himself of the opportunity!

"This is not a case in which you have clear proofs before you. It is a case of circumstance only, as the counsel for the prosecution has told you, and therefore every minute observation with which it might be my unpleasant duty to trouble you, will, I am sure, be taken into consideration. It is not my case; it is your own case. My duty performed, not upon my feeble breath, thank God, will the irrevocable doom depend; upon yours it will, and therefore, when the arduous task committed to my friends and me is performed, our consciences will be clear.

"I have demonstrated to you what the counsel for the prosecution was obliged to admit—that not only no adequate, but no assignable, motive for the murder on the part of the prisoner can be discovered. Did this man, then, commit the murder without a motive?

"The counsel for the prosecution has been driven to declare that there is no necessity for a motive for the commission of crime. That, it appears to me, is a contradiction of common sense.

"But the counsel for the prosecution has undertaken to prove that the crime was committed by the prisoner. I believe it will be laid down by the learned Judges as a doctrine not to be controverted, that it is the duty of the prosecutors to bring home to the prisoner, without any reasonable doubt whatever, the commission of this offense. It is not my business to prove who did it. That is the task they have undertaken. They must prove that the murder has been committed by Courvoisier, and unless they do so, he must be acquitted. Unless that is proved, I beseech you to be cautious how you imbrue your hands in this man's blood. The Omniscient God alone knows who did this crime. I am not called on to rend asunder the dark mantle of the night and throw light upon this deed of darkness. They are bound to show the prisoner's guilt, not by inference, by reasoning, by that subtle and refined ingenuity which I was shocked to hear exercised in the opening address of my friend, but to prove it by downright, clear, open, palpable demonstration.

"Now, gentlemen, how do they seek to do so? In the first place, what said Mr. Adolphus and his witness Sarah Mancer? But let me do myself justice and others justice, by now stating that in the whole course of the narrative with which I must trouble you, I must beg that you will not suppose that I am, in the least degree, seeking to cast the crime upon either of the female servants of the deceased nobleman. It is not at all necessary to my case to do so. I wish not to asperse them. God forbid that any breath of mine should send tainted into the world persons perhaps depending for their subsistence upon their character. It is not my duty, nor my interest, nor my policy to do so.

"Now the first imputation cast upon this man by Mr. Adolphus was his agitation. Try that by the test of your own hearts and consciences. Here he is. The prisoner having seen his master retire to his peaceful bed, and having gone in quiet to his own bed, in the morning he is alarmed by the housemaid, who was up before him, with an outcry of 'Robbery!', and some dark, mysterious suggestions of murder. 'Let us go,' said she, 'and see where my Lord is.'

"Gentlemen, I must confess that that expression struck me as very extraordinary. If she had said, 'Let us go and tell my Lord that the house is plundered,' that would have been natural. But why should she suspect that anything had happened to his Lordship? She saw her fellow servant safe, no taint of blood about the house. And where did she expect to find her master? Why, in the bedroom, to be sure. What was there to lead to a suspicion that he was hurt? Courvoisier was safe. The cook was safe. And why should she suspect that her master was not safe too? If I have heard the character of that nobleman rightly, there was never a man breathed who had less reason to suspect or dread a foe.

"To continue, however, on the alarm Courvoisier did as he was desired. He preceded the woman down stairs. As was his custom, he was the first person to enter his master's bed-room. And what did he do? You can see whether there was anything unnatural in it. The room was in darkness. Every window was closed. What would any one of you have done upon such an occasion? The prisoner walked up to the window, which he was in the habit of opening. He opened a shutter. And then this female servant sees a speck of blood on the pillow, and runs screaming out of the room.

"I put a question to the witness respecting the account she gave before the coroner. The depositions taken before the coroner are now before the learned judges, and perhaps they will consider it their bounden duty to tell the jury whether that woman swore before the coroner as she did before the court. My conscience is clear; I have discharged my duty by throwing out that suggestion. The question I put to the witness was this —'Upon the oath you have taken, did you not tell the coroner that you saw—instead of some blood on the pillow—his Lordship murdered on the bed?' That is matter for the jury to consider; I will now pass on.

"The windows were thrown open, and the daylight was let in upon the dreadful spectacle. Could you expect Courvoisier, or any human being, who did not disguise within a human shape the heart of a wild beast, to remain unmoved at the dreadful exhibition? To see rank, age, a nobleman of seventy-three, in the enjoyment of good health, having respectable friends around him, having as much happiness as wealth, rank, and respectability could procure him, with his throat cut, weltering in his blood—how do you think you could have borne the spectacle? Mr. Adolphus says that you must show no agitation at such a sight, and if you do, it is to be taken a proof of guilt. What, I should like to know, would Mr. Adolphus have inferred from it if the man had remained calm, and looked on unmoved? Would you not have thought, and thought justly, that the man who was unmoved, who did not shudder with agitation at such a sight, was himself capable of committing the deed? But when Mr. Adolphus called on you to mark the agitation of the prisoner as a proof of guilt, what became of the women who showed the very same feelings? I think the better of those women for it. God forbid I should insinuate it was a proof of their guilt. It would appear to me, on the contrary, to be a proof of their innocence.

"I wish my friend had been where I happened to be by accident, in Hyde Park, some days since, when the murderous attempt on the life of our gracious Queen was made. I wish my friend could have seen the countenances of the bystanders when it became known; how the stoutest man stood appalled, and every face betrayed the most painful agitation. If agitation were a proof of guilt, I should say that there was not a man in the Park who might not have been convicted of an attempt to murder the Queen. Agitation, indeed! Thank God I have not yet met with that demon in the shape of man who can look on murder without agitation.

"Then my friend said that the prisoner had given no assistance. Gentlemen, the fact is not so. The assertion has been disproved by the witnesses for the prosecution . . . [A]s soon as he recovered himself from the shock which he had sustained, it has been proved that the prisoner did what was the most natural of all things for him to do. Lord William Russell had a son, the sole remnant of his admirable family, a friend of mine, with whose great loss I most deeply sympathize. The prisoner sat down, and instantly began to write to this gentleman to tell him what had occurred. He was in the act of doing so, when the maid-servant accosted him—feminine exclamation! —with 'Why, what the Devil are you doing there?' And told him that Mr. Russell must be sent for. The prisoner rushed downstairs, and in the agitation of the moment stopped the first man, in order to send him to Mr. Russell. 'What do you mean by sending such a man as that?" said the [maid-servant] to him. In the name of Heaven, was that a time to look minutely at the exterior of the messenger? Would not any human being who had sense enough to recollect the number of the house in which Mr. Russell lived do as well as the profoundest philosopher in the country? Everything the prisoner attempted to do was objected to, and yet it is made a complaint against him that he did nothing!

"The housemaid suggested that he should have mounted a horse and rode off to Mr. Russell, with the melancholy intelligence. And here, let me ask whether, if the prisoner had been guilty of the crime alleged against him, he would not have gladly availed himself of the means of escape which was suggested to him by the housemaid? . . . Is not that the course which in all human probability a guilty man would have adopted? . . .

"Instead, however, of escaping, as he might have done, he remained in the house.

"He answered every question that was put to him by the numerous policemen and others by whom he was surrounded. Of the conduct of the police on the occasion I shall have a word or two to say presently. A multiplicity of questions were put to the prisoner, every one of which he answered truly, and without hesitation or delay. His replies to each question were prompt, and what is of more importance, they were also true. I implore [you] not to forget that. . . .

"Is it not remarkable that the cause of the prisoner's being taken into custody at all proved to be quite groundless? At this time he was no more in custody than any of the other servants in the house. But at length a locket was found upon his person that the police supposed to be the property of the deceased, and Courvoisier was questioned respecting it. And what was his reply. Why, that it was his own. His assertion was not believed by the police, and the former valet, Ellis, an honest man I believe, was called in, who very fairly said he could not swear the locket was his lordship's. Well, after all the suspicion that had been so unjustly excited against the prisoner, what was the fact? Why the search went on, and Lord William Russell's locket was found, and the account given by the prisoner was proved to be true. . . . Suppose it could have been proved that he told a falsehood instead. My learned friend Mr. Adolphus would have a right to say it was to cover his guilt. But Courvoisier having told the truth when interrogated, I have a right to say it was a proof of his innocence. . . .

"Then, said my learned friend, the prisoner's trunk had been searched, and—to be sure—nothing suspicious was found in it. But do you think, said he, that the prisoner would have been fool enough to put the evidence of his guilt into his own trunk? I do not think he would. He must have been either a fool or a madman to have done it. It was searched by Inspector Tedman on the morning of the 6th—an officer who gave his evidence most fairly, his object being, as he stated, to ascertain if any stolen property or suspicious article could be found in it. He searched it minutely, taking out and unfolding article by article, but without detecting anything to incriminate or make him suspect the prisoner. Of course not, said my learned friend, Courvoisier was not such a fool as to put into his own trunk the evidence of his guilt.

"Well, but that trunk having been minutely searched by Tedman, what in fairness to the prisoner should have been done with it? What would a practised policeman of the old school have done   .   .   . ? Having once satisfied himself, as Tedman had done, that there was nothing in the trunk to criminate the prisoner, he ought instantly, for the interests of justice and the interests of the prisoner—if the interests of a prisoner ever enter into the calculations of a policeman—he ought instantly have locked and sealed that trunk. And sent it to a place of safety, where no miscreant, speculating on his share of [a] £450.0.0 reward, could have tampered with it in order to insure the conviction of the unfortunate man at the bar. But instead of that it was left open, in a room accessible to the female servants and to the whole gang of the police.

"And then what did they do? Having examined it on the 6th, they went to it again on the 8th [and found nothing suspicious]. The same policeman, Tedman, who had examined it on the 6th, again examined it on the [14th]. Why? He gave an honest reason for it. Courvoisier's uncle went to the house of Lord William with a message from the prisoner, who had been committed on the 10th. He sent for a shirt on the 13th. The man who was supposed to be conscious of having perpetrated this horrid deed sent his uncle to get linen out of his trunk, which was in the custody of the police. Did he know that in that very trunk evidence of the murder was to be found? [On the 14th], Tedman unfolded a shirt the same way he had done on the 6th, and then out dropped the gloves spotted with blood. Who put them there between the 6th and the 14th? My learned friend (Mr. Adolphus) asks, 'Who murdered Lord William Russell?' I am not bound to show that. But I have a right to ask, 'Who put these bloody gloves in the prisoner's trunk between the 6th and 14th of May, after the first minute examination by Tedman, and the prisoner had been already three days in gaol?' I say openly and fearlessly that these articles were placed there by some of the police for reasons best known to themselves.

" 'Thus bad begins, but worse remains behind.' This man, it was evidently determined, should be made the victim of some foul contrivance.

"Now I beg you to call in mind what Inspector Tedman said. He told us that he minutely examined the trunk on the 6th of May, and, notwithstanding all his vigilance, neither gloves nor handkerchiefs were found. The contents of the trunk were actually ransacked over and over to find evidence against the prisoner. Yet Mr. Collier, the constable, who, for reasons best known to himself would not go to the trunk without a witness (and, to make sure of his witness, took a brother policeman), Collier went to the trunk after it had been already three times examined, and found—as he tells us—on the very top of the things [in the] trunk two handkerchiefs spotted with blood. [These handkerchiefs], he took care to inform you, lest the fact of being found there should not be considered sufficient, had the prisoner's initials upon them. But the trunk had been examined not only once, but three times before Mr. Collier says he found the [shirt front] and handkerchiefs in it.

"But why, I would ask, was it necessary to repeat the searches so often? Why should these policemen go to the prisoner's trunk days after the unfortunate man was sent to a gloomy dungeon at least three miles distant? For the purpose of doing what? Of producing evidence against him which was not in existence before? I will suppose for a moment that the gloves might have been overlooked on the 6th and the [8th] of May. But what can be said about the handkerchiefs? And how did it happen that they should be placed on the very top of the very articles which had been previously turned over and ransacked again and again? Now, I ask this question: 'Who put these things in the trunk, and for what purpose?' They were not there on the 6th. It is clear Courvoisier could not have put them there, even if for a moment supposing that he would have risked his neck by so doing. It was physically impossible. He was in his dungeon at the time, three miles distant. Some villains must have been at work here to provide proofs of guilt against the prisoner, and endeavour to make you instrumental in rendering him the victim, not of his own guilt, but of their own foul machinations. It is clear beyond a doubt that the handkerchiefs were placed in the trunk after Courvoisier was sent to his gloomy dungeon. And I suppose no man will charge me with going too far in saying there exists a strong suspicion, if not actual proof, that the trunk has been practiced on.

"But I leave this part of the subject, and shall turn now to the conduct of Mr. Inspector Pearce—that merciful and exemplary officer, who would not, of course, attempt to intimidate a poor wretch in the fangs of the police, trembling for his life, [and] would make no suggestion to extort the confession that might hang him! Now let us see what was the conduct of this man.

"Finding some things, forsooth, in Courvoisier's pantry, he takes them up to the parlour and places them before the prisoner's face. Now, if the prisoner had been guilty of this crime, had he one particle of guilt upon his conscience, would he not have shrunk back in fear and horror on beholding these silent proofs, dug from the earth as it were on purpose to confront him and call to his mind the dreadful crime he had committed? It would have required no speech to intimidate him. His manner would at once have indicated what he felt. But the policeman was too cunning. His manner in court under the control of the bench, and under the eye of the jury, was very different from what it must have been when he had his anticipated victim alone. 'Look here, sir,' says he to the prisoner. 'Dare you now look me in the face?'

"Merciful GOD! gentlemen, was this an expression to be used by an officer of justice to an unfortunate man like the prisoner? Was there any exhibition on earth so likely to strike him dumb with horror as the proofs of murder lying before him, and that miscreant challenging Cou 'voisier to look him in the face? But he did look Mr. Pear e in the face, and answered him, 'I know nothing about these things. My conscience is clear. I am innocent.'   .   .   .

"Would it not have been more prudent, and more just to the prisoner, to have merely placed these things before him, and then said, 'These things were found in your pantry. Have you anything to say about them?' But no, that course would not suit Mr. Pearce, who was anxious—of course in pursuance of his duty merely—to get a confession from the prisoner. Was it right of Mr. Mayne, the Commissioner of Police, and a magistrate to boot, to send this inquisitorial ruffian Pearce to a private room with the prisoner, in order to brow-beat and frighten him into an admission of his guilt?   Such treatment is worthy only of the Inquisition.

"Yet the fellow who did all this told you he expected to share in the plunder, the £450.0.0 reward.   Yes, gentlemen of the jury, the money is to be divided upon the coffin of my unfortunate client should you pronounce him guilty.   And Mr. Inspector Pearce, and the rest of the police myrmidons, will, when they receive their respective shares, write the receipt in the blood of the prisoner.   I had hoped, gentlemen of the jury, that the days of blood-money had passed away .   .   .   [B]ut I am afraid that I am mistaken, and that the system is about to be revived again .   .   .   [R]ewards might be offered by the Government from the purest motives.   They might induce men to hunt out evidence.   But the effect also is to make them invent, fabricate, colour, distort, and exaggerate it to attain the end they have in view.

"Next came Mr. Baldwin, the constable, who did his best in the work of conspiracy to earn the wages of blood.   He swore well and to the purpose.   He did all he could to send a fellow-creature 'unhouseled, unanointed, unaneled' before his God.   That man equivocated and shuffled, and lied on his oath as long as he could, pretending never to have heard of the reward because he was no scholar, although every wall in London was blazoned with it.   Do you remember how he gave his evidence?   When I asked him about the reward, do you not recollect the manner in which he attempted to baffle my question?   Poor man!   He did not know how to read, and he never heard about a reward.   And yet that miscreant bloodhound was obliged afterwards to admit to me that he heard the placard offering the reward read at the station-house over and over again.   Was there no practice here?   It stands detected at once.

"Now, I tell the commissioners of police, and I tell the Government from this place—I tell them with the freedom and independence of a man who has nothing to fear or expect from them —that they are acting upon a bad and vicious system in offering rewards to their men for hunting out the blood of their fellow-creatures.   After this, and the case of Gould, I shall consider any Government that offers rewards accessory to murder.

"There is an expression of the prisoner which is supposed to operate to his prejudice.   But, to my mind, I cannot imagine anything more natural than the expression to which I am going to refer. And I would remind the jury that you are not to canvass too strictly the expressions of a foreigner. The expression to which I allude is this—'It would not go so hard against me if these things were not found in my pantry.'

"Then comes the question, 'Who hid them there?' You are asked to say that Courvoisier hid these things in the pantry, [and] that therefore he is guilty. But is not the fact of these things being found in the pantry a proof that they were not put there by the prisoner? What! he who, if the statement made be correct, was up all night roaming about the house—who had bed-rooms and passages, and other places to conceal those things —could he be supposed to be the person to go and place these things in his own pantry? Could he have selected this place in particular in order that he might the more securely place a rope about his own neck? Who hid the handkerchiefs? Who hid the gloves? The pantry, you will recollect, was open to every one. And was it not the very place where every one wishing to place the crime at the prisoner's door would hide the things which were found there?   .   .   .

"Another expression of the prisoner's has been caught at with a view to his prejudice. They can find no trace of actions, and so they are obliged to fly to words. The slightest expression is fastened upon. The prisoner is reported to have said, 'I wish I had old Billy's money; I would not be long in this country.'

"This expression he used in the presence of the two female servants, so [the prosecution] want to say that the prisoner premeditated robbery and murder, and that he did so in the presence of two witnesses, and those witnesses his fellow-servants. I will do the witnesses the justice to admit that the prisoner did make use of these words. But unless you can believe him to be insane, you cannot suppose that in using them he was influenced by any improper or base motives. They are perfectly consistent with the views and feelings of an innocent man. You, gentlemen, are fond of the land that gave you birth. But supposing you were far from [it], and, toiling with industry and zeal for daily sustenance, but away from all those whom you loved most dear, and anxiously desiring to return home to the land that you loved, the friends of your youth, and the companions of your childhood—what more natural for you to exclaim, if you saw a rich man passing, 'I wish I had that man's money, and I would not be long away from my own country.' . . . There never dropped from human lips a more innocent or natural expression, 'I wish I had old Billy's money; I would soon be in my own country,' an expression upon which the prosecution in this case has caught at with so much avidity. . . .

"Over every portion of this case doubt and darkness rest, and you will come to a conclusion against this man at the peril of your souls. It is assumed that because of the stain of blood upon the white gloves, that therefore the prisoner is guilty of murder. What! is it usual for a man to commit the crime of murder in white gloves? Then, again, a part of a shirt was discovered in the prisoner's trunk, and this circumstance is fixed upon as operating to the prisoner's prejudice. What! is a man to commit murder, and because spots of blood might appear upon a part of his shirt he is so to economise his linen, that he would throw a portion of it away, and keep another portion, and then, in order that he might give every chance against himself, he is to place the reserved part in his own trunk [along with a sixpenny pair of gloves] where it is sure to be found by any person looking over it? Why the thing is absurd . . .

"But are you, upon the facts stated in reference to the gloves, [to the handkerchiefs], to his shirt front, to impute to the prisoner the crime of murder? Courvoisier was apprehended in the house. That house is searched. The police, according to their account, so watched the house that nobody could have gone out. Is it not singular, then, that in no part of the property belonging to Courvoisier, or on his person, was one spot of blood discovered? If he murdered the man, do you think it possible that he should have no taint of blood, either on his person or clothes? Would not there have been an appearance of bloody water if he had washed himself? Where were the stains of blood under the fingernails, which, like the damned spot on *Lady Macbeth's* hand, no water could wash out? When was it, too, that any articles, even of the slightest suspicion, were found in the prisoner's trunk? Not until the 14th of May, eight or nine days after the commission of the murder, at a time when the prisoner was far removed from the premises where his trunk [was] deposited, and while he was confined within the walls of a prison.

"You are aware that a great many observations have been made upon the subject of the walls and the back area door. On seeing these marks Courvoisier observed that whoever committed the murder must have come in at a certain place. And such was the impression of Tedman and two other policemen, though, on re-examination, they found that this could not have been the case. Did they give Courvoisier an opportunity of correcting his error also? They took means to correct their own error; but he was bound by an observation he made at the moment, and in which they all concurred at the first superficial glance.
.   .   .

"I have now described to you this case as it was laid before the magistrates [at the preliminary examination], and as up to the close of yesterday, I was prepared to meet it. I now come to a portion of the case of which I have reason loudly to complain. I allude to the evidence which was adduced against the prisoner for the first time yesterday. Is it not most extraordinary, that although this murder has been rumoured about the whole metropolis for so many weeks past, after it has been frequently brought under the consideration of the police magistrates, yet up to the night of Thursday last nothing was known about the missing plate? I have my strong suspicions about it. I think nothing could be more shameful than that after the arrival in this court of Cumming, who admitted that he knew I was counsel for the prisoner, no intimation of the nature of his evidence should have been given to the prisoner. I admit that the names of other witnesses not examined before the magistrates have been very fairly communicated to the prisoner's counsel. I think that a night at least should have been given to allow inquiries to be made into the character of the persons coming up against the prisoner. This new evidence was sprung upon us like a mine under our feet. I know nothing about Mrs. Piolaine. How should I? The prosecution have taken care that I should know nothing about her. But let us examine her testimony. If that woman did not tell the truth distinctly, the persons who were called to corroborate her prove nothing at all.

"I hope you know something of Leicester Place. If you do, you know the character of this foreign hotel, with a billiard room attached to it, where, unlike at a respectable hotel, any stranger, not being a guest, may enter and gamble. This is the resi-

dence of Mrs. Piolaine, who though she heard of the murder of
Lord William Russell on the day after it occurred, did not for
three long weeks, whilst her husband was remaining in this
country, speak a word respecting it to the partner of her bed.
And never once thinks of looking into the parcel left her, as she
says, by the prisoner, until the day previous to that upon which
she is made a witness. Gentlemen, I ask this question, 'Did you,
in the whole course of your existence, ever hear of such a singular circumstance?'

"It was not until the middle of this long investigation, and after the prisoner had undergone the agonizing ordeal of standing a
whole day in that dock, that this new evidence was brought into
court, though it has been proved that for some time previously a
reward of £50.0.0 had been offered for the discovery of the
plate. And was it not an odd time for such a discovery to have
been made? They kept it to themselves all night, and sprung
[it] upon us in the morning, when every moment of ours was
engaged with the other part of the proceedings. The prisoner
ought at least to have had one night afforded him to make inquiries upon the subject.

"What was Mrs. Piolaine's evidence? A French paper, forsooth, was translated to the lady (and I beg the particular attention of your lordships and of you gentlemen of the jury to this
circumstance) and then, in some unaccountable manner, it puts
her in mind of a parcel having been left with her by Courvoisier,
whom she had never known by the name of 'Courvoisier,' but
by the name of 'Jean.' How on earth could a French paper
have directed her suspicions against the prisoner? I have no
right to speculate upon what the paper contained. But how
could a French paper have made her suspect a man of whom she
had never heard?"

Here Mr. Baron Parke interrupted to say that if "learned
counsel wished to raise a doubt or contradiction on the point, he
might have called for the paper and examined its contents."
Phillips barely paused:

"I have a right to say that there is little or no proof how that
paper directed her suspicions against Courvoisier. Neither is
there any proof that she ever knew Courvoisier to be a servant
of Lord William Russell. This most important part of the case
depends upon the testimony of that woman. Except through

her they don't trace [the parcel] to Courvoisier. She says that
it was Courvoisier who brought the parcel a week or a fortnight
before the murder. She knew nothing about the man. She remembered so little about the man that she did not know him
when he came in. And she says that . . . after the
trial [started] she opened up the parcel at last, in the presence
of some half-dozen persons, who in a most extraordinary manner
signed every one of them a kind of roundrobin of an inventory
of what it contained.

"This is all very well. But it is perfectly consistent to suppose
that Courvoisier was not the man who brought this property to
her. The prosecution told you that they would identify the
property in the parcel as Lord William Russell's. They went
further. They said they would identify the clothes which the
parcel contained as being those of the prisoner. They called the
housemaid and the man Ellis [the former valet]. But they
could only say they had seen the prisoner in a jacket similar to
the one found in the paper parcel. Neither could swear that the
jacket belonged to Courvoisier. The prosecutors went further,
and they called the prisoner's washerwoman, whose testimony
was to this effect:

> 'Upon my oath, no sock of Courvoisier's that I ever
> washed—and I have washed many—was ever marked
> in the heel as this is. They were marked at the top,
> and the letters also were different. He did not mark
> them with a "C" as this is marked, but with the letters
> "B.F.C." '

"Why this is disproof, if anything, of the fact which they
wished to establish.

"But supposing all this were admitted (and I am sure you will
pay attention to what I am saying, and if you can find your way
out of this case consistently with the ends of justice without
shedding the prisoner's blood you will be glad to do so), and that
this mysterious evidence about the plate were as clear as it is
doubtful, that the clothes in the parcel belonged to Courvoisier,
and that the parcel itself was deposited by the prisoner with
Mrs. Piolaine. Supposing all this admitted, is it conclusive of
murder?

"Gentlemen, this is a question upon which his Lordship will
give his most valuable opinion. But I might venture to say that

though this evidence, if true, would be conclusive of robbery, and of that robbery the prisoner might hereafter be convicted, if guilty, and upon conviction, transported for the term of his natural life to undergo a lingering death in exile in Norfolk Island; yet it is by no means conclusive of murder. Therefore, in acquitting the prisoner of the murder you will have still this reflection, that if guilty of the robbery, he will be liable to a heavy and dreadful punishment. With respect to the commission of murder, you may have a strong suspicion, or even a moral conviction; but it is not [on] a strong suspicion or a moral conviction that a man is to be declared guilty of murder. If, notwithstanding that suspicion, you feel bound to acquit the prisoner, he is still answerable to the law of this country for the robbery, if guilty.

"And, even supposing him guilty of the murder, which indeed is known to the Almighty God alone, and of which for the sake of his eternal soul, I hope he is innocent, it is better far that in the dreadful solitude of exile he should, though not in the sight of man, yet before the presence of God, atone by lingering repentance for the deed, than that he should now be sent in the dawning of his manhood to an ignominious death in a case where the truth is not clear. I say that the proof adduced is not conclusive of murder, though it may be of dishonesty on the part of the prisoner, with which latter crime he does not at present stand charged.

"And now, gentlemen, having traveled through this case of mystery and darkness, my anxious and painful task is done. But, gentlemen, yours is about to commence. May the Almighty God guide you to a just conclusion. One of the attributes of the Almighty is this day given to you. The issue of life and death is in your hands. To you it is given to restore this man once more to the enjoyments of existence and the dignity of freedom, or to consign him to an ignominious death, and to brand upon his grave the awful epithet of 'Murderer.' Gentlemen, mine has been a painful and awful task, but still more awful is your responsibility. To violate the living temple which the Lord hath made, to quench the fire that His breath [hath] given, is an awful and tremendous responsibility. And the word 'Guilty' once pronounced, let me remind you, is irrevocable. Speak not that word lightly. Speak it not on suspicion, however strong, upon moral conviction, however apparently well grounded—upon inference, upon doubt—nor upon anything but a clear, irresistible, bright noonday certainty of the truth of what is alleged.

"I speak to you in no spirit of hostile admonition. Heaven knows I do not. I speak to you in the spirit of a friend and fellow Christian. And in that spirit I tell you that if you pronounce the word lightly, its memory will never die within you. It will accompany you in your walks. It will follow you in your solitary retirements like a shadow. It will haunt you in your sleep and hover round your bed. It will take the shape of an accusing spirit, and confront and condemn you before the judgment seat of your God. So beware what you do."

The end was jolting. Phillips had been speaking for three hours. Three hours of solemn quiet except for the melodic voice pleading for justice and mercy for Courvoisier. Tears touched even whiskered cheeks. Tears in the jury box. Those whose minds had been already made up now wondered if they had not judged too soon and too harshly. Shaken, they listened to the brief testimony of five witnesses, including Lady Julia Lockwood, that spoke to Courvoisier's good character for kind heartedness, humanity, and inoffensive disposition. If the vote had been taken then   .   .   .   but it was not.

For three and a half hours, Lord Chief Justice Nicholas Tindal charged the jury, counseling them with the full latitude that England gives her judges, analyzing for them the evidence, telling them the law, drying every tear and resolving every doubt. "You are not," he said, "to administer mercy but justice." At the same time, "it will not be enough that such facts and circumstances should in your minds be consistent with the guilt of the prisoner; they must be such as to exclude from your mind all reasonable doubt upon the question as to whether or no the prisoner committed the dreadful crime charged against him."

He chopped away impartially to right and to left. The jury should not give a "strict interpretation" to words used "in a moment of anxiety," such as Sarah Mancer's "Let us go and see where his Lordship is," or her statement that she had seen Lord Russell "murdered in bed." Nor, similarly, to Courvoisier's offhand remark to fellow servants about Old Billy's money.

Of Inspector Pearce's "Can you look me in the face?" he told them: "Perhaps the observation might as well not have been made, but I am bound to tell you I believe the officer made it honestly, and without any improper intention; and therefore I do not think he is deserving of the blame that has been attempted to be cast upon him."

Constable Baldwin was a different matter. They should disregard the whole of his testimony about no prints in the dust, for "he gave his testimony in such a way that it would be dangerous in such a serious inquiry as this to give any credit to it." But they should not forget that others had given testimony on the same point.

As to the unlikelihood of Courvoisier hiding stolen property in his own pantry, the judge suggested the jury consider that the thief doubtless thought the property was well concealed. And of the possibility that a stranger had been thief and murderer, they should consider "how any stranger, after taking" the various articles, "could think of putting them where they were found."

In determining whether there was a police conspiracy against Courvoisier, "the jury should consider whether, if the policemen could be capable of committing such an act for such a purpose, it was not likely that they would for the same object have done something which would be more effective in inculpating the prisoner. The gloves, after all, were but very slightly marked with blood, and they were things in which it was not probable that a person would invest himself who would be about to engage in so bloody a transaction."   .   .   .   "The observations were applicable to the finding of the two handkerchiefs."

The Chief Justice told them that but for the finding of the silver, "the case might have been open to some conjecture favourable to the prisoner. The person who committed the robbery might have been disturbed, and it could have been said that he only succeeded in carrying off those fourteen articles; but these articles being afterwards found where the prisoner himself left them, and when it turns out that they were not carried off by a stranger, this conjecture falls to the ground. The evidence respecting these articles is only legitimate for the purpose of doing away with this conjecture. At the same time that I feel it my duty to make this observation, I am bound to caution you not to mix up the crime of murder with that of robbery. Many a man might be guilty of robbery who would shrink with horror from the perpetration of the more dreadful crime of murder; but, at the same time, you will perceive that this additional evidence is calculated to throw a general light on the whole transaction."

Finally, he rubbed the bloom off the testimony of Courvoisier's only witnesses—his character witnesses. " . . . I may here observe that it is clear he had forfeited the good character that had been given him by his having removed from his master's house a quantity of plate several days before the murder."

The charge had been in keeping with the judge's personal reputation for fairness on the bench. The jury went to their deliberations, returning to the courtroom an hour and 25 minutes later.

"How say you, gentlemen," asked the court clerk, "have you agreed on your verdict; do you find the prisoner guilty or not guilty of the felony of murder with which he is charged?"

The hushed tension of the moment returns in the Victorian journalese: "The foreman of the jury, in a suppressed tone, which however was distinctly audible in the most distant part of the crowded court, so breathless was the anxiety which prevailed, replied, 'We find him *Guilty*' ".

Minutes later, the clerk spoke to Courvoisier:

> "François Benjamin Courvoisier, you have been found guilty of the wilful murder of William Russell, Esquire, commonly called Lord William Russell. What have you to say why the Court should not give you sentence to die according to law?"

Courvoisier said nothing, "nor did he betray the slightest visible emotion."

In a silent courtroom, the Lord Chief Justice, now in his black cap, spoke, his voice betraying an emotion long restrained:

> "François Benjamin Courvoisier, you have been found guilty by the unanimous verdict of an intelligent, a patient, and an impartial jury of the crime of wilful murder. That crime has been established against you, not indeed by the testimony of eye-witnesses, but by the no less unerring certainty of circumstances all pointing to your guilt, and sufficient to remove any

doubt from the minds of the jury and those who heard this trial.

"It is ordained by God that the murderer shall not go unpunished, and that divine ordination has been exemplified and made manifest in the course of this trial, for, although your crime was committed in the dark and lonely time of night, when no eye but that of a watchful Providence could see the deed, it has nevertheless been brought to light in a manner clear and convincing to all. The murder in itself, with the single exception of one direct circumstance against you which subsequently appeared in the course of the trial, was involved in mystery. It was committed in the dark, and planned by you with so much secrecy and cunning, aided by the peculiar facilities of which you took advantage, that you considered yourself secure from the consequences of your crime. You felt no compunction for your helpless and unconscious victim, who at the time was buried in repose, in the sanctity and security of his own dwelling. You felt no regard for that sacred duty which a servant owes to his master, and that master a kind and indulgent one. You selected the dark hour of night to deprive an innocent and unoffending nobleman, aged and infirm, of his property and life, and thereby destroyed, for a period, the domestic and social comfort of the members of his noble family who have sustained a shock almost unparalleled, and which has been communicated to the whole community. The motive which induced you to commit this guilty and atrocious act can only be known to God and your own conscience, but it is to be feared that the base love of gain first induced you to break through the law of God and man, and led you to destroy your master, whom you were bound to protect and to defend.

"It therefore becomes necessary, in order to hold out a warning to others in your situation, that your life be forfeited, and that the law should take its course. I can hold out no hope of mercy to you in this world, but I implore you to employ the few short days you have to live in prayer and sincere repentance, and an earnest appeal for mercy to that beneficent and Almighty God from whom alone you can expect or hope for mercy.

"It now only remains for me to pass upon you the sentence of the law, which is, That you, François Benjamin Courvoisier, be taken from this gaol to a place of execution, and that you there be hanged by the neck until you be dead, and that your body be afterwards buried within the precincts of the prison, and may God Almighty have compassion on your sinful soul."

Chapter VII

THE CONFESSIONS OF COURVOISIER

If, to a reporter watching him led from the dock, Courvoisier appeared unmoved either by the prospect of hanging or repentance, it could only have been a momentary appearance. The last choked up words of the Lord Chief Justice ended Courvoisier's silent period. Ordinarily an outgoing, talkative man, at least for the last 40 days since he had the advice of counsel Courvoisier had said very little about what concerned him most. Now, even before he left the holding cell at the Old Bailey to be returned to Newgate prison, Courvoisier began talking, anxious to be talking, to have people listen to something different every time. Each day a new confession right down to the night before he was hanged 16 days later before more than 20,000 spectators, crowding streets, windows, rooftops for a better view of the gallows erected just outside the prison wall. William Makepeace Thackeray got up at three in the morning to be present at the event he described as "Going to See a Man Hanged;" he estimated the crowd at 40,000,[1] at the last moment turning away his face in horror,[2] yet leaving he said, "with a disgust for murder, but it was for *the murder I saw done*." [3]

The confessions of Courvoisier had in them enough of variety to satisfy every curiosity and every theory of the crime—social, moral, theological. He told his jailers he started stealing silverware from the dining-room sometime after Lord Russell went to bed on the night of May 5–6; he was surprised at this work by the old man himself on the way to the bathroom; in the ensuing row Lord Russell said he would fire Courvoisier in the morning, and went back to bed; "roused to a state of phrensy" by this encounter, Courvoisier took a large ivory-handled, damascus carving knife from the dining-room supply, and when snores once again sounded through the bedroom door he quietly entered the room and cut Lord Russell's throat without waking him.

Again, Courvoisier said Lord Russell threatened to take away his character; his master was about to give him a bad character

1. [W. M. Thackeray], "Going to See a Man Hanged," 22 Fraser's Magazine 150, 153 (1840).

2. *Id.* 156.

3. *Id.* 158.

for being inattentive, forgetting to send the coach to Brookes' on time on May 5th was but one example; and so Courvoisier killed him.

Again, he said he had planned the murder for the previous night, to cover up various thefts, but abandoned the enterprise until early Tuesday. In one version of this, he said it was God who stayed his hand.

As the end approached, the confessions became more vivid, more breast beating, more Victorian. He had planned the killing and robbery a week before; he had violated all 10 Commandments, had been under the dominion of Satan, and been enjoying his sins; he berated himself for fouling the good name of Courvoisier, and prayed for salvation through Christ. He acknowledged that "[c]ondemnation and eternal sufferings are the portion I deserve."

Each of these variations of motivation and sequence was accompanied by equally inventive versions of the details of the crime itself, and of the hiding of the stolen property, bringing excited denials from the police. The exasperated Sheriff Evans told the press Courvoisier had contradicted himself so often no credit could be given to anything the wretch said other than that he had killed Lord Russell with a knife. Nonetheless, Courvoisier's inexhaustible flow of detail was sufficiently needling to the police that they felt obliged to dig up the floor of Courvoisier's Bow-street cell, and drain a toilet in a search for more stolen property; results zero.

In one of his more colorful tales, Courvoisier said that with the exception of some trifling thefts from a former employer he had led an upright life, until a visit to Richmond attending Lord Russell, when he was corrupted by a book. The Duke of Bedford's valet had loaned him the novel *Jack Sheppard*, and fascinated with the hero's life of crime he had launched his own by stealing Lord Russell's locket. Since then he had also seen a performance of the play *Jack Sheppard*. Elaborating on the theme, Courvoisier said the inspiration for murdering Lord Russell had come from the book; he was sorry he read it. This report brought an angry letter to *The Times* from W. Harrison Ainsworth, author of the best selling fictionized version of the Jack Sheppard story,[4] saying that "the assassin Courvoisier"

4. W. H. Ainsworth, Jack Sheppard
[1839].

had denied the whole report and had never read his book. The Sheriff, in the public interest, repeated that the report was true; Courvoisier had told him it was the book that did it. The volatile weekly *Examiner* denounced the evil tendencies of this sort of literature; it carefully paralleled the language of one of Courvoisier's confessions—"I went to the side of the bed and drew the knife across his throat," with similar language in the Ainsworth romance, describing a killing by Jack Sheppard's lieutenant Blueskin—"Seizing her by the hair, he pulled back her head, and drew the knife with all his force across her throat." [5] Whether the comparison proved that Courvoisier or those reporting his confession had read Ainsworth, the *Examiner* said it expected "that detestable book" would now be advertised as *"The Cutthroat's Manual,* or *The Mid-night Assassin's vade mecum"* and "If ever there was a publication that deserved to be burnt by the hands of the common hangman it is *Jack Sheppard."* [6]

Though their understanding of the details varied, the public eagerly snapped up the demoralizing influence of bad literature as a moral to be gained from the fall of Courvoisier. The star of the Dublin performance of "Jack Sheppard" later recalled:

> "The very night we opened, Courvoisier's confession was published. In this he says that the first idea of crime which he ever had came to him while he was witnessing the play of 'Jack Sheppard' at the Adelphi, and he had been really led into cutting Lord William Russell's throat through that play. That settled our business, for although we fulfilled every night of our engagement, I remember the houses were very poor." [7]

Satirical doggerel attacked Ainsworth, a prospective victim saying he has "misgivings of the 'gentle Sheppard's' razor

.   .   .

> "For he had read his several tales of severing bone and muscle

5. Examiner (London), June 28, 1840, No. 1691, page 402; *cf.* W. H. Ainsworth, Jack Sheppard 181 [1839].

6. Examiner (London), *supra* note 5.

7. H. W. Bleackley, Jack Sheppard 105 (1929).

("So had the late Courvoisier, who killed Lord William Russell.)" [8]

This explanation of Courvoisier's ruin was coupled with a rebuke to Charles Phillips for his warning to the Courvoisier jury "to be cautious how you imbrue your hands in this man's blood." It was hawked even in the shadow of the gallows to the crowds awaiting Courvoisier's execution, in a broadsheet that included *The Lament of Francis Courvoisier* (to the tune of "Bank of Primroses"):

"To the Surrey for to see Jack Sheppard
  To beguile the time I went one night,

But I little thought that fatal evening
  That it would all my prospects blight.

"Alas! that night has proved my ruin,
  In innocent blood I have my hands imbued,

I was unworthy of such a master,
  Who to me was always kind and good.

"For a whole week I planned the murder,
  It engaged my mind by day and night,

I felt no remorse, but like a demon
  It seemed to me a source of great delight." [9]

Throughout his ordeal of confessing, Courvoisier insisted that he had not put the bloody gloves or handkerchiefs in his trunk, that he knew nothing about the gloves, that any spotting of the handkerchiefs would be from a nosebleed having no connection with the murder, that he knew nothing about the torn shirt. He said he rolled up his sleeves before the killing. (Years later, this led to a picturesque if confused explanation of the absence of blood on Courvoisier's clothing; he had stripped, and at the time of the murder was "in a complete state of nudity," except for a pair of white cotton gloves.) [10]

---

8. *Id.* 106.

9. The Execution of Francis Courvoisier for the Murder of Lord William Russell, opposite the debtor's door, this day, (broadsheet, [1840]); and *see*, H. W. Bleackley, Jack Sheppard 107–108 (1929).

10. Henderson, *supra* ch. III, note 7, at 155, and *cf.* J. B. Atlay, Famous Trials 62 (1899), C. Biron, Without Prejudice 147 (1936), Y. Bridges, Two Studies in Crime 121, and app. II (1959), A. Brock, A Casebook of Crime 23 (1948), M. Frewen, Melton Mowbray 19–20 (1924), H. M. Walbrook, Murders and Murder Trials viii, 79 (1932).

Several times Courvoisier went out of his way to exonerate the cook and the housemaid; they had nothing to do with the murder; he was sorry he had caused them any grief. His own feelings of remorse were strongly reinforced for him in the Reverend Mr. Carver's "condemned sermon" delivered to a record attendance of inmates and distinguished visitors—nobles, Members of Parliament, ladies—in the Newgate chapel the day before the hanging. Addressing a dejected Courvoisier, who sat on a bench directly before the pulpit, as "you, the midnight assassin of an aged, amiable, and unoffending master," the Ordinary of Newgate reminded him:

> "You had almost reached the very verge of a triumph that would have included the deepest sorrow to the guiltless .   .   . So strong was the impression of your innocence, from your long-established character for mildness and probity, that a mortal stab was about to be inflicted upon the reputation of your fellow-domestics and other innocent persons. You reposed in quiescent security of acquittal. At the critical juncture, God, in the wonderful working of His Providence, by a marvellous chain of circumstantial evidence, with unerring certainty, fixed upon you the guilt of murdering one whom every tie of religion and morality bound you to love, reverence, and respect, yea, to peril your own life, if necessary, to save that of your master from the assassin's blow."

The minister suggested to Courvoisier that private reflection would be more productive than "on this exciting occasion, before a large and public assembly," that there was still time for a more satisfactory confession of each "horrid and loathsome detail," and even a possibility of having his scarlet sins "made white as snow." Courvoisier considered the suggestion. Sarah Mancer and Mary Hannell were on his mind the night before he died:

> "I still think of those poor servants whom I have had the heart to treat so cruelly. I doubt not that they will pardon me. I pray to God that he may bless them, and make them prosper in this world, and promote their salvation."

In the days following his conviction and sentence to death, one additional confession of Courvoisier led all the rest. It is even now not completely clear how this confession first came to public notice, whether from an eavesdropper, from someone who broke a confidence, from Courvoisier's own fast moving lips, or from Charles Phillips himself. But in the same Monday morning newspapers carrying the story of Courvoisier's conviction and the first accounts of his confession of guilt, the word was out that before Charles Phillips spoke to the jury Courvoisier had confessed his guilt to his counsel. Of all the confessions of Courvoisier, this one was to have the most lasting effects, surviving Courvoisier's making peace with man and God, clouding the remaining years of Charles Phillips, following Phillips into the final estimate of his contemporaries, stirring controversy over the role of Courvoisier's counsel and counsel in general, and ultimately influencing the ethical canons of lawyers in England, America, and wherever the Anglo-American system of legal representation has taken hold.

The exact moment and content of Courvoisier's confession to his lawyer are not agreed upon. One version has it that Courvoisier merely confessed to Phillips the theft of the Russell silver, and that this occurred on Saturday—the last day of the trial. But this account is based almost entirely on a jumbled interpretation of an ambiguous recollection of Mr. Serjeant Ballantine almost a half century after the event,[11] and is not consistent with allusions to the confession in the press or with other contemporary accounts. There is, for example, solicitor Hobler's unseemly jubilation to his client The Commissioners of Metropolitan Police right after the jury came in on Saturday:

> "I have the satisfaction of acquainting you that the Prisoner Courvoisier has been found guilty & sentenced to die—
>
> "I am well pleased to hear from Mr. Phillips's own lips that yesterday, the Prisoner after he had seen my female witness Madam Piolaine yesterday morning con-

11. Y. Bridges, Two Studies in Crime, *supra* note 10, at 87–89; Ballantine, *supra* ch. III, note 7, at 61–63; *cf.* Robinson, *supra* ch. III, note 7, at 60–61.

fessed to Mr. Phillips & Clarkson that he did the murder   .   ." [12]

There is also the detailed public statement made by Charles
Phillips nine years after the trial, a statement attested to by a
number of lawyers present at the trial, and—on this point—not
contradicted by the numerous people then alive and in a position
to know.[13] Phillips' statement is likewise accepted here as fixing the place where he heard the confession, in—rather than out
of court as some have speculated.[14]

Piecing together newspaper and other contemporary accounts,
including Phillips' version, I think this is what probably happened:

When, on Friday morning, before the start of the second day
of the trial, Charlotte Piolaine identified Courvoisier in the
Newgate prison yard as the "Jean" who had left the package of
silver with her, Courvoisier also saw Mrs. Piolaine. At the first
opportunity, which was after he was in the dock that morning,
the courtroom filling with spectators but the judges not yet on
the bench, Courvoisier sent word that he wanted to talk to his
counsel. Mr. Phillips and Mr. Clarkson came to their client in the
courtroom. As Mr. Phillips tells it in his own language (which
has a Phillips ring whoever is doing the talking):

"   .   .   Up to this morning I believed most firmly in his innocence; and so did many others as well as
myself.

" 'I have sent for you, gentlemen,' said he, 'to tell you
I committed the murder!'

---

12. Letter, Hobler to The Commissioners of Metropolitan Police,
dated "Old Court Saturday 10
m[?] to 7," [June 20, 1840].

13. *Compare* Y. Bridges, Two Studies in Crime, *supra* note 10, at
87–89, *with* Henderson, *supra* ch.
III, note 7, at 205–206; Report of
the Trial of Courvoisier vi–vii,
40–41, 66–69 (1918); The Times
(London), Herald (London), Chronicle (London), Post (London), all
June 22, 1840; Warren-Phillips,

supra ch. III, note 75, generally,
and especially at 11; see also 12
Central Criminal Court Sessions
Papers 266–269 (1840), and Regina
v. Courvoisier, 9 Car. & P. 362
[1841], 173 Eng.Rep. 869, 870
(1840).

14. Robinson, *supra* ch. III, note 7,
at 60; Y. Bridges, Two Studies in
Crime, *supra* note 10, at 89; see,
Ballantine, *supra* ch. III, note 7, at
61–62.

"When I could speak, which was not immediately, I said, 'Of course, then, you are going to plead guilty?'

" 'No, sir,' was the reply, 'I expect you to defend me to the utmost.'

"We returned to our seats   .   .   ." [15]

15. Warren-Phillips, *supra* ch. III, note 75, at 11.

Chapter VIII

IN CONFIDENCE

Mr. Phillips and Mr. Clarkson had not long to remain in their seats if something were to be done about the startling news they had just received from their client. Shortly the judges would take the bench, and the trial would again be under way. Courvoisier's solicitor Mr. Flower had informed Phillips when he was employed that the defense of the case rested on Courvoisier's innocence. The previous day's vigorous cross-examination of prosecution witnesses, notably Sarah Mancer and Constable Baldwin, had been dictated by the defense of innocence. What now? A matter of legal ethics?

As with trial lawyers yesterday and today, confronting the necessity of response in the heat of conflict, Phillips' dilemma could not be continued for philosophical speculation. It was now. An overpowering immediacy. In the moments that remained, a practical decision had to be made that could affect the life of his client, and his own career at the bar. Does professional duty require me to stick with Courvoisier? Would it be even proper to continue to defend such a man? If I stay on, how do I conduct such a defense? If the defense continues, not one, but a succession of hard decisions, each with its own refined pricking at the conscience of a lawyer.

What do you do when your client tells you in mid-trial that he is "guilty" ? The answer to that one Phillips had not learned at Trinity College, Dublin, nor at his Inn of Court the Middle Temple, nor in 28 years of practice. But it had to be answered now. As Phillips later said, "My position at this moment was, I believe, without parallel in the annals of the profession." [1] Sad day for any lawyer. No precedent.

Phillips was leading counsel; the decision was his. As he recalled it, "I at once came to the resolution of abandoning the case, and so I told my colleague." Junior counsel Mr. Clarkson rebelled at the suggestion. "He strongly and urgently remonstrated against it, but in vain. At last he suggested our obtaining the opinion of *the learned judge who was not trying the*

---

1. Warren-Phillips, *supra* ch. III, note 75, at 11–12.

cause upon what he considered to be the professional etiquette under circumstances so embarrassing." [2]

This was desperate and bad advice. No one fitted the description of the words here italicized. There were two judges in the case. Mr. Baron Parke was not the presiding judge, was not to charge the jury, nor to impose the mandatory death sentence if the jury found Courvoisier guilty, but under the English practice at the time he was "trying the cause" in every other sense of the words. He assisted Lord Chief Justice Tindal in reading evidence to the jury, made some comments to the jury, and made some rulings on questions of law. He was there as an essential figure in the trial to assist the Chief Justice. A law report published the year after the trial describes the case as *Regina v. Courvoisier*, "Before Lord Chief Justice Tindal and Mr. Baron Parke." [3]

It was desperate and bad advice, but Phillips in desperation took it. His statement years later that one of the judges was "not trying the cause" can only have been a rationalization of his conduct under stress. It was perhaps an indirect statement of what Phillips could not bring himself to confess—that even if Mr. Baron Parke were one of the judges, since he was not the principal one, it would still be a good bet that Parke would say nothing to the Chief Justice. (From the available evidence it is still unclear exactly when Lord Chief Justice Tindal was informed of Courvoisier's confession to Mr. Phillips.) [4]

In any event, at that moment in the rapidly filling courtroom, Phillips felt the need of advice as urgently as Courvoisier felt the need for a lawyer. He "very willingly acquiesced" [5] in Mr. Clarkson's suggestion. Together, they went to see Mr. Baron Parke, and told him what had happened. Phillips' decision under these circumstances, said a hostile contemporary, "showed

---

2. *Id.* 12.

3. 9 Car. & P. 362 [1841], 173 Eng. Rep. 869 (1840); *cf.* 12 Central Criminal Court Sessions Papers, title page, and page 216 (1840); *see* also, Henderson, *supra* ch. III, note 7, at 204; Chronicle (London), June 22, 1840; and generally, Report of the Trial of Courvoisier vii–viii (1918).

4. *Compare* Warren-Phillips, *supra* ch. III, note 75, at 14, *with* S. Warren, *The Mystery of Murder, and its Defence*, in 2 Miscellanies Critical, Imaginative, and Juridical 1, 61, and 61n., and 62 (1855).

5. Warren-Phillips, *supra* ch. III, note 75, at 12.

the inherent weakness of his character. It was peculiarly a situation for self-reliance and sound judgment." [6]

We do not have Mr. Baron Parke's own version of what took place. His trial notes, once in the Inner Temple Library,[7] are nowhere to be found, thought destroyed in an air raid that scored a direct hit on the Library during World War II. But lawyers who speak as from personal knowledge tell us the judge was "much annoyed" [8] with Phillips, one saying "[t]he baron very naturally rebuked him for making him acquainted with the confession." [9] What is known of the judge's respect for the legal proprieties give these comments the ring of understatement.[10]

Criticism of Charles Phillips for telling it to the judge has come principally from lawyers. His very human feeling of need for advice in an emergency, and getting it where he could, take on a serious aspect in the context of the trial under way and Phillips' relationship to court and client. In the same moment, he compromised a judge's at best difficult duty to let nothing but the law and the evidence in court affect his conduct of a trial, and broke the confidence in which he was bound to hold the communication of his client. Later, he compounded his indiscretions, incurring the further wrath of old Serjeant Ballantine:

> ".   .   . and certainly no censure can be too severe upon the conduct of Phillips, who, when assailed for his mismanagement of the case, violated the confidence that his interview with Baron Parke demanded, and endeavoured to excuse himself by saying he had acted under that learned judge's advice." [11]

If Phillips' actions on these points were not model, something may still be said for what he did, at the time he did it.

Unless it is clear that no confidence is intended, a lawyer is required to treat as confidential communications from his client,

---

6. Ballantine, *supra* ch. III, note 7, at 62; *see* also C. Biron, Without Prejudice 144–145 (1936).

7. Report of the Trial of Courvoisier viii (1918).

8. *Id.*

9. Robinson, *supra* ch. III, note 7, at 61.

10. 15 Holdsworth, A History of English Law 486–492 (1965); 9 *id.* 414 (1926).

11. Ballantine, *supra* ch. III, note 7, at 62.

indeed from anyone consulting him for legal advice even though the lawyer decides not to take the case. The lawyer is bound by the rule of his profession to maintain the confidence in court or out of court, and the law goes even further. Under the attorney-client privilege, the lawyer cannot be forced to testify to what has been told to him in confidence.[12] It is the lawyer's duty to preserve that confidence "at every peril to himself," [13] resolving doubts in favor of keeping the confidence, resisting every attempt to squeeze out of him a confidence that ought to be kept. As an old judge wrote of a young lawyer who crumbled under the threat of contempt if he refused to tell what his client had told him:

> Defendant's attorney should have chosen to go to jail and take his chances of release by a higher court. This is not intended as a criticism of the action of the attorney. It is, however, a suggestion to any and all attorneys who may have the same or a similar problem.[14]

The rule of confidence and the attorney-client privilege are for the benefit of the client; the confidence may not be revealed without the client's consent. The confidential relationship rests on the notion that unless a man can talk freely with a lawyer, the lawyer cannot properly advise him as to his rights and duties, or properly represent him in court. The client often does not know what is and what is not of legal significance; that is why he consults a lawyer; to this end he must be able to tell all to his lawyer—the dribs and drabs, the unsorted details of his life, without fear that anyone else—not even the state—will ever become privy to his personal and business secrets, his indiscretions, his sins, for all he knows perhaps his crimes. This right to speak to someone in private, one mark of a free man, is our way of assuring every man access to the law, a right the Anglo-

---

12. For the rule of confidence and the privilege, see generally, 8 Wigmore, Evidence §§ 2290–2292, and especially pages 542–554, also § 2286, and especially pages 530–531 (1961); and 58 Am.Jur. "Witnesses," §§ 460–548, pages 259–306, 1971 Cum.Supp. 53–66; see also ABA Old Canons, *supra* Intro. note 29, Canon 37, and Code of Professional Responsibility, Canon 4 (1969–1970) [hereafter cited as ABA CPR].

13. West's Ann.Calif.Bus. & Prof. Code § 6068(e).

14. Shinn, J., concurring, in People v. Kor, 129 Cal.App.2d 436, 447, 277 P.2d 94, 101 (1954), hearing in Sup.Ct., *denied* (1955).

American system of justice deems more compelling than whatever is lost in not being able to find out in court just what it is a man has told his lawyer.

The rules of confidence began to take shape in 16th century England, but for more than 200 years the confidential nature of lawyer-client talk rested not on benefit to the client but on protection of the lawyer's honor. What sort of a man is it who would break a confidence? Later, the courts declined to enforce a private code of morality. If a lawyer were indeed the sort who could not be trusted with a confidence, the law would not stop him from talking, even though gentlemen might stop talking to him. The modern theory of protecting client rather than lawyer took hold in the course of the 18th century, but the detailed working out of the rules governing the attorney-client privilege ". . . were still in the formative stage in the first half of the 1800s," [15] when Courvoisier's case was tried.

Two exceptions to the rule of confidence are generally recognized: the lawyer is not required to keep confidential a client's announced intention to commit a crime, nor need he remain silent about confidences when the client attacks his conduct [16] (usually manifested by refusing to pay a fee.)

Though not a recognized exception, another circumstance often puts the confidence in hazard. The sometimes difficult problems in ending a strained lawyer-client relationship can directly or indirectly involve a nibbling away at the confidences exchanged between client and lawyer during friendlier moments. Once a lawyer undertakes to represent a client in court, if, like Phillips, he later comes "to the resolution of abandoning the case," he cannot simply drop it, without permission of the court. In order to obtain the court's permission to withdraw from a case, the lawyer has got to convince the judge there is a good reason for it. Often this can be hedged with sufficient buzfuz to make the judge realize something drastic is afoot, without telling him explicitly anything the lawyer has learned in

---

15. 8 Wigmore, Evidence § 2290, page 543 (1961).

16. ABA Old Canons, *supra* Intro. note 29, Canon 37; *see* ABA CPR, *supra* note 12, DR 4–101(C) (3), (4).

confidence. Irreconcilable differences between lawyer and client in the conduct of the case is a euphemism that will sometimes move a judge. But when a trial has already started, and a change of lawyers will mean not only an apparent embarrassment to the client's cause, but justice delayed, added expense, and loss of time for everyone—judge, jurors, other parties to the litigation, a court is very properly loathe to permit a lawyer out for trivial reasons.[17] How do you convince a court the reason is substantial without invading the area of confidence? How do you convince the court the case is such that a self-respecting lawyer may not properly proceed with the case?

If a client insists on perjuring himself and wants the lawyer to stand by and watch him do it, since the intention to commit a crime cannot be confidential the lawyer may tell it to the judge and be relieved of his client.[18] If the case is not that clear, the lawyer struggles with his conscience, getting advice if time permits by putting hypothetical cases to brother lawyers. In case of doubt, the lawyer's duty to his client will dictate that he keep his own counsel, and continue the representation. It may be said for Charles Phillips that he was not the only lawyer in 1840 or since who wondered where his duty lay to client, to court, to society, to himself. It was a decision under pressure; the circumstances were unique. Some decision was called for; he made his; he went in and told it to the judge.

Whatever Mr. Baron Parke's feelings about being made an unwilling party to the terrible secret, there is no reason to doubt that his advice to Phillips has been accurately reported. Phillips says the judge "requested to know distinctly whether the prisoner insisted on my defending him; and, on hearing that he did,

---

17. ABA Old Canons, *supra* Intro. note 29, Canon 44; ABA CPR, *supra* note 12, EC 2–32, EC 5–15, EC 5–19, EC 5–21, EC 7–8, DR 2–110, DR 5–102; H. Drinker, Legal Ethics 140–142 (1953) [hereafter cited as Drinker].

18. McKissick v. United States, 379 F.2d 754 (5th Cir. 1967); *appeal after remand*, 398 F.2d 342 (5th Cir. 1968); In re Branch, 70 Cal.2d 200, 210–211, 74 Cal.Rptr. 238, 245, 449 P.2d 174, 181 (1969); *see* In re Atchley, 48 Cal.2d 408, 310 P.2d 15 (1957); *cert. denied*, 355 U.S. 899, 78 S.Ct. 273, 2 L.Ed.2d 195; *cf.* M. Freedman, "Professional Responsibility of the Criminal Defense Lawyer: The Three Hardest Questions," 64 Mich.L.Rev. 1469, 1475–1478 (1966), Formal Opinion no. 287 (1953) in Opinions of the Committee on Professional Ethics 633 (ABA 1967 ed.).

said I was bound to do so, and to use all fair arguments arising on the evidence. I therefore retained the brief   .   .   ." [19]

It was not till much later that this interview became public knowledge. The storm that broke over Charles Phillips' head was not because he told it to the judge.

19. Warren-Phillips, *supra* ch. III,
       note 75, at 12.

Chapter IX

TO DEFEND A GUILTY MAN

1. PUBLIC REACTION

The first reaction to the news that Charles Phillips had addressed the jury, his conscience burdened with the confidential confession of Courvoisier's guilt, was the reaction of the working press, newspapermen who had seen Phillips in action before, veterans of the criminal trial. Their reaction was that of the understanding pro. What a horrible thing to happen to a lawyer! What was the guy to do? How had he behaved in a tight spot? Very well, they thought. A typical account read:

> "We presume that this communication on the part of the prisoner entirely changed the line of defence intended to be taken by his counsel; for it was generally rumoured that a severe attack would be made on the fellow-servants of the prisoner, and also on the police who were engaged in the investigation. We must, however, do Mr. Phillips the justice to state that with that honourable zeal which always distinguishes him for his clients, he made the best of a very bad cause; and, although surrounded by difficulties, his speech for the prisoner was most energetic and impressive." [1]

Although one might have thought Phillips' attack on the police severe enough, another reporter joined in, saying Phillips had done "the best he could for his unfortunate client, at the same time abstaining from indulging in insinuations respecting the prisoner's fellow-servants or the police, which he knew at the time he was addressing the jury were altogether without foundation." [2]

That was Phillips' best press for a long time. The English public were appalled. Without bothering for the moment with the details of exactly what it was that Phillips had said to the jury, some immediately struck out at the fundamental horror, as repellant to Victorian London as to many today: Phillips had

1. Chronicle (London), June 22, 2. Herald (London), June 22, 1840.
   1840.

141

been trying to persuade a jury to acquit a man he knew was guilty.

"One of the Profession" summed up the public's outrage in a letter to *The Times*:

> "Sir,—After reading the eloquent and impassioned address of Mr. C. Phillips in defence of Courvoisier, a doubt suggested itself to my mind whether a profession in which a man employs his talent 'to screen the guilty, and to varnish crime', can be considered honourable.
>
> "The culprit had avowed his guilt, and in the course of his speech Mr. Phillips stated to the jury 'that the prisoner was accused of murdering a member of the admirable Russell family, and the only son of the deceased victim he was proud to call his friend.' At that time he was pleading the cause of the assassin of his friend's father: and, had his eloquence prevailed, the result would have been, that through his instrumentality a confessed murderer would have been turned loose upon society, perhaps again to imbrue his hands in the blood of the sleeping, and to be again rescued by the ingenuity and astuteness of counsel from the justly offended laws of his country.
>
> "I seek not to impeach Mr. Phillips' character, which, from report, I believe to be of a high order, nor that of counsel in general pursuing the same line of conduct. They may be, and possibly are, 'all honourable men,' but looking at the thing abstractedly, and without reference to the existing and sanctioned abuse of professional talent, I am simple enough to consider that he who defends the guilty, knowing him to be so, forgets alike honour and honesty, and is false to God and man!
>
> "If my friend is to protect the butcher of my sleeping parent, though conscious of his guilt, Lord save me from my friends.
>
> "Let any man make the case his own, and there will be an echo in every heart deprecating the system I now decry." [3]

3. The Times (London), June 25, 1840.

A legal periodical *The Jurist* tackled the "grave and difficult question" raised by Courvoisier's case. It editorialized that the customary rule of the English bar requiring counsel to defend regardless of his opinion as to guilt or innocence is "inconsistent with the laws of morality, since it amounts to neither more nor less than that a man is bound to deceive, if it be for the interest of his client." To Lord Erskine's argument that "[i]f the advocate refuses to defend, he assumes the character of the judge; nay, he assumes it before the hour of judgment . . .", *The Jurist* replied that in the unlikely event that no lawyer would take a man's case, he would have himself to thank for it that "the evidence . . . on his own shewing, was so strong as to afford irresistible inference of his guilt." "We contend," *The Jurist* bluntly concluded, "that if an accused person be really guilty, he has no moral right to any defence." [4]

The Bishop of London brought the moral issue (in "what had occurred on a late most melancholy and remarkable occasion") onto the floor of the House of Lords. He presented a petition from "the inhabitants of London" asking that the legislation of 1836 giving prisoner's counsel a right to address the jury be now reconsidered, as being "a principle of exceedingly questionable propriety." Without attacking the profession as such, it was, the Bishop, said, a "question that really concerned the character of the community at large." He found himself unable to reconcile some "passages of God's word . . . with the propriety of any man taking a reward to prove that to be otherwise which the accused himself had distinctly confessed." [5]

In the Lords when the Bishop of London spoke was Charles Phillips' friend Lord Brougham, who two decades earlier in the same chamber had successfully defended Queen Caroline against a charge of adultery, and in doing so had pulled out the last stop in speaking of the zeal a lawyer must bring to his client's cause. He now found himself at "some loss to understand the grounds upon which the petitioners rest their prayer."

> "The privilege," he said of which they and the Bishop were complaining, ". . . is not that of the counsel but of the prisoner: it is a privilege upon which the elucidation of truth, the prevention of injus-

---

4. 4 The Jurist, No. 184, pages 593–594, July 18, 1840.

5. 55 Parl.Deb., H.L. (5th ser.) 1401 (Aug. 10, 1840).

tice depend, and the life, liberties, and property of the subject are not worth an hour's purchase if the freest scope, I will say more, the most unrestrained license is not given to the bar. Whether in a case which is right or wrong, this is the rule, the sacred rule of the profession, and it is one upon which the safety of the administration of justice depends.

"With regard to the judgment of counsel, as to the propriety or impropriety of taking any case in hand, how, I ask, can any man know a case to be a bad one before it is tried? Is he to enter into an investigation of it, sitting in his chambers, upon an *ex parte* statement? Supposing he did so, and should then refuse to enter upon the defence, what would be the consequence? The door would be opened to the possibility of a refusal being given to be counsel in a case, and if a man has a right to refuse to act in one case, the same right might be exercised in others."

By way of peroration, Lord Brougham then delivered a resounding restatement of the views of Erskine defending the unpopular defendant Thomas Paine in 1792:

"If once a barrister is to be allowed to refuse a brief, and to say he will not defend a man because he is in the wrong, many will be found who will refuse to defend men, not on account of the case, but because they are weak men, under the pressure of unpopularity, against whom power has set its mark, because they are the victims of oppression, or are about to be made so, or because it will not be convenient for parties at all times to beard power on behalf of individuals in the situation of prisoners." [6]

Strawmen, said the Bishop. True, "[i]t is not competent for a counsel to refuse a brief, but I lament the hardship of the law, which, since the recent alteration which has been made in its provisions, might compel a man to do that which is against his own conscience, namely defend by a speech a man whom he knows to be guilty." [7]

6. *Id.* 1401–1402.   7. *Id.* 1402.

The argument between the Bishop of London and Lord Brougham has been continued in a thousand forums since, and has not ended. It renewed not only the fundamental questioning of the morality of the profession of law, but even more basic questions of the purpose of the system of justice.

2.   THE RELIGIOUS INFLUENCE

The Bishop of London's immediate concern, like the concern of the older Church and of the moralists, was the morality of each man's conduct as the route to his own salvation, in this instance—concern for the soul of the man who becomes lawyer. How save the soul of the man if the soul of the lawyer is lost? [8] To the Bishop of London, Courvoisier damned himself when he murdered Lord William Russell. A priest might help him; he was no longer deserving of a lawyer's help, lest another soul be jeopardized. The soul of Charles Phillips was threatened but not doomed as long as he believed Courvoisier innocent. "If . . .", St. Thomas Aquinas had written of the 13th century advocate, "he defends an unjust cause unknowingly, thinking it just, he is excused according to the measure in which ignorance is excusable." But, said Aquinas, "If knowingly he defends an unjust cause, without doubt he sins grievously . . ." [9]

The earliest English lawyers were churchmen. And centuries before Blackstone introduced his influential *Commentaries* with a note on the supremacy of "divine law," [10] the stern moralist teaching of Catholic England had been reinforced for all lawyers with a strong religious flavor in the books that explained and expanded the common law. In *Glanvil* (12th century) and in *Bracton* (13th), and in the writings of Fortescue and Littleton (15th) and St. Germain (16th).

In his *Doctor and Student*, barrister Christopher St. Germain told the English lawyer he ". . . may give no counsel (saving his oath) neither against the law of God nor the law of

---

8. See letter, "The License of Counsel," from "A Well-Meaning Person," (June 29, 1840), in Chronicle (London), June 30, 1840.

9. 2 Aquinas, Summa Theologica, Part 2–2, Question 71, Article 3, page 1499 (1st Complete Am. ed. Benziger Bros., 1947; written 1265–1274) [hereafter cited as Aquinas].

10. 1 Blackstone, Commentaries *41–*43.

reason," [11] and that to advise a client against what the lawyer knew to be the truth was a double fault, putting ". . . himself in jeopardy of another man's conscience." Doctor reminded Student of the Bible's warning, "He that wilfully will put himself in jeopardy to offend shall perish therein." [12]

Following the separation of England from the church at Rome, fierce backward longings for Catholicism joined with an enthusiasm for Reformation in numerous schismatic shapes to force hard religious and moral decisions into the daily lives of otherwise peaceful men. For centuries England bubbled with an intense, brawling, religious fervor. "O sinful! O miserable Land!" called out the nonconformist Richard Baxter, "Who kindled all the hellish flames of thy malignity and mad divisions? And who continued them, and for what? What cloven foot hath entrd and expelled concord? " [13]

No one, least of all lawyers, could remain unaffected. A continuous struggle ensues to save the souls of lawyers, individually and as a profession. Men must live by law, and the law must live by lawyers. But lawyers are constantly being reminded that righteousness is their true mission on earth. The mission is not always joyously accepted. Over the years there is tugging and hauling, some cutting and trimming, to reconcile speaking for clients with speaking for truth.

In the early 17th century, the King's Attorney-General for Ireland dropped into the Preface of a volume of reports some moral tonic for his professional readers. "But good lawyers," wrote Sir John Davies, "have not with us that liberty which good Physicians have: for a good Physician may lawfully undertake the cure of a foul and desperate disease, but a good lawyer cannot undertake the defence of a foul and desperate Cause. But if he fortune to be ingaged in a cause, which seeming honest in the beginning, doth in the proceeding appear to be unjust, he followeth the good counsel of the School-man *Thomas Aquinas* . . ." [14]

---

11. St. Germain, *supra* ch. III, note 34, Dialogue II, ch. 6, page 119.

12. *Id.* ch. 5, page 117.

13. R. Baxter, Cain and Abel 12 (1689).

14. J. Davies, A Report of Cases, Preface, page 20 (1762; 1st publ. 1615).

In the Latin Davies quoted, Aquinas moved an inch towards an understanding of Phillips' dilemma, taking note of professional duty, yet ultimately leaving him perspiring and squirming, with no choice but to get out:

> [H]e ought not to throw up his brief in such a way as to help the other side, or so as to reveal the secrets of his client to the other party. But he can and must give up the case, or induce his client to give way, or make some compromise without prejudice to the opposing party.[15]

A barrister of the Commonwealth period summed up the case for the personal morality of lawyers with a righteous pungency:

> [T]o speak well in a bad cause is but to goe to Hell with a little better grace but without repentance . . . .[16]

Despite such prompting from within the profession, it is a reasonable inference that more than one lawyer was on his way to the perpetual fires, for the clergy kept up a continuous exhortation. The preacher Thomas Fuller (1642) epitomized *The good Advocate* as "one that will not plead that cause wherein his tongue must be confuted by his conscience." [17] And the eloquent Bishop of Lincoln Robert Sanderson addressed himself specially to the lawyers assembled for the start of the court term at Lincoln on August 4, 1625. Do not, said the Bishop, count it as "the glory of thy profession, by subtilty of wit and volubility of tongue to make the worse cause the better," but rather to "use the power of thy tongue and wit to shame impudence and protect innocency, to crush oppressors and succour the afflicted, to advance Justice and Equity, and to help them to right that suffer wrong." [18]

Robert Hale, barrister of Lincoln's Inn, gave up the law because "things commonly practised . . . seemed to him contrary to that exactness of Truth and Justice which became

---

15. Aquinas, *supra* note 9.

16. J. Cooke, The Vindication of the Professors 8 (1646).

17. T. Fuller, The Holy State 51, Book 2, ch. I (1642).

18. R. Sanderson, XXXVI Sermons 148, § 34 (8th ed. 1686); 2 R. Sanderson, Works 269 (1854).

a Christian . . . ." [19]   His son Matthew, still remembered as a scourge of witches, stuck by the law to become Lord
Chief Justice of England.   In a final *Great Audit* . . .
of the Good Steward, Sir Matthew Hale assured his Maker he
had taken the Bishop of Lincoln's advice.   He examined his own
books and certified himself free of the taint that might mark
less righteous members of the profession.   Never, never, never!
"I never," he reported, "used the advantage of my Elocution, either to maintain a falshood, or to abuse credulity into foolish
opinion or perswasion."   And again, "I never used the advantage
of Eloquence or Rhetorick to deceive people, or to cousen them
into any thing.   My heart always went along with my tongue
. . .   I never used my Elocution to give credit to an ill
cause; to justifie that which deserved blame; to justifie the
Wicked, or to condemn the Righteous; to make any thing appear more specious or enormous than it deserved . . .
When the cause was good, and fully so appeared to me, I
thought then was that season that the use of that ability was my
duty . . ." [20]

A friendly biographer Bishop Burnet (1682) shades the spot-
lessness of this self-appraisal ever so slightly.   As Hale grew
more experienced in the practice, and came to learn that a cause
which first appeared "very bad" might turn out to be "really
very good and just," ". . . he abated some of the Scru-
pulosity he had about Causes that appeared at *first view* Injust
. . ." [21]

The religious insistence that the lawyer use his talents only in
the cause of Right reflects concerns beyond that felt for ordinary members of the flock.   The lawyer who defends a guilty
man harms not only himself but society, increasing the risk that
a guilty man will escape earthly punishment, and decreasing respect for a system of justice that countenances intimacy with a
profession even suspect of immorality.   The lawyer engages in
friendly conversation with his professional adversary.   His
former colleague at the bar is now on the bench.   Attending to a

---

19. G. Burnet, Life and Death of
   Sir Matthew Hale, Kt. 2 (2d ed.
   1682).

20. 1 [M. Hale], Contemplations
   Moral and Divine 459–460 (1676).

21. G. Burnet, Life and Death of
   Sir Matthew Hale, Kt., *supra* note
   19, at 144, 143.

thousand mysterious details of the law, the lawyer goes in and out of court, in and out of the chambers of the judge himself. While lay eyes stare and lay ears strain, the lawyer approaches the bench and whispers to other counsel, to the judge, his clerk, his bailiff. What schemes are not concocted? What results not predetermined? The lawyer's words move justice into action. His intervention unsheathes the sword or stays it. Is it not important that one so close to the fountain of justice be, and appear to be, morally pure? Can he be either, if it is accepted that he will use his talents in behalf of the man who has said to him privately and quietly, "I am guilty" ?

3.　WHEN IS A MAN GUILTY?

The Bishop of London and *The Jurist* aghast alike at Courvoisier's crime and his callousness in waiting out a verdict, gambling on an acquittal that would accuse the innocent, had cast a cold and jaundiced eye on Charles Phillips as if a party to his client's depravity. Lord Brougham, as he said, was looking at "the administration of justice," the practical working of a system of continuous justice, the day to day reconciliation of abstract principles of morality and justice with the necessary generality of laws and the particular acts of particular men. More than Courvoisier's guilt or Phillips' moral complicity were at issue. How surely keep justice open to all men if counsel be denied to some of them?

To the working of that system of continuous justice it is commonly said that the lawyer must defend the apparently guilty to make certain the innocent is defended; the truth cannot be known until a court has determined it; [22] even a confession of guilt does not always mean a man is guilty.[23]

A man may confess guilt to shield another, "take the rap." He may confess guilt through mental aberration; each unsolved

22. ABA Old Canons, *supra* Intro., note 29, Canon 5; Drinker, *supra* ch. VIII, note 17, at 142–144.

23. 2 S. Romilly, Memoirs 182–184 (1840); S. Rogers, "The Ethics of Advocacy," 15 L.Q.Rev. 259, 261 n. 1 (1899); G. Sharswood, Essay on Professional Ethics 105 (5th ed. 1884); G. Warvelle, Essays in Legal Ethics 138 n. 28 (1902); see 4 Blackstone, Commentaries *329, and C. Darrow, The Story of My Life 134–135 (1932), and [C. Darrow], Attorney for the Damned 427–433, 438 (A. Weinberg ed. 1957).

killing in the morning newspaper is followed by distraught or delighted telephone calls to the police insisting "It was one of my best murders." He may confess guilt through ignorance of the critical fact: the man he struggled with and left for dead, recovered. He may confess guilt in desperation—alone, impoverished, overawed by the power aligned against him, incapable of defending himself, nothing left but to confess, hoping and begging for mercy. He may confess under pressures that stronger, bolder, more hardened, guiltier men might resist.

More often, I believe, a man confesses guilt because he is guilty. Even if he fights down the urge to unburden himself to someone, many a man walks through the shadows "feeling" guilty because he is guilty. But whether we confess or merely feel ourselves guilty, most of us in judging ourselves pass moral not legal judgments. Similarly, we shout out our innocence or "feel" innocent (by which we mean not fit for punishment) by the same sort of personal standard, a moral not a legal judgment.

These personal moral judgments, whether or not revealed to anyone else, do not always coincide with the generalizations we call law. The guilty man often believes himself legally innocent, the innocent man sometimes believes himself legally guilty, because by his own standards he is morally innocent or guilty; yet he may be far from that point of innocence or guilt where the law, making one rule for an infinite number of occasions, says "Not guilty," or "Guilty."

A part of the study of law is a study of the rules, and the long range reasons for the rules, the law uses as a method of formalizing the usual. They are rules that lawyers and judges have to wrestle with to find in them the sense that fits a particular case; sometimes there are disharmonies. Sometimes in single instances, in the important cases—your case or mine, the rules let pass a moral wrong that is no legal wrong; sometimes the rules find legal wrong where no man in his right mind can find moral wrong.

It remains one of the burdens of living in our society that whether or not my personal morality condemns me for parking in red zones or mercy killing, for enjoying pot or polygamy, I am held to the law's dim view of the matter. On the other hand, as a compensating blessing, though my conscience be stricter than either my conduct or the law, I may claim the benefit of the law's view of the matter. It becomes important in any case to find out just what is the law's view of the matter.

It takes a lawyer to convince a would-be rapist that he is not guilty, because for all his moral guilt, all his lecherous striving, there was, alas, no penetration. Maybe attempted rape, but not rape. Perhaps no moral difference, but a legal difference of many man years in prison.

A man may flee from the law knowing he owes a gambling debt, though it is not the law that pursues him, for the gambling debt is illegal (even in wide-open Nevada) and there is no legal guilt at all in refusing payment.

In our society we leave much to the goodwill of men and to their decency, the law encouraging very generalized notions of "good," but not designed to punish "bad" people nor even all conduct that is "bad". The law, for example, draws distinctions between civil and criminal wrongs, recommending neither but condemning the criminal wrong the more severely. The ordinary, inexperienced, moral man gives little thought to such distinctions, trying as best he can to avoid both civil and criminal wrongs. Trapped by misfortune, and for that reason unable to make a payment he knows is rightly due, the uncounseled moral man flogs his conscience with his own moral judgment on himself—"Guilty!", "Guilty!", "Guilty!" He may even confess himself an embezzler or defrauder, unless, instructed in the law, he is advised there is no crime at all, only a civil liability.

For the sake of saying something that at least another lawyer might understand, particular laws attempt to draw lines, marking off the point of no return—where a man's conduct becomes sufficiently objectionable to his neighbors that something ought to be done about it. The man who tiptoes to within an inch of the line may be a moral delinquent though he stays "legal;" his neighbor just over the line may be no devil though clearly "illegal." Approaching the line a man may feel a twinge of excitement, or conscience, or even moral guilt. Just over the line he may feel a sense of moral indignation, even outraged innocence, that such a small step could ever be considered illegal. Yet somewhere, the law, if it is to be at all recognizable as law, has got to say, ".   .   .   but here you stop!" So the law draws its distinctions for the better and for the worse, a guide alike to the pure of heart, the occasional backslider, and (in Phillips words) the "demon in the shape of man." It draws a line between 60 miles per hour and 65 miles per hour, between avoiding taxes and evading taxes, between reneging on a promise you once intended to keep and reneging on a promise you never intended to keep, between planning to kill someone and intentionally killing him. The man who stops just short of violating the law may get no medals for morality but he also gets no time in prison. In the wide open space between the medals and the prison a man is left to his own conscience and the opinion of his neighbors.

The law intended to stop sharpers from claiming money that is not owed (the Statute of Frauds) may sometimes defeat a just debt, because the claim was not in writing.

The law intended to stop a man from holding off suit until defense becomes impossible—memories grown dim, witnesses dead or missing (the Statute of Limitations) may sometimes defeat a just suit, because it was not filed fast enough.

The law intended to prevent designing grownups from imposing on children (the defense of infancy) may defeat a just claim, because the man who signed the contract was 20 instead of 21.

The law intended to give a man, for all his misfortunes, a new start in life (the bankruptcy laws) may defeat a widow's just claim for the money she needs to live on.

These, and a thousand other rules—some broad enough to go by the name of principle, express in combination what we know as the rule of law as opposed to chaos. Until the rules are changed, the law will judge men by them rather than some absolute or personal standard of morality. As Thomas Gisborne wrote almost two centuries ago, "Let it be remembered, that the standard to which the advocate refers the cause of his client is not the law of Reason, or the law of God, but the law of the Land . . . "[24] Clouded in controversy as it may sometimes be, there is a clearer, more general agreement on what the law of the land is than there is on either the law of reason or the law of God. The generality of that legal judgment is enough

24. T. Gisborne, An Enquiry into the Duties of Men, ch. 9, page 319 (2d ed. 1795).

to keep our society from coming unglued, even though it does not always suffice to free us of personal feelings of moral guilt.

Some men, perhaps most, who confess or even "feel" guilty are guilty, morally and legally. Yet it is not invariably so. And it is some mark of a civilized society that it will take pains to make sure before condemning anyone. The pains that we take to make sure go by the lawyer's name of "procedure," to some by the dirty word "technicalities" (as indeed they are) as though a legal technicality like a technical knockout were a poor substitute for the genuine article. Any system of justice has its procedures, its technicalities, the details by which it takes laws out of the books and puts them to work. It is often only a choice of procedures that separates savagery or tyranny from civilized life. Head-hunting is a procedure; so is the rack. Whether you are presumed guilty when charged with crime or presumed innocent until proved guilty is a technicality.

Our particular choice of technicalities distinguishes us from men who are not free. "[T]he most celebrated writ in the English law," [25] "the great and efficacious writ," of habeas corpus is a technicality.[26] For want of it men in our English past and men in other lands today have been kept caged without conviction of any crime, often without even being told why they are deprived of their liberty.

There are other procedures of the law which may delay the day of reckoning for a guilty man as surely as they preserve the liberty of an innocent one. The privilege against self-incrimination,[27] for example, which some ignorant men continue to discuss in underworld terms like "taking it on the lam," "taking a powder," or "taking the Fifth." The privilege reinforces the presumption of innocence, requiring the accuser to gather evidence to prove a man guilty rather than resort to the simpler, faster expedient of squeezing his genitals until he confesses. A technicality.

The suspicion of gossip formalized in the rules against hearsay testimony. The right to confront one's accusers, and to cross-examine them, born of an ancient distrust of weak or corrupt

---

25. 3 Blackstone, Commentaries *129.

26. *Id.* *131.

27. See generally, L. Levy, Origins of the Fifth Amendment (1968).

men bearing "false witness." Technicalities. Technicalities learned the hard way of history. Many of them written into the Constitution in the Fourth, Fifth, Sixth, Seventh, and Eighth Amendments to remind us that the procedures, the technicalities by which we do justice are not trifles.

These together with other technicalities of procedure, one of them the right to counsel, are a recognition of the importance of every solitary human being, irrespective of his "image" in a status conscious society. A recognition too of human fallibility, the disinclination of civilized men to arrive at harsh, irrevocable conclusions (such as death) until all the possibilities have been exhausted. That is the meaning of the insistence on a verdict of "Guilty" before a man is condemned. This is what Lord Brougham was talking about in his debate with the Bishop of London. A restatement of the principle came from Mr. Phillips' own Middle Temple, signed only "Templar." (Was it Charles Phillips himself?) He wrote with some heat to the editor of the *Chronicle*:

> Though a man be guilty, that is no reason that he should be convicted contrary to law. To warrant a conviction a man must not only be guilty, but his guilt must be legally proved; if that is not done, and yet, nevertheless, the man be convicted, he is as equally murdered as if he were perfectly innocent.[28]

It would make for a much healthier condition of our thinking about the role of the lawyer, if we said as plainly as "Templar" that guilty or not, we refuse to punish a man except through an orderly process, and that not the sham process of a kangaroo court nor a pretended defense couched in the forms of the law as a polite prelude to a predetermined judgment. It is not a lawyer's quibble that a man is not guilty until a judge or a jury say so. The "Guilty" verdict is the demonstration to the accused, and to those who still love him, as well as to ourselves, that a process of justice has been at work, and having seriously considered the possibilities of error, has come to a deliberate conclusion that here is a man who ought to be punished.

It might be easier for some of us to swallow if we added to the absolute distinction between "Guilty" and "Not guilty," the

---

28.   Letter dated June 23, in Chronicle (London), June 25, 1840.

Scot's alternative of "Not proven" (often interpreted as "Not guilty, but don't do it again"), or the distinction that some have made between those who are "Not guilty" and those who are innocent.[29]   By whatever semantic device, the principle in fact adhered to ought to be more often and more publicly stated, that our legal process is on trial with every trial, not merely the question of guilt or innocence, and that we refuse to destroy our legal process even at the expense of occasionally letting a guilty man go free.

4.   TO SEE THAT A MAN GETS WHAT THE LAW GIVES

This doctrine of liberty under laws by which we live has roots in a day of sterner religious strictures, harsher moral judgments, and a cruder justice than we now know.   Despite his religious and moral concern for the personal jeopardy of the lawyer who counsels a cause he knows is bad, St. Germain more than four centuries ago—consistently or not—was certain that every man is entitled to his law.   In *Doctor and Student*, written at a time counsel was denied those indicted for felony and the court was thought to be counsel for the prisoner, St. Germain tells us that a man known to the judges to be guilty still cannot be condemned out of hand.   The accused, he maintained, cannot be permitted to enter a technically incorrect plea, which in the 16th century would seal his doom as a matter of law:

> [F]or though he be a common offender, or that he be guilty, yet he ought to have that the law giveth him .   .   ..   And also sometime a man by examination, and by witness, may appear guilty that is not; and in like wise there may be a vehement suspicion that he is guilty, and yet he is not guilty: and therefore for such suspicion or vehement presumptions methinketh a man may not with conscience be put from that he ought to have by the law, ne yet although the judges knew it of their own knowledge.[30]

29. A. Holtzoff, "Ethics of Advocacy," 16 Buffalo L.Rev. 583, 586 (1967).

30. St. Germain, *supra* ch. III, note 34, Dialogue II, ch. 49, page 258.

And if it were an appeal of felony where the defendant (called the appellee) was permitted a lawyer:

> [I]f the appellee be poor, and have no counsel, the court must assign him counsel, if he ask for it, as they must do in all other pleas: and that methinketh they are bound to do in conscience, though the appellee were never so great an offender, and though the judges knew never so certainly that he were guilty, for the law bindeth them to do it.[31]

A wholesome thought that: that every man, even a guilty one "ought to have that the law giveth him." So it is not the lawyer who is to determine that a man is guilty, not he alone to decide that a man just possibly innocent will or will not have a voice to speak for him. If the lawyer were to become the arbiter, to decide in advance of trial:

This man is "Guilty" because he himself says so;

This man is "Guilty" though he doesn't say so;

This man is "Not guilty" because I think so,
and only him will I represent, not much would be left of our system of justice. As lawyer Erskine told the court in 1792:

> From the moment that any advocate can be permitted to say that he will or will not stand between the Crown and the subject arraigned in the court where he daily sits to practice, from that moment the liberties of England are at an end. If the advocate refuses to defend, from what he may think of the charge or of the defence, he assumes the character of the judge; nay, he assumes it before the hour of judgment; and in proportion to his rank and reputation, puts the heavy influence of perhaps a mistaken opinion into the scale against the accused, in whose favour the benevolent principle of English law makes all presumptions, and which commands the very judge to be his counsel.[32]

No one, least of all those most critical of the profession, has yet had the temerity to suggest that our system of justice sub-

---

31. *Id.*

32. Rex v. Paine (1792), 22 How.St. Tr. 412 (1816–1826); 1 Erskine, Speeches 474 (J. High ed. 1876).

stitute trial by lawyer for trial by judge or trial by jury. A hundred years ago Mr. Justice Branwell made the point with an uncommon bluntness:

> A man's rights [he said] are to be determined by the Court, not by his attorney or counsel. It is for want of remembering this that foolish people object to lawyers that they will advocate a case against their own opinions. A client is entitled to say to his counsel, 'I want your advocacy, not your judgment; I prefer that of the Court.' [33]

The function of the lawyer then is not to condemn men but to put into practice for all of us what we have decided on as abstract principle, that no man "be put from that he ought to have by the law." It is the lawyer's important task to see to it that the principle is adhered to despite public excitement, and without regard to personal enthusiasm or hate for the particular litigant, even for the man who tells his counsel (as Courvoisier did) that he is guilty. The lawyer who does his duty advises by the law of the land, seeing to it that his clients receive that measure of shelter the law says they are entitled to. This is a large and essential assignment. If, in addition, the lawyer can encourage a client to a higher view of things, so much the better. But as a lawyer his expertise is law not morality, and it is the client who must live and die with the client's conscience. The lawyer presents the case at law, leaving to judges and juries the final determination of whether or not a client's moral judgments on himself are consistent with our system of justice.

The great function of the lawyer in our society is not to establish or disprove guilt, but to see to it that an orderly process of justice is indeed continuous. He is an equalizer, cutting down to legal size the man "above the law," increasing the stature of the man who doesn't "know" anybody, so that each may approach the law as an ordinary man. To write it down that "all men are created equal," [34] and that everyone is entitled to "the equal protection of the laws" [35] does not make it so at 42nd and Broad-

---

33. Johnson v. Emerson, L.R. 6 Ex. 329, 367 (1871).

34. Declaration of Independence, in Documents Illustrative of the For-

mation of the Union of Am. States 22 (C. Tansill ed. 1927).

35. U.S.C.A.Const. Amend. Art. XIV § 1.

way. It takes more than divine revelation to enable one to understand let alone enforce his legal right. It is the lawyer who makes as much of reality as we know of equality before the law.

So the questions for the lawyer are not "Shall I defend a guilty man?", not "How can I argue for acquittal if I 'know' he is guilty?" The lawyer asks himself, "What is this man entitled to under the law?", "Under the established system of justice is there the required proof that this man is to be punished?" Neither judge nor jury, legislator nor moralist, the lawyer is required to insist that his client be given what he is entitled to under the law, and that he not be punished unless there is the proof that our system of justice requires. That is the lawyer's part of the system of justice in his prime role as the representative at law of another, less informed human being who places his life, liberty, or property in the lawyer's care. On other occasions, when he has not assumed that representative role, the lawyer as legislator or citizen joins with others in attempting to improve the laws. And at whatever level, if the system of justice as we know it and practice it ultimately does not achieve justice as we come to believe it, the system of justice will be in for change.

In the meantime, the lawyer must be there to present a case for decision by others, advising according to the law, advising the witness, "Answer what you are asked!" The law and the evidence. Those are the lawyer's truths. Certainly not "truth" in an absolute sense. But close enough to "truth" to permit an orderly system of continuous justice to operate. The language of "determination of truth" as the purpose of a trial confuses the public into believing that it is the will-o'-the-wisp we are after, God's truth, some sort of pure reason, as distinct from the truths that men live by.

Whatever the torments of his private morality, the lawyer has got to know what the law of the land requires. When Edward Coke fought his historic battle with King James over whether the law or the King ruled England, the King—so Coke later reported,

> said that he thought the law was founded upon reason, and that he and others had reason, as well as the Judges: to which it was answered by me, that true it was, that God had endowed His Majesty with excellent

science [i. e. knowledge], and great endowments of nature; but His Majesty was not learned in the laws of his realm of England, and causes which concern the life, or inheritance, or goods, or fortunes of his subjects, are not to be decided by natural reason but by the artificial reason and judgment of law, which law is an act which requires long study and experience, before that a man can attain to the cognizance of it: that the law was the golden met-wand and measure to try the causes of the subjects; and which protected His Majesty in safety and peace; with which the King was greatly offended, and said, that then he should be under the law, which was treason to affirm, as he said; to which I said, that Bracton saith, *quod Rex non debet esse sub homine, sed sub Deo et lege.* [that the King should not be under any man, but under God and the law.] [36]

The lawyer's conscience like his law is a learned thing, not intuitive, untutored, abstract; it is not everyman's conscience. Applied to a specific case, the lawyer's conscience is a reflection of an educated sense of justice under law and of a thorough awareness of a lawyer's role in the system of continuing justice. The lawyer has got to know deep inside that even a guilty man is entitled to justice. To paraphrase what a California judge once said of the right of a drunken man to a safe street,[37] a guilty man is as much entitled to a fair trial as an innocent one, and much more in need of it. In insisting that if even a guilty man is condemned it must be according to the regular forms that we have established, the lawyer serves his client today and the innocent tomorrow, and adds his passing encouragement to the old hope for a just society.

5. IF A CLIENT TELLS HIS LAWYER . . .

Charles Phillips has told us of his anguish after deciding to go on with the defense of Courvoisier:

"At the close of the, to me, most wretched day on which the confession was made, the prisoner sent me this astounding message by his solicitor—'Tell Mr. Phillips, my counsel, that I consider he has my life in

---

36. Prohibitions Del Roy, 12 Coke 63, 77 Eng.Rep. 1342 (1608).

37. Robinson v. Pioche, Bayerque & Co., 5 Cal. 460, 461 (1855).

his hands.' My answer was, that as he must be present himself, he would have an opportunity of seeing whether I deserted him or not. I was to speak the next morning! Fevered and horror-stricken, I could find no repose. If I slumbered for a moment, the murderer's form arose before me, scaring sleep away; now muttering his awful crime, and now shrieking to me to save his life! I did try to save it .   .. I have since pondered much upon this subject, and I am satisfied that my original impression was erroneous. I had no right to throw up my brief, and turn traitor to the wretch, wretch though he was, who had confided in me." [38]

What Charles Phillips has not told us is what went through his mind when he first decided to abandon Courvoisier.

Was it anger that a client had been false to his own lawyer? Hardly that. For though Phillips has insisted that up to the moment of confession he believed as did many others in Courvoisier's innocence, it is a common experience of trial lawyers— criminal and civil—that a client does not always tell his lawyer the truth. The most dismal and persistent refrain in the lawyer's post-mortem on the lost case is "I learned about my case in court." As one of Phillips' critics later remarked:

"I suppose few counsel have defended more accused persons than myself, and I must allow that innocence was not the characteristic feature of the majority of my clients; but I cannot remember any case in which I received an unqualified admission of guilt. The utmost that approached to it was a mild suggestion that if the evidence was too strong for me to obtain an aquittal, it was hoped that I would save my client from transportation." [39]

Was Mr. Phillips horrified that a man who had had the temerity to plead "Not guilty" was not really innocent? Certainly not. A hardshell 17th century theologian might insist that it was "not lawful for a guilty prisoner to say 'Not guilty,' when he

38. Warren-Phillips, *supra* ch. III, note 75, at 14–15.

39. Ballantine, *supra* ch. III, note 7, at 64.

is justly interrogated," [40] "rather be disgraced than damned." [41]
But an older rule against self-incrimination prevailed,[42] and
it had long been recognized in court practice that the plea of
"Not guilty" meant nothing more than that it was for the state
(not the accused) to prove a man guilty. Something more than
a decade before Courvoisier was tried, an English statute even
said that if a prisoner refused to plead, a plea of "Not guilty"
would be entered for him.[43] So Courvoisier's "Not guilty" misled no one, least of all the court or experienced trial counsel; it
was the signal for the prosecution to begin its case.

Was Phillips suddenly struck with the brazen effrontery of
Courvoisier, a murderer, refusing to plead guilty, yet forcing his
guilty knowledge upon his counsel, disturbing the peace of innocence. It is possible. As we shall see in a moment, the English
bar still achieves a certain bliss from this sort of ignorance.
And to the many criticisms of Courvoisier has been added one
that could only strike a cutthroat as nitpicking, i. e., that he had
no business telling his lawyer he was guilty.[44] Phillips might
question his client's wisdom but hardly his propriety; especially
when, as we now know, but a few minutes later he was to follow
Courvoisier down the sawdust trail and tell it to the judge.

Was Phillips thinking of himself—the cause half-won now
appearing almost hopeless, his carefully prepared speech now in
need of serious revision, the embarrassment now of cross-examining witnesses and speaking to the jury, his reputation at the
bar now in jeopardy? Human frailty built into any system of
justice.

Too many crossed strands for any man to sort out for himself.
Best perhaps to lay it to the law, and the uncertainty of the
direction of duty. All we may be sure of is that if Courvoisier
had said nothing to his counsel on that 19th of June, Charles
Phillips would have gone ahead with the same eloquence and a
less troubled conscience giving the same guilty man the defense

40. 13 J. Taylor, Works 362 (3d ed.
R. Heber ed. 1839).

41. *Id.* 367.

42. See 13 J. Taylor, Works, *supra*
note 40, at 365, and L. Levy, Origins of the Fifth Amendment
(1968).

43. 7 & 8 George IV, ch. 28, § 2
(1827).

44. 1 W. Townsend, Modern State
Trials 247–248 (1850); see "Licence of Counsel," in The Law
Magazine, vol. 39 Old Series, vol.
8 New Series, pages 53, 60 (1848).

the law allows him. Continue or throw up the brief? Do we decide that only the innocent are deserving of counsel, and that an accused man may have a lawyer only so long as the lawyer guesses right on innocence or remains ignorant of guilt? If the right to counsel were to hang by so fine a thread, we must revise our entire thinking about the importance of ordinary people receiving guidance through the maze of the law. If the predilections of the individual lawyer determine the issue, we must tell Lord Brougham that he was wrong, that the *right to counsel* is the right of the lawyer to give counsel, not the right of the accused to have it.

If before he came to trial Courvoisier had told his solicitor Mr. Flower that he was guilty, his chances of obtaining trial counsel, competent counsel, would have been seriously reduced. The press generated prejudice against him would have been the same whether he was guilty or innocent. In the state of "loyal excitement" that pervaded London a week before the trial of Courvoisier, the madman Edward Oxford who had attempted to assassinate the Queen was having difficulty getting a lawyer. An uncle who went looking for "professional assistance" for his troubled nephew sought out the solicitor Mr. Hobler. ".   .   .   [B]ut he declined, having the prosecution of Gould and Courvoisier on his hands." [45] This is a common experience of the unpopular litigant, civil or criminal, whether his cause is just or unjust; he is confronted with a bar that is suddenly very busy. As it turned out, both Courvoisier and Oxford got lawyers. Courvoisier was convicted, Oxford acquitted by reason of insanity, yet the result in each case balanced on a hairline, possibly influenced by the sequence of the trials. In his diary, John Hobhouse (Lord Broughton) noted:

> "At the Cabinet on July 11, many of us expressed regret at the acquittal of Oxford; but the Lord Chancellor said it had saved the Government from much embarrassment, as it would have been difficult to execute him. Lord Melbourne said that he considered Oxford half-witted at his examination before the Privy Council.
>
> "I had some talk, privately, with Lord John Russell [Lord William Russell's nephew] on the subject. He

45. The Annual Register (1840) 245–247.

agreed with me that Oxford had been acquitted because Courvoisier had been condemned; and that, perhaps, the next culprit would be convicted. For my own part, I remarked that I should not be the least surprised if some great catastrophe was caused by this verdict." [46]

The defendant, with more knowledge of the facts but much less knowledge of the law, is less equipped than his lawyer to decide whether he is indeed legally guilty, and whether he should or should not plead guilty, or even acknowledge his guilt. If making those preliminary, too often borderline, judgments of himself might affect his opportunity to be well defended, it is a foolish man that would condemn himself in advance.

Yet if the accused is bothered over the proper course of action, he does not stand alone in his misery of conscience. The struggle of centuries has resulted in a rule that no man may be imprisoned unless he has had the opportunity to be "represented by counsel at his trial." [47]   But that recognition of principle is

46. 5 Broughton, Recollections of a Long Life 278–279 (Lady Dorchester ed. 1911).

47. Argersinger v. Hamlin, 407 U.S. 25, 92 S.Ct. 2006, 2012, 32 L.Ed.2d 530 (1972); and see also Powell v. Alabama, 287 U.S. 45, 53 S.Ct. 55, 77 L.Ed. 158 (1932); Johnson v. Zerbst, 304 U.S. 458, 58 S.Ct. 1019, 82 L.Ed. 1461 (1938); Ferguson v. Georgia, 365 U.S. 570, 596, 81 S.Ct. 756, 770, 5 L.Ed.2d 783, 798 (1961); Gideon v. Wainwright, 372 U.S. 335, 83 S.Ct. 792, 9 L.Ed. 2d 799 (1963); *overruling* Betts v. Brady, 316 U.S. 455, 62 S.Ct. 1252, 86 L.Ed. 1595 (1942); Douglas v. California, 372 U.S. 353, 83 S.Ct. 814, 9 L.Ed.2d 811 (1963); White v. Maryland, 373 U.S. 59, 83 S.Ct. 1050, 10 L.Ed.2d 193 (1963); Massiah v. United States, 377 U.S. 201, 84 S.Ct. 1199, 12 L.Ed.2d 246 (1964); Escobedo v. Illinois, 378 U.S. 478, 84 S.Ct. 1758, 12 L.Ed.2d 977 (1964); Pointer v. Texas, 380 U.S. 400, 85 S.Ct. 1065, 13 L.Ed.2d 923 (1965); Miranda v. Arizona, 384 U.S. 436, 469–474, 480, 86 S. Ct. 1602, 16 L.Ed.2d 694 (1966); *reh. denied,* 385 U.S. 890, 87 S.Ct. 11, 17 L.Ed.2d 121; Anders v. California, 386 U.S. 738, 87 S.Ct. 1396, 18 L.Ed.2d 493 (1967); *reh. denied,* 388 U.S. 924, 87 S.Ct. 2094, 18 L.Ed.2d 1377; United States v. Wade, 388 U.S. 218, 87 S.Ct. 1926, 18 L.Ed.2d 1149 (1967) and Gilbert v. California, 388 U.S. 263, 87 S.Ct. 1951, 18 L.Ed.2d 1178 (1967), *but cf.* Kirby v. Illinois, 406 U.S. 682, 92 S.Ct. 1877, 32 L. Ed.2d 411 (1972); Burgett v. Texas, 389 U.S. 109, 88 S.Ct. 258, 19 L.Ed.2d 319 (1967); Mempa v. Rhay, 389 U.S. 128, 88 S.Ct. 254, 19 L.Ed.2d 336 (1967); Mathis v. United States, 391 U.S. 1, 88 S.Ct. 1503, 20 L.Ed.2d 381 (1968); Coleman v. Alabama, 399 U.S. 1, 90 S. Ct. 1999, 26 L.Ed.2d 387 (1970); Kitchens v. Smith, 401 U.S. 847, 91 S.Ct. 1089, 28 L.Ed.2d 519 (1971); see Statement of Black, J. dissenting from adoption of "Rules of Procedure for the Trial of Minor Offenses Before United States Magistrates," in 400 U.S. 1031– 1036, 27 L.Ed.2d lviii–lx (1971);

not self-executing. It does not end qualms over the application of the principle in the minds of those who must apply it as distinguished from those who only write about it. The persistent conflict that has always been felt to exist between the moral and the legally right thing to do continues to trouble the profession of lawyers.

A man is not reared with the conscience of a lawyer, and there are few lawyers who have not at some time felt old misgivings not readily disposed of by abstract legal principle. Many a lawyer has asked himself Boswell's famous question, "But what do you think of supporting a cause which you know to be bad? " And not all have been able to tell themselves with Johnson's quick self-assurance: "Sir, you do not know it to be good or bad till the Judge determines it." [48]

6. LAWYER'S DILEMMA: THE ENGLISH RULES

Faced with the difficulty of reconciling duty-to-counsel and self-respect (conscience, morality), the English bar does what it can to keep counsel ready, able, and innocent.

Taking more literally than others do the notion that the law is a "public profession," the English barrister operates under the so-called "taxi-cab rule." Within the limits of his competence and the pressure of other commitments, he is bound to serve all comers who pay his fee (with special provision made for legal aid for those unable to pay fees).[49] The rule is explicit, and the conflicts of interest which will justify a refusal to accept a case are also explicit; personal predilections are not among them. The rule exists on paper and in practice. On the other hand, the barrister's direct contact with the client is deliberately minimal; that dirty function is performed by the solicitor, who is not bound to accept all comers.[50] So that the "taxi-cab rule" for the barrister means that a choosy solicitor must hail the cab.

Criminal Justice Act of 1964, 18 U.S.C.A. § 3006A (amended 1968, 1970).

48. 2 Boswell's Life of Johnson 47 (G. B. Hill ed. 1887).

49. W. W. Boulton, A Guide to Conduct and Etiquette at the Bar of England and Wales 17, 21, 25, 83 (4th ed. 1965) [hereafter cited as Boulton]; R. E. Megarry, Lawyer and Litigant in England 32–33 (1962).

50. T. Lund, A Guide to the Professional Conduct and Etiquette of Solicitors 82 (1960) [hereafter cited as Lund].

If somehow the barrister has been contaminated by hearing a confession "before the proceedings have been commenced, it is," the governing Council of the Bar has said for more than half a century, "most undesirable that *an advocate to whom the confession has been made* should undertake the defence, as he would certainly be seriously embarrassed in the conduct of the case, and no harm can be done to the accused by requesting him to obtain another advocate." The advice stops short of saying, "And be sure you don't tell the second barrister you did it!" The words I have italicized make it clear that the English bar is concerned with the ticklish practicalities of the moral question rather than with the ultimate question of conviction or acquittal of confessed murderers, thus satisfying the Bishop of London to a point. If the confession comes during the trial, the English barrister is to proceed with the defense of his Courvoisier, but under wraps (as will be discussed in the next chapter).[51] The English bar even recommends this before-and-during trial rule to English lawyers practicing where the profession is not split into barristers and solicitors.[52]

Unlike the barrister, the English solicitor (governed by The Law Society rather than the Council of the Bar) is free to proceed with the case whether the confession comes before or during the trial. The solicitor is enjoined "to bear in mind in these circumstances that it is for the prosecution to establish their case in accordance with the rules of evidence and for the prosecution to prove that the accused is guilty of the offence charged; it is not for him to establish his client's innocence." [53] But again, as with the barrister, knowledge limits the defense.

7.   LAWYER'S DILEMMA: THE AMERICAN EXPERIENCE

a.   RIGHT TO COUNSEL IF YOU CAN FIND ONE

For the American lawyer whose client quietly confesses himself guilty, the path of duty is not so clearly marked.

The colonists brought with them from England a strong distrust of paid lawyers, so much so that some of the American col-

---

51. Boulton, *supra* note 49, at 70–71; *cf.* M. Hilbery, Duty and Art in Advocacy 8–10 (1959), Shawcross, The Functions and Responsibilities of an Advocate 27 (1958).

52. Annual Statement of the General Council of the Bar 14 (1915).

53. Lund, *supra* note 50, at 106–107.

onies experimented briefly with prohibition of the profession.[54] Yet if Americans took a dim view of lawyers they took an even dimmer view of Crown judges. From a very early date, in some instances even before the Revolution, they rejected the British practice that told a man indicted for felony he could have no lawyer since "the court is counsel for the prisoner." [55] Some of them had had a court as their counsel, William Penn, for ·instance. His judges doggedly tried to browbeat an even more stubborn English jury into convicting Penn and William Mead of "tumultuous assembly" for Penn's preaching in the streets of London. When the Recorder asked Mead if he had been at the scene of the crime, Mead replied he was not bound to accuse himself, adding: "And why dost thou offer to insnare me with such a Question? Doth not this show thy Malice? Is this like unto a Judge, that ought to be Counsel for the Prisoner at the Bar? " [56] Thirty years later Penn made certain that in his colony at least there would be an even contest. In his Charter of Privileges for Pennsylvania, Penn wrote:

> That all Criminals shall have the same Privileges of
>
> Witnesses and Council as their Prosecutors.[57]

Following this tradition Pennsylvania was one of the earliest of the colonies to provide for assignment of counsel in capital cases.

The American colonists had a well founded suspicion that the court might not be a very good counsel for a man being prosecuted by the King who appointed the court. They complained to the world in the Declaration of Independence, "He has made Judges dependent on his Will alone, for the tenure of their offices, and the amount and payment of their salaries." [58] Accordingly, they wrote into the Sixth Amendment to the Constitution what had already become the general practice in America before

54. D. Mellinkoff, Language of the Law 208–210; 219–220 (1963).

55. Powell v. Alabama, 287 U.S. 45, 61–65, 53 S.Ct. 55, 61–62, 77 L.Ed. 158, 166–168 (1932); see also 2 Legal Papers of John Adams 402–403 n. 40 (L. Wroth & H. Zobel ed. 1965).

56. Rex v. Penn and Mead (1670), 6 How.St.Tr. 951, 957 (1816–1826).

57. 5 F. N. Thorpe, ed., American Charters 3079 (Article V), and see also 3060 (Article VI).

58. Documents Illustrative of The Formation of the Union of Am. States 22, 23 (C. Tansill ed. 1927).

the Constitution that "In all criminal prosecutions, the accused shall enjoy the right . . . to have the assistance of counsel for his defense."

It took another 141 years to find out for sure that those words of the Constitution did something more than change the old English rule forbidding counsel to address a jury on behalf of an indicted defendant. As usual, constitutional principle was established in a case where the men on trial were not pillars of the community; in this instance illiterate, black hoboes, riding the rails, found guilty of gang raping two white women hoboes in an open freight gondola. Death sentences followed perfunctory trials with representation so perfunctory they "were not accorded the right to counsel in any substantial sense," [59] the liquorish hack who put in an ambiguous sort of token appearance himself telling the trial judge, "[I] think the boys would be better off if I step entirely out of the case according to my way of looking at it and according to my lack of preparation of it and not being familiar with the procedure in Alabama . . ." [60] This was the *Scottsboro Case*, cause celebre of the '30's, which settled it that a constitutional right to "effective" counsel applies to trials in state as well as federal courts. Beyond that, where helpless defendants face the death penalty, "the right . . . to have the assistance of counsel" means not only that the accused is *permitted* a lawyer, but that as "a logical corollary" [61] he has a right to have counsel appointed to defend him. In words quoted ever since, a staunch conservative Mr. Justice Sutherland wrote:

> The right to be heard would be, in many cases, of little avail if it did not comprehend the right to be heard by counsel. Even the intelligent and educated layman has small and sometimes no skill in the science of law. If charged with crime, he is incapable, generally, of determining for himself whether the indictment is good or bad. He is unfamiliar with the rules of evidence. Left

---

59. Powell v. Alabama, 287 U.S. 45, 58, 53 S.Ct. 55, 60, 77 L.Ed. 158, 165 (1932).

60. *Id.* 55, 53 S.Ct. at 59, 77 L.Ed. at 163; see also D. Carter, Scottsboro 19, 22 (1969).

61. Powell v. Alabama, 287 U.S. 45, 72, 53 S.Ct. 55, 65, 77 L.Ed. 158, 172 (1932).

without the aid of counsel he may be put on trial without a proper charge, and convicted upon incompetent evidence, or evidence irrelevant to the issue or otherwise inadmissible. He lacks both the skill and knowledge adequately to prepare his defense, even though he have a perfect one. He requires the guiding hand of counsel at every step in the proceedings against him. Without it, though he be not guilty, he faces the danger of conviction because he does not know how to establish his innocence.[62]

Those words of Mr. Justice Sutherland make almost as much sense when the stakes are not life but livelihood (i. e. property), and certainly as much sense when not life but liberty is on the line. Of this latter fact we have had to be reminded by another of society's derelicts, this time a white man Clarence Earl Gideon, who mustered up the remnants of his self-respect to scribble out a complaint to the Supreme Court of the United States that he was being unjustifiably held in prison, convicted without a lawyer to speak for him. From *Gideon v. Wainwright*,[63] decided in 1963, we start from the premise that every man tried for a serious crime in this country must have a lawyer appointed to represent him, if he doesn't have the money to hire one. Nine years later, and the Supreme Court has extended the coverage, so "that absent a knowing and intelligent waiver, no person may be imprisoned for any offense, whether classified as petty, misdemeanor, or felony, unless he was represented by counsel at his trial; "[64] as the dissenters in the state court phrased it, "From the inside all jails look alike."[65] It is the sense of our time that only with counsel will every man be accorded that "due process of law" that a system of continuous justice requires.

If the accused is entitled to a lawyer, is the coin blank on the other side? Or is it also "a logical corollary" that an American lawyer has a duty to defend? And that, regardless of what he thinks of the man or his cause?

---

62. *Id.* 68–69, 53 S.Ct. at 64, 77 L. Ed. at 170–171.

63. 372 U.S. 335, 83 S.Ct. 792, 9 L. Ed.2d 799 (1963), and cases cited *supra* note 47.

64. Argersinger v. Hamlin, 407 U.S. 25, 92 S.Ct. 2006, 2012, 32 L.Ed.2d 530 (1972).

65. State *ex rel.* Argersinger v. Hamlin, 236 So.2d 442, 445 (Fla. 1970); *cert. granted*, 401 U.S. 908, 91 S.Ct. 887, 27 L.Ed.2d 805.

Some American lawyers winced at the sharp prick of those questions long before the Supreme Court decisions of this century. In the Massachusetts colony, for instance, an indicted defendant was permitted trial counsel despite the contrary rule in the mother country.[66] Yet in the turbulent days immediately preceding the Revolution, a loyalist charged with murdering a "patriot" learned very quickly that being permitted counsel and getting counsel were not the same.

That was the case with Ebenezer Richardson, dubbed "The Informer." He told a Boston court he had "made application to almost every Lawyer in town to undertake his cause, which no one would do . . ." After all the lawyers present declined requests from the bench to become counsel for "The Informer," the court "asserted their Authority and order'd Mr. Fitch the advocate General" into service. Fitch tried in vain to argue himself out of the assignment, finally, to keep the record straight for the locals, "saying that since the Court had peremptorily ordered him, he would undertake it, but not otherways." When *Rex v. Richardson* was called for trial, Fitch was sick, and the case was postponed. When he was again sick at the next trial date, the court appointed Josiah Quincy, who took the defense.[67]

Quincy was also scheduled to be co-counsel with John Adams and Robert Auchmuty for Captain Thomas Preston, indicted with eight men of his command for five murders in what has become known as "the Boston Massacre" of March 5, 1770. Word of this professional engagement reaching Quincy's father, he wrote:

> My Dear Son, I am under great affliction at hearing the bitterest reproaches uttered against you, for having become an advocate for those criminals who are charged with the murder of their fellow-citizens. Good God! Is it possible? I will not believe it. . . .[68]

Here is a small portion of the son's reply:

> Let such be told, Sir that these criminals, charged with murder, are *not yet legally proved guilty*, and

---

66. 2 Legal Papers of John Adams, *supra* note 55.

67. *Id.* 396, 401–402.

68. 3 Legal Papers of John Adams, *supra* note 55, at 1, 5–6.

therefore, however criminal, are entitled, by the laws of God and man, to all legal counsel and aid . . . and I dare affirm that you and this whole people will one day REJOICE that I became an advocate for the aforesaid 'criminals' *charged* with the murder of our fellow-citizens.[69]

As it turned out, Quincy did not take part in the Preston trial but was co-counsel for the defense in the trial of the soldiers.[70] John Adams did represent both Captain Preston and his men. Years later he recalled how he came to take the case. On the morning after the shootings a Boston merchant of his acquaintance Mr. James Forrest came to Adams' office:

With tears streaming from his Eyes, he said I am come with a very solemn Message from a very unfortunate Man, Captain Preston in Prison. He wishes for Council, and can get none. I have waited on Mr. Quincy, who says he will engage if you will give him your Assistance: without it positively he will not. Even Mr. Auchmuty declines unless you will engage. . . . I had no hesitation in answering that Council ought to be the very last thing that an accused Person should want in a free Country. That the Bar ought in my opinion to be independent and impartial at all Times And in every Circumstance. And that Persons whose Lives were at Stake ought to have the Council they preferred: But he must be sensible this would be as important a Cause as was tryed in any Court or Country of the World: and that every Lawyer must hold himself responsible not only to his Country, but to the highest and most infallible of all Trybunals for the Part he should Act. He must therefore expect from me no Art or Address, No Sophistry or Prevarication in such a Cause; nor any thing more than Fact, Evidence and Law would justify. Captain Preston he said requested and desired no more: and that he had such an Opinion, from all he had heard from all Parties of me, that he could chearfully trust his Life with me, upon those Principles. And said Forrest, as God almighty is my

69. *Id.* 7.   70. 3 Legal Papers of John Adams, *supra* note 55, at 22, 101.

Judge I believe him an innocent Man. I replied that must be ascertained by his Tryal, and if he thinks he cannot have a fair Tryal of that issue without my Assistance, without hesitation he shall have it. Upon this, Forrest offered me a single Guinea as a retaining fee and I readily accepted it.[71]

Though in the best tradition of the English bar, in the path of Erskine and Brougham, John Adams' and Josiah Quincy's legal ethics at that moment were their own. When the going got rough, there was no consensus among the lawyers in America.

b. THE SHAPERS OF LEGAL ETHICS

The first influential American attempts to give ethical guidance to a scattered profession, of only more or less educated individual practitioners and of requestionable repute,[72] did not come until the 19th century.

David Hoffman, born three years before the adoption of the Constitution, turned his attention from a lucrative practice at the Maryland bar to become professor of law at the University of Maryland in 1816. As some others before and since, he found the study of the law uplifting, its practice corrupting. He proposed to keep lawyers from the pit with a series of "Resolutions In Regard To Professional Deportment" addressed chiefly to law students. Published in 1836, the same year England at last removed the ban against trial counsel for those indicted for felony, the credo sounded a note of moral uplift for a profession little regulated from within or without.[73]

Hoffman loped over a wide range of professional sin from excessive zeal (Resolution 1) to "Avarice . . . one of the most dangerous and disgusting of vices"(Resolution 49), with a bracing fiftieth "LAST RESOLUTION. I will read the foregoing forty-nine resolutions, twice every year, during my professional life." In between he warned against such diverse vices as failing to answer letters (No. 36) and prolonging litigation for personal profit (No. 19). Some of "Hoffman's Resolutions" have become standard with the profession, e. g. "I will espouse

---

71. 3 Diary and Autobiography of John Adams 292–293 (L. H. Butterfield ed. 1961); cf. 3 Legal Papers of John Adams, *supra* note 55, at 22 n.72.

72. D. Mellinkoff, Language of the Law 219–229 (1963).

73. D. Hoffman, A Course of Legal Study 744, 752 (2d ed. 1836).

no man's cause out of envy, hatred or malice, towards his antag-
onist" (No. 2).   Others, e. g. resolving not to plead the Statute
of Limitations (No. 12) or the defense of Infancy (No. 13) to
defeat a debt, would today involve a lawyer in serious questions
of professional misconduct, denying to a litigant his rights under
the law.   Hoffman said it was "dishonourable" for a lawyer to
lend himself to a claim or defense the lawyer felt "ought not, to
be sustained" (No. 11), but as best one may gather, this resolve,
for Hoffman as for lawyers today, was a rule for civil cases (No.
14).   In a special resolution (No. 15), one of his longest, perhaps reflecting his troubled thoughts, he approached, wobbled,
and did not squarely confront the tough decision that faced
Charles Phillips:

> When employed to defend those charged with crimes
> of the deepest dye, and the evidence against them,
> whether legal, or moral, be such as to leave no just
> doubt of their guilt, I shall not hold myself privileged,
> much less obliged, to use my endeavours to arrest, or to
> impede the course of justice, by special resorts to inge-
> nuity—to the artifices of eloquence—to appeals to the
> morbid and fleeting sympathies of weak juries, or of
> temporizing courts—to my own personal weight of
> character—nor finally, to any of the overweening influ-
> ences I may possess, from popular manners, eminent
> talents, exalted learning &c.   Persons of atrocious char-
> acter, who have violated the laws of God and man, are
> entitled to no such special exertions from any member
> of our pure and honourable profession; and indeed, to
> no intervention beyond securing to them a fair and dis-
> passionate investigation of the *facts* of their cause, and
> the due application of the law; all that goes beyond
> this, either in manner or substance, is unprofessional,
> and proceeds, either from a mistaken view of the rela-
> tion of client and counsel, or from some unworthy and
> selfish motive, which sets a higher value on profession-
> al display and success, than on truth and justice, and
> the substantial interests of the community.   Such an
> inordinate ambition, I shall ever regard as a most dan-
> gerous perversion of talents, and a shameful abuse of
> an exalted station.   The parricide, the gratuitous mur-
> derer, or other perpetrator of like revolting crimes, has

surely no such claim on the commanding talents of a profession, whose object and pride should be the suppression of all vice, by the vindication and enforcement of the laws. Those, therefore, who wrest their proud knowledge from its legitimate purposes, to pollute the streams of justice, and to screen such foul offenders from merited penalties, should be regarded by all, (and certainly shall be by me,) as ministers at a holy altar, full of high pretension, and apparent sanctity, but inwardly base, unworthy, and hypocritical—dangerous in the precise ratio of their commanding talents, and exalted learning.[74]

Hoffman's advice in this critical area wavers between an abhorrence of any defense for "atrocious" criminals, and a possible distinction between the use of "commanding talents" and ordinary talents. There is a suggestion that a man whose lawyer has already convicted him may be entitled to a defense, but only a second class defense, without "special exertions," with the implication that in other cases a lawyer's duty might carry him beyond seeing to it that there be a trial by the established rules, "a fair and dispassionate investigation of the *facts* of their cause, and the due application of the law . . ." Hoffman did not come to grips with the question of a quiet confession, nor did he bring himself to say as simply and bluntly as Mr. Baron Parke to Phillips, that a lawyer is bound to defend "and to use all fair arguments arising on the evidence." But Hoffman wrote four years before Courvoisier's Case.

In the year Hoffman died, 1854, another lawyer turned law professor, Judge George Sharswood (later Chief Justice of the Pennsylvania Supreme Court) published his University of Pennsylvania ". . . Lectures on the Aims and Duties of the Profession of Law." While not naming "Hoffman's Resolutions" as a source of misapprehended duty, Judge Sharswood went straight to the point of Hoffman's dudgeon over lawyers who "screen such foul offenders from merited penalties." He stated plainly that even a guilty man "has a constitutional right to a trial according to law . . . It is not to be termed screening the guilty from punishment, for the advocate to exert all his ability, learning, and ingenuity in such a defence, even if

74. *Id.* 755–757.

he should be perfectly assured in his own mind of the actual guilt of the prisoner." He continued, ". . . if it were considered that a lawyer was bound or even had a right to refuse to undertake the defence of a man because he thought him guilty; if the rule were universally adopted, the effect would be to deprive a defendant, in such cases, of the benefit of counsel altogether." [75]

Queen v. Courvoisier was a case in point. When Judge Sharswood wrote, François Benjamin Courvoisier was hanged and dead 14 years, but his counsel Charles Phillips was still around, and the controversy over Courvoisier's Case had not been permitted to die. Just five years earlier, a galling press reference to Courvoisier's counsel as a "marked" man had goaded Phillips into making a full scale defense of his conduct; the pot was still boiling. Sharswood reviewed the case at some length. Putting to one side the separate question of the scope of legitimate defense after a confession of guilt, Sharswood addressed himself to the fundamental issue:

> But there were [he said] those on this side of the Atlantic, who demurred to the conclusion, that an advocate is under a moral obligation to maintain the defence of a man who has admitted to him his guilt. Men have been known, however, under the influence of some delusion, to confess themselves guilty of crimes which they had not committed: and hence, to decline even such a defence, is a dangerous refinement in morals. Nothing seems plainer than the proposition, that a person accused of a crime is to be tried and convicted, if convicted at all, *upon evidence,* and *whether guilty or not guilty,* if the evidence is insufficient to convict him, he has a *legal right* to be acquitted. The tribunal that convicts without sufficient evidence may decide according to the fact; but the next jury, acting on the same principle, may condemn an innocent man. If this is so, is not the prisoner in every case entitled to have the evidence carefully sifted, the weak points of the prosecution exposed, the reasonable doubts presented which should weigh in his favor? And what offence to truth

---

75. G. Sharswood, A Compend of Lectures on the Aims and Duties   of the Profession of the Law 31–33 (1854).

or morality does his advocate commit in discharging that duty to the best of his learning and ability? What apology can he make for throwing up his brief? The truth he cannot disclose; the law seals his lips as to what has been communicated to him in confidence by his client. He has no alternative, then, but to perform his duty. It is his duty, however, as an advocate merely, as Baron Parke has well expressed it, to use ALL FAIR ARGUMENTS ARISING ON THE EVIDENCE. Beyond that, he is not bound to go in any case; in a case in which he is satisfied in his own mind of the guilt of the accused, he is not justified in going.[76]

About 50 years later, George Warvelle, looking over the field, found the full burden of Sharswood's stern professionalism somewhat excessive. At the same time Hoffman's moral klaxons were too raucous. In his *Essays in Legal Ethics* (1902), Warvelle elaborated his own middle view.

Whatever Warvelle believed, he believed emphatically. He believed we were right in rejecting the older "barbarous practice" of England that denied counsel to the indicted accused. "The popular clamor," he said, "so often heard, concerning the loopholes in the meshes of the law, whereby criminals go unpunished, is but the veriest bosh, and it is immaterial that much of this clamor originates with men who assume to be teachers of morals. That our criminal law is perfect and our legal machinery without defect, no one asserts; but we have made a great advance over the 'good old days' when poor and decrepit women [i. e. witches] were ruthlessly and brutally sacrificed on the altar of justice by pious and God-fearing men." [77]

On the other hand he advised young lawyers against specializing in the practice of criminal law, for the biblical reason that if you handle pitch you will get dirty; [78] " . . . a man cannot continually stand as an apologist for crime and a defender of criminals without having his own moral sensibilities sadly blunted." [79] Warvelle thought one should not "decline a retainer

---

76. *Id.* 42–44; see T. Cooley, A Treatise on the Constitutional Limitations 703 (1868).

77. G. Warvelle, Essays in Legal Ethics 130–132 (1902).

78. Eccl. (Apoc.) 13:1.

79. G. Warvelle, Essays in Legal Ethics 144 (1902).

merely because he may believe the accused to be guilty," [80] but he insisted a lawyer had neither a legal nor an ethical duty to take any criminal case. Except when ordered by a court to defend a poor man, he said, the lawyer " . . . is under no obligation to palliate and defend iniquity of any kind in a court of justice, or to undertake a cause which his soul abhors, and his condition would be that of an abject and miserable slave if, as some would contend, he were to be at the command of every miscreant who might choose to employ him." [81]

According to Warvelle, a confession might give a lawyer pause about taking a case in the first place, but—unless ordered by the court to defend—the lawyer might decline or "with the utmost propriety" defend. General condemnation of such a defense, Warvelle said, was inspired by ". . . the professional moralist [who] is usually a very one-sided person with a narrow mental horizon, and his disciples, as a rule, tend to develop the same characteristics." The lawyer, he thought, "has a far wider ranger of mental vision and a better knowledge of applied ethics." Moral guilt was not a jury question, and an accused must have counsel to test the evidence of guilt. "This in itself is sound morality, and its denial now would rend the bonds of society." Once having taken the case, Warvelle continued, if "knowledge of his client's guilt only comes to counsel after the trial has made considerable progress," the lawyer was bound to defend. The "psuedo-moralists" who said the lawyer must withdraw would have him "break faith with the prisoner . . ." "This phase of our subject," he noted, "was definitely settled during the first half of the last century, the principal precedent being an English state trial, now known as the Courvoisier Case . . . ." [82]

c. THE BAR ASSOCIATION CODES

The first *Code of Ethics* for lawyers in the United States was adopted in 1887 by the Alabama State Bar Association. This was before George Warvelle had been heard from, and it took its cue from Judge Sharswood. The Alabama *Code* quoted Sharswood's observations that no other profession was beset with so many temptations "to swerve from the lines of strict integrity,"

---

80. *Id.* 133.

81. *Id.* 132.

82. *Id.* 134–138, and 138 n. 27.

and that against the "pitfalls and mantraps" athwart the path of the young lawyer "[h]igh moral principle is his only safe guide . . ." [83] On defense of the guilty, Alabama lawyers adopted Rule 13 as a clear distillate of Sharswood principle:

> An attorney *can not reject the defense* of a person accused of a criminal offense, because he knows or believes him guilty. It is his duty by all fair and honorable means to present such defenses as the law of the land permits; to the end that no one may be deprived of life or liberty, but by due process of law.[84]

In the next two decades, the lawyers of eight states took as their own the substance of Alabama's *Code* on the duty to defend the guilty. In two other states, Wisconsin (1901) and Kentucky (1903), they made a small verbal change with profound implications; they changed the words "can not reject the defense" to read "is not bound to reject the defense;" [85] it was Warvelle's free choice.

The American Bar Association worked on its own *Canons of Professional Ethics* for three years, with the Alabama *Code of Ethics* as the model and its draftsman Judge Thomas Goode Jones a member of the Association's committee.[86] But if Judge Jones had a hand in drafting the Association's rule on defense of the guilty, the voice the committee heard was the voice of Warvelle. When Alabama's Rule 13 emerged from committee in 1908, it had undergone a reverse metamorphosis; the butterfly had changed into a worm. Canon 5 read:

> It is the right of the lawyer to undertake the defense of a person accused of crime, regardless of his personal opinion as to the guilt of the accused; otherwise innocent persons, victims only of suspicious circumstances, might be denied proper defense. Having undertaken such defense, the lawyer is bound, by all fair and honorable means, to present every defense that the law of

---

83. Proceedings, Ala. State Bar Assn, appendix (1887); Proceedings, Ala. State Bar Assn. (1895) cxii; 35 Rep. of Ala. State Bar Assn. (1912) 139.

84. Proceedings, Ala.State Bar Assn. (1895) cxvii; 35 Rep. of Ala.

State Bar Assn. (1912) 144; emphasis supplied.

85. 31 A.B.A.Rep. 695 (1907).

86. 33 A.B.A.Rep. 567–573 (1908); Drinker, *supra* ch. VIII, note 17, at 23–26.

the land permits, to the end that no person may be deprived of life or liberty, but by due process of law.

(A concluding paragraph contrasted the duty of the prosecutor, "not to convict, but to see that justice is done.") [87]

The provenance of Canon 5 was clear, but the spirit had changed. The "can not reject" had become "the right of the lawyer to undertake;" the duty to undertake had changed to a duty to continue, as in Courvoisier's Case. A separate Canon (No. 4) said that "A lawyer assigned as counsel for an indigent prisoner ought not to ask to be excused for any trivial reason, and should always exert his best efforts in his behalf." [88] The committee did not linger over trifles, and re-emphasized in another Canon (No. 31) that a lawyer "has a right to decline employment." [89]

A lone member objected to Canon 5 even in its watered down form, objected that it required him to continue in the face of a confession he believed. "True morals," he argued, "proper regard for justice and the execution of the law, ought to teach me to make known to the court the confession that has been made and leave the court to deal with it. I say I should not defend the criminal." From a Minnesota delegate came the acid response that no lawyer was bound to defend criminals, " . . . but if any lawyer should reveal, or attempt to reveal, either to the court or to the prosecuting officer any information obtained in his professional capacity, such a lawyer in Minnesota would be subject to disbarment, and I am frank to say that I would see to it that the charge of unprofessional conduct was pressed to the utmost." [90]

With that, Canon 5 was adopted (1908), leaving it unclear exactly how "innocent persons, victims only of suspicious circumstances" were to be assured a "proper defense," if it was the right but not the duty of lawyers to defend.

---

87. 33 A.B.A.Rep. 576 (1908); ABA Old Canons, *supra* Intro., note 29, Canon 5; cf. Code of Trial Conduct, § 3 (1963 and 1972).

88. 33 A.B.A.Rep. 576 (1908); ABA Old Canons, *supra* Intro., note 29, Canon 4.

89. 33 A.B.A.Rep. 583 (1908); ABA Old Canons, *supra* Intro., note 29, Canon 31.

90. 33 A.B.A.Rep. 59–61 (1908).

Within the very restricted constitutional requirements of the day, and in an easygoing, haphazardly voluntary way, counsel were often appointed to defend those unable to afford a lawyer. Beyond that, the American Bar Association (and in a slightly variant form the laws of a number of the states) commended to the profession as a general principle of the practice the lawyer's oath of the State of Washington, including the ringing final paragraph:

> I will never reject, from any consideration personal to myself, the cause of the defenseless or oppressed, or delay any man's cause for lucre or malice. SO HELP ME GOD.[91]

If that was somewhat preachy, it did restate an old ideal of the high calling of the advocate; it touched some hearts and perhaps some young minds.

Nonetheless, numerous causes of the defenseless and oppressed were rejected, if not for personal considerations then for impersonal considerations, coldly impersonal ones, such as a routine "Sorry, but our office doesn't handle that sort of case." There was also still a note of relevance in the 1902 remarks of the great criminal lawyer Clarence Darrow to assembled prisoners in Cook County jail, that " .   .   .   nine tenths of you are in jail because you did not have a good lawyer, and, of course, you did not have a good lawyer because you did not have enough money to pay a good lawyer." [92] There was more to it than that. Law schools of the period and for long years after the adoption of the *Canons of Professional Ethics* were urging their students to shun the criminal law as a disease of the lowest classes of mankind and the bar, like the equally unthinkable and morally suspect syphillis. The reasons were much the same that George Warvelle had given. Decent people ought to leave it to someone else, lest you be contaminated.

As a practical matter, Canon 5 was not intended to convince lawyers to defend anyone who wanted a defense, but to remind non-lawyers that a lawyer was not necessarily a moral delin-

---

91. *Id.* 584–585; see e. g. West's Ann.Calif.Bus. & Prof.Code § 6068 (h); see also La.Bar Assn. Code of Ethics (1899), Art. II, § 7, in App. "C" to Report of Committee on Code of Professional Ethics, 31 A.B.A.Rep. 676, 714 (1907), and see also App. "E", pages 715–716.

92. [C. Darrow], Attorney for the Damned 7 (A. Weinberg ed. 1957).

quent if he did. Occasionally lawyers would speak of a "right and obligation to defend persons charged with crime." [93] What they were really trying to tell the world in Canon 5 was that lawyers had a right to defend, regardless of what they or the community thought of an accused man, and that a system of continuous justice required at least that much.

The American College of Trial Lawyers went a step further. By way of "supplement" to the Canons, it took a position half-way between Alabama's old Rule 13 *can not reject* and Canon 5's *right . . . to undertake* saying a lawyer *should not decline to undertake* the defense of criminal cases because of personal opinion as to guilt. It recognized in such cases a "duty of service on the legal profession," and though a lawyer was not bound to take a particular case, he "should not lightly" decline because of "his or public opinion concerning . . . guilt." Once undertaken, the case is not to be dropped on the basis of the lawyer's opinion; and—somewhat ambiguously— "confidential disclosure of guilt alone does not require a withdrawal from the case," though it would limit the nature of the defense.[94]

Amended piecemeal over the years, the *Canons of Professional Ethics* were looked to for guidance by lawyers throughout the United States. They were interpreted in advisory opinions by national and local committees on professional ethics, and were relied on in countless disciplinary proceedings. In some states they became law; in others they had moral and persuasive force.[95] Then, in the hot summer of 1969, the American Bar

93. Code of Legal Ethics, Calif.Bar Assn. § XI.

94. Code of Trial Conduct, §§ 3 and 4 (1963); see and cf. 1972 Revision.

95. See generally, Drinker, *supra* ch. VIII, note 17. And see also, Advisory Opinions of the Board of Governors, State Bar of Okla. [1936]; Ethics Opinions, Los Angeles County Bar Association (1968, 1972); Opinions, Va. State Bar (1965); Opinions of the Committee on Professional Ethics, A.B.A. (1967); Opinions of the Committee on Professional Ethics, The Association of the Bar of the City of New York (1947); Opinions of the Committees on Professional Ethics of the Association of the Bar of the City of New York and the New York County Lawyers' Association (1956); Oregon State Bar "Bluebook" (1954–1960); O. Phillips & P. McCoy, Conduct of Judges and Lawyers 7–20 (1952); Privileges and Responsibilities of Lawyers in Arizona (1958); Rules and Canons of Ethics, State Bar of Texas (1958, 1961); Selected Opinions of the Committee on Professional Ethics of the Fla. Bar (1969).

Association junked the old *Canons*, as being disorganized, over-lapping, unenforceable, and mostly the " 'generalizations designed for an earlier era.' " " . . . [M]any abound with quaint expressions of the past." The Association adopted instead, effective with the new year, a work five years in the making, a spanking new *Code of Professional Responsibility*, intended to cure the ills of the Canons while keeping the "many provisions that are sound in substance." [96] The plan of the *Code* is a body of nine "axiomatic norms," (i. e. the new *Canons*), followed in each case by supporting "Ethical Considerations" that are "aspirational in character," and "Disciplinary Rules" that are "mandatory." [97]

One of the "quaint expressions of the past" that went overboard in the process was the exhortation to lawyers never to reject "the cause of the defenseless or oppressed . . ." Another was old Canon 5's declaration that it is "the right of the lawyer to undertake the defense of a person accused of crime, regardless of his personal opinion as to the guilt of the accused; otherwise innocent persons, victims only of suspicious circumstances, might be denied proper defense."

For these particular disorganized, unenforceable generalties of a bygone era, the *Code* substituted some well organized, unenforceable generalties of the latter 20th century. Here is the new Canon 2:

> A Lawyer Should Assist the Legal Profession in Fulfilling Its Duty to Make Legal Counsel Available.

Among the Ethical Considerations supporting new Canon 2 is one telling a lawyer that while he isn't required to accept clients, he should not "lightly decline proferred employment," and ought to take his share of cases that "may be unattractive both to him and the bar generally." [98] Another says that a "personal preference" against bucking other lawyers, judges, officials, "or influential members of the community" does not jus-

---

96. ABA CPR, *supra* ch. VIII, note 12, Preface, page i.

97. *Id.*, Preliminary Statement, page 1.

98. *Id.*, EC 2–26.

tify refusal to become a man's lawyer.[99]   Others, with their own quota of "quaint expressions" begin by recalling that:

> History is replete with instances of distinguished and sacrificial services by lawyers who have represented unpopular clients and causes. Regardless of his personal feelings, a lawyer should not decline representation because a client or cause is unpopular or community reaction is adverse.[1]

Even so, "[A] lawyer should decline employment if the intensity of his personal feeling, as distinguished from a community attitude, may impair his effective representation of a prospective client."[2]   In the bewildering nightmare world where "personal feeling" and "community attitude" coincide, it's every man for himself; the contingency is not covered.

The closest the new *Code* comes to direct guidance on defense of the "guilty" is this Ethical Consideration:

> When a lawyer is appointed by a court or requested by a bar association to undertake representation of a person unable to obtain counsel, whether for financial or other reasons, he should not seek to be excused from undertaking the representation except for compelling reasons. Compelling reasons do not include such factors as the repugnance of the subject matter of the proceeding, the identity or position of a person involved in the case, the belief of the lawyer that the defendant in a criminal proceeding is guilty, or the belief of the lawyer regarding the merits of the civil case.[3]

It is to be noted that a lawyer's belief in the guilt of the accused is not a "compelling reason" to beg off—only when a court or bar association has requested a lawyer to take the case. The negative inference is that absent such a request, a lawyer's belief in the guilt of the accused is a "compelling reason" to beg off. Nothing is now even mentioned about the centuries old *right* of the lawyer to take a case regardless of his own belief as

99. *Id.*, EC 2–28.

1. *Id.*, EC 2–27.

2. *Id.*, EC 2–30.

3. *Id.*, EC 2–29; cf. Code of Trial Conduct, §§ 3 and 4 (1972 Revision).

to guilt or innocence. For lack of the new *Code* saying, as the old *Canons* did, that the right exists, some may now conclude that the right has sunk without trace. To the extent that lawyers are concerned over the omission, there is an invisible yet substantial obstacle in the path of the unpopular defendant searching for counsel to defend him. The difficulty is resolved only in last extremity by court appointment or the request of a bar association. The individual right, if not the individual duty, of a lawyer to make his services available to anyone in trouble, has now been befuzzed with a last ditch corporate responsibility. This is something less than the traditional unencumbered independence of the lawyer, a retreat from the vigor of old Canon 5, an erosion of the hard-earned right to counsel.

The lawyer is still enjoined under the new *Code of Professional Responsibility* to preserve confidences; [4] that much of tradition has been explicitly saved. On withdrawal from a case: there is a redundant reminder that a lawyer can't withdraw without court permission if court rules say he can't.[5] He may ask for permission to withdraw if his client insists on an unwarranted defense,[6] but defense under the plea of "Not guilty," simply requiring the state to prove its case, is of course not unwarranted. The lawyer may also ask to withdraw when his client "By other conduct renders it unreasonably difficult for the lawyer to carry out his employment effectively." [7] Charles Phillips, untutored by Mr. Baron Parke, might have found a refuge there.

By January of 1972, various forms of the *Code of Professional Responsibility* had been adopted in 40 states and by the District of Columbia Court of Appeals for the District. In seven more states (Connecticut, Rhode Island, South Carolina, Massachusetts, Montana, Wyoming, and Texas) state bar associations had recommended to their state supreme courts that the *Code* be adopted; no public announcement of action had yet been made in Alabama, California, and North Carolina.[8] Whatever uncertainties may exist about the language of the *Code*, on defense of those who say they are guilty the uncertainties affect only the

---

4. ABA CPR, *supra* ch. VIII, note 12, Canon 4.

5. *Id.*, DR 2–110(A)(1).

6. *Id.*, DR 2–110(C)(1)(a).

7. *Id.*, DR 2–110(C)(1)(b).

8. 17 Am.Bar News, no. 1, page 15 (Jan., 1972).

lawyer who ponders the question of voluntarily undertaking such a case, not his acting in response to appointment by court nor at the request of a bar association, and certainly not his action once the case has been undertaken. On this the bar's tradition and rule remain quite clear. As of this moment, we may be certain, thanks in part to the troubles of Charles Phillips, that any American lawyer receiving a quiet confession during trial would—without consulting the judge—proceed to give his client the best defense he knew how.

Important ethical choices remain. The one that plagued Mr. Phillips to the grave was not his decision to defend Courvoisier, but how he went about doing it—after he knew. What did he know? Not positively that his client was guilty (a jury would decide that), but enough to shake any lawyer—that Courvoisier at least did not believe in Courvoisier's innocence.

Chapter X

HOW FAR FOR A CLIENT?

1. PRINCIPLE AND CIRCUMSTANCE

If Charles Phillips' continuing to defend a confessed killer was itself disturbing enough to the Bishop of London and some others who shared the Bishop's views, most of the contemporary bar and many of the public were ready to grant as an abstract proposition that a conscientious lawyer might have something to say even for a sinner, whose cause he had undertaken in ignorance. They agreed that the system of justice required it. "He was bound to continue the defence . . ."[1]

It was a "Yes, but . . ." Yes, say something. But look what the man has said!

They reviewed Phillips' words that seemed movingly eloquent uttered on behalf of a man they had thought he believed innocent of murder. In the light of the "confession" to counsel, the admiration turned to horror and anger, and the question of any defense for the guilty merged in the public's thinking with the kind of defense that had been made.

What was it that Phillips had intended to convey to the jury? Though repeatedly disclaiming any intention of casting the guilt on the "female servants," he had asked:

> "But was it necessary or expedient for Courvoisier to break into the house [in which he lived], to rob where he had daily and hourly opportunity of plunder—the suspicion not cast upon him at all, but if cast upon him, shared with others?"

With that small seed planted, Phillips had reviewed the happenings of the evening before and of the morning of the discovery of Lord Russell's body:

> "The prisoner having seen his master retire to his peaceful bed, and having gone in quiet to his own bed, in the morning he is alarmed by the housemaid, who

---

1. Ballantine, *supra* ch. III, note 7, at 62.

was up before him, with an outcry of 'Robbery!', and
some dark, mysterious suggestions of murder. 'Let us
go,' said she, 'and see where my Lord is.'

"Gentlemen, I must confess that that expression
struck me as very extraordinary. If she had said, 'Let
us go and tell my Lord that the house is plundered,'
that would have been natural. But why should she suspect that anything had happened to his Lordship?
She saw her fellow servant safe, no taint of blood about
the house. And where did she expect to find her master? Why, in the bedroom, to be sure. What was
there to lead to a suspicion that he was hurt? Courvoisier was safe. The cook was safe. And why should
she suspect that her master was not safe too?
.   .   ."

Was not Phillips deliberately suggesting to the jury (in a case
that was almost certainly an inside job) that there was some
reason to think Sarah Mancer had some foreknowledge of the
crime that Courvoisier did not have? And, ultimately, that
Courvoisier was not guilty and Sarah Mancer was?

Again, what could Phillips have intended by his free swinging
attack on the police?

Inspector Pearce was an "inquisitorial ruffian," trying "to intimidate a poor wretch in the fangs of the police, trembling for
his life," "to brow-beat and frighten him into an admission of
his guilt." Constable Baldwin was a "miscreant bloodhound,"
"who did his best in the work of conspiracy to earn the wages of
blood," his share of the reward which the police would split and
write their "receipt in the blood of the prisoner." "Some villains must have been at work here," Phillips had told the jury,
"to provide proofs of guilt against the prisoner, and endeavour
to make you instrumental in rendering him the victim, not of
his own guilt, but of their own foul machinations."

Could this have been understood in any way but a charge that
the whole prosecution was a brazen, bought attempt to frame an
innocent man?

And what of the merciless attack in cross-examination and argument on the credibility of Mrs. Piolaine, whose testimony it
was that hanged Courvoisier? She enters the courtroom an

unknown innkeeper of London, and she leaves—after performing a public service—accused of keeping a disreputable house, her sex life made public, and her integrity suspect, her whole narrative held up to public ridicule. "Gentlemen, I ask this question, 'Did you, in the whole course of your existence, ever hear of such a singular circumstance?' "

Having had Courvoisier's confession, could Phillips have thought otherwise than that Charlotte Piolaine was an honest witness?   And was he not attempting to make her out a liar?

There were other troubling passages in Phillips' speech to the jury (some of them discussed in the next chapter), the overall impression now one of revulsion.   What Phillips knew was weighed, and not too finely, against what he had said.   The popular conclusion was that Charles Phillips as a man and a lawyer had done a despicable thing.

Lord Broughton thought Phillips' conduct "outrageous;" [2] Solicitor-General Wilde told a friend it was "infamous;" [3] someone else thought that Phillips' "wild flowers of speech . . . [were]easily grown, but have a very rank and foul smell in the nostrils of honest men." [4]   The least harsh comment was that he had gone too far.[5]   His most persistent and acid critic, the editor of *The Examiner*, wrote nine years after the trial:

> "And what is the essential difference, in point of sentiment between aiding and assisting by such means in the escape of an assassin from the hands of justice, and aiding and assisting in his escape before he falls into the hands of justice . . .. We know how Mr. Phillips would act if a wretch accosted him with the red hand, saying, 'I have just cut my sleeping master's throat, help me to escape from pursuit of justice, and here are five blood stained guineas for the service': and in point of sentiment, how is the case altered when the escape desired is from the verdict of a jury, instead of the hands of the police . . .. The only answer is that all his sympathies and all his faculties were bought and paid for; that he was hired for the

2.   5 Broughton, Recollections of a Long Life 275 (1911).

3.   *Id.* 293.

4.   Chronicle (London), "The License of Counsel," June 23, 1840.

5.   25 The Law Magazine 238 (Aug. 1840).

job of effecting a cut-throat's escape; and he belonged for the nonce, morally and intellectually, out and out, to the assassin." [6]

This was *The Examiner* making the worst of Phillips' own gross version of Lord Brougham on the duty of counsel. Goaded into public reply by intermittent attack on his conduct in Courvoisier's Case, Phillips had just broken silence in a letter to *The Times*, followed by an explanatory pamphlet that included lawyers' indorsements. He defended his defense of Courvoisier. Phillips now said that his first impulse to desert Courvoisier on hearing the confession had been wrong. "I had no right to throw up my brief, and turn traitor to the wretch, wretch though he was, who had confided in me. The counsel for a prisoner has no option. The moment he accepts his brief, every faculty he possesses becomes his client's property." [7]

That final hard line was a crude adaptation of something Phillips' friend Henry (later Lord) Brougham had said as one of counsel for Queen Caroline in 1820. George IV, a notorious lecher, was trying to rid himself of the Queen, accusing her of adultery with the Italian Bartolomo Pergami. The Queen's men (ultimately successful) were attempting to encourage the Government to drop the charge. As he opened for the defense in the House of Lords, Brougham had said "that the cause of the Queen . . . did not require recrimination at present," that he was not now called upon "to utter one whisper against the conduct of her illustrious consort." He nonetheless warned the Lords that if such a defense became necessary to his case, neither he nor "even the youngest member in the profession, would hesitate to resort to such a course, and fearlessly perform his duty." [8] Brougham had in mind not merely the King's liaisons with Lady Jersey and others, but also a secret marriage to the Roman Catholic Mrs. Fitzherbert, which under the Act of Settlement could result in a forfeiture of the crown. Public charges of adultery against the King were alarming enough, and that was the threat understood by Brougham's audience.[9] In that setting, he went on to remind "their lordships"

6. Examiner (London), No. 2,184, page 770, Dec. 8, 1849.

7. Warren-Phillips, *supra* ch. III, note 75, at 15.

8. 2 Trial of Queen Caroline 7–8 (1821).

9. 2 Brougham, Life and Times of Henry Lord Brougham 308–310

—that an advocate, in the discharge of his duty, knows but one person in all the world, and that person is his client. To save that client by all means and expedients, and at all hazards and costs to other persons, and, amongst them, to himself, is his first and only duty; and in performing this duty he must not regard the alarm, the torments, the destruction which he may bring upon others. Separating the duty of a patriot from that of an advocate, he must go on reckless of consequences, though it should be his unhappy fate to involve his country in confusion.[10]

Brougham's effective speech had been controversial from the moment of delivery; he himself was proud enough of it to polish it, and republish it.[11] D'Israeli, no lawyer and no lover of lawyers, on trial for libeling one of them, had professed to find in Brougham's words the claim of a lawyer's duty "even to commit treason" to save a client.[12] Years later, Lord Halsbury thought "Lord Brougham's overstatement . . . much nearer the truth than the tone of advocacy which should take into account . . . what the newspapers would say of the advocate next day." [13] Wrenched out of its context, Brougham's extreme credo had been made the more extreme by Phillips and extremest of all by *The Examiner*. The effect was violent enough to heat up a stew still bubbling: Just how far ought a lawyer to go for a client?

Granted a guilty man is entitled to a defense, how does a decent lawyer go about defending him? Granted a confidence must be kept within the limits already discussed, how is one to act after receiving a confidence? Those who are not lawyers have ready and varied answers. Pray for Divine mercy. Keep your lip zipped. Act honorably. Etc. For the lawyer, these will

(1871–1872); 9 Brougham, Works 83 n. (1872); W. Forsyth, Hortensius 389 n. 1 (2d ed. 1874; 1st ed. 1849); S. Rogers, "The Ethics of Advocacy," 15 L.Q.Rev. 259, 270, and n. 2 (1899); cf. 1 W. C. Townsend, Modern State Trials 259 (1850).

10. 2 Trial of Queen Caroline 8 (1821).

11. 9 Brougham, Works 83 (1872); cf. W. Forsyth, Hortensius, *supra* note 9.

12. J. Stammers, The Case of the Queen v. D'Israeli 11 (1838).

13. Private letter of Lord Halsbury [1893], quoted in S. Rogers, "The Ethics of Advocacy," 15 I.Q.Rev. 259, 271 (1899).

not suffice. The need to do something, the utter lack of abstractness, strains the lawyer's conscience at every turning. Read me no riddles. Come to the point: Did the confidence of Courvoisier's confession either require or permit Charles Phillips to act publicly as though he had never heard it?

Even stated that concretely, the question still has in it an element of abstraction unpalatable to the trial lawyer. It ignores some further turning of the screw.

Courvoisier had not confessed to counsel until after a full day of trial. That first day Phillips had sharply cross-examined both Sarah Mancer and Constable Baldwin. Bits and pieces of Sarah Mancer's testimony had enough of the curious in them to raise the stray thought that she herself might not be beyond suspicion. In Constable Baldwin's answers to questions about the reward he had shown himself capable of perjury. That much was in record before Courvoisier confessed to Phillips, and could not be rubbed out. The jury had heard it, had watched a frightened Sarah Mancer and the lying, evasive Constable Baldwin on the witness stand. In light of the confession, should these points of weakness in the prosecution case be ignored? Could they be?

Samuel Warren, a barrister and writer of distinction and a friend of Charles Phillips, gave his own short answer. Phillips, he said, was "bound to act as though he were not the depositary of the fatal secret confided to him . . . " This alone would satisfy the system of justice—the attorney-client confidence kept, the jury decide as it is sworn to do, "according to the evidence." [14]

William Townsend (1850) summed it up:

> If burdened by a confession which he cannot divulge, he will betray it, should the counsel's speech abstain from urging those remarks on defective testimony which he would have made irrespective of the confession.[15]

14. S. Warren, *The Mystery of Murder and its Defence* in 2 Miscellanies Critical, Imaginative, and Juridical 42 (1855).

15. 1 W. C. Townsend, Modern State Trials 254-255 (1850).

If the peculiarity of Sarah Mancer's early morning responses to the discovery of the corpse had passed unnoticed in Phillips' argument, if Constable Baldwin's deliberate efforts to conceal his knowledge of the reward had not been mentioned, everyone in the world (except Courvoisier and those who had his confidence) would have thought the omissions strange.

Juries are alert to sense a lack of enthusiasm on the part of counsel. In the first round of appeals in the *Scottsboro Case,* Chief Justice Anderson of the Supreme Court of Alabama dissented from the conclusion of his fellow judges that the defendants had been adequately represented. He could "appreciate the position of a lawyer appointed to defend an indigent defendant whom he may feel is guilty and as against whom public sentiment is at fever heat," but in his opinion the performance of counsel "was rather pro forma than zealous and active and which is indicated by a declination on the part of counsel to argue the case," though there was abundant argument for the prosecution. He thought that counsel's inaction was "bound to make an unfavorable impression on the jury." [16]

The conscientious juror compliments himself on detecting points for the accused. If the lawyer does not argue the force of that evidence, the juror readily comes to the conclusion that the lawyer is holding back deliberately, that the accused's own lawyer has no faith in the innocence of his client. That indeed was the very position of defense counsel in *Johns v. Smyth* (1959): [17] a penitentiary killing; a signed confession in which the killer says he knifed his cellmate on the provocation of a homosexual embrace; assigned defense counsel after talking with his client does not believe the story of provocation, and does not argue it to the jury though the prosecution introduces the whole confession as evidence of guilt. The client is found guilty of first degree murder, and is given a new trial for failure of counsel to perform his duty. The lawyer has permitted his own conscientious scruples to stand in the way of a proper defense for his client.

16. Powell v. State, 224 Ala. 540, 555, 141 So. 201, 214 (1932) (dissenting opinion).

17. 176 F.Supp. 949 (E.D.Va.1959).

2.   "CASTING THE GUILT UPON THE INNOCENT"

The *Smyth Case* involves the lawyer's conscience in concern for his own moral integrity at the expense of his client. It does not touch the further refinement of the anguish of Charles Phillips.

With Sarah Mancer's testimony his problem was most acute, for argument about her testimony would tend not only to weaken the case against Courvoisier but call her own innocence into question.   She is not on trial, and cannot be convicted at this trial whatever suspicion is aroused against her.   Yet because of what is said today, on another day she may be on trial.   And even if not, it goes against the grain of decency to stir up suspicion against someone you have reason to believe beyond it.

Could Phillips continue to act as though he had never heard Courvoisier's confession, even to the point of leaving the jury to infer from what he said that Sarah Mancer was guilty of murder?   The tug of conscience urges some compromise with the confidence, against the risk of helping to condemn the innocent. Phillips' speech itself demonstrates that struggle, not one but two suggestions of the innocence of the female servants, though at the same time not turning loose of the doubts surrounding Mancer's testimony.

In his own belated defense, Phillips denied that his lawyer's obligation to Courvoisier gave him the right of "casting the guilt upon the innocent," but he denied that he had done it.[18] Some newspapers felt the disclaimers of that intent in Phillips' speech had been too carefully worded: "It is not my duty, nor my interest, nor my policy   .   .   ." " "to cast the crime" on Mancer or Hannell.   "God forbid" that he should do so.   Sly insinuations, they thought.   Like the rabble rouser urging on the mob, shouting to them not to heat up the tar their victim so richly deserves.[19]

Besides, in retrospect, the event proved that Phillips had been defending a guilty man.   Phillips' critics were not attuned to fine distinctions between arguing the evidence and implying guilt, between argument on testimony given before or after the confession, nor even between Phillips' vigorous cross-examina-

---

18. Warren-Phillips, *supra* ch. III,   19. Examiner (London), No. 2,183,
     note 75, at 15–18.   pages 755, 756, Dec. 1, 1849.

tion before the confession and his argument to the jury after he had Courvoisier's confession. *The Examiner* found monstrous the whole of Lord Brougham's view of the advocate's role, which Phillips had taken for a cover motto on his pamphlet of defense. "An advocate . . . knows . . . but one person in the world, that client, and none other . . ." It was, wrote the editor, a "detestable doctrine," that the lawyer " 'must not regard the alarm, the suffering, the torment, the destruction, which he may bring upon any other.' " [20] *The Examiner* noted that these last words of Brougham doctrine were not included in Phillips' pamphlet. He "strangely omits the part which makes it so closely applicable to his own conduct." [21] The paper recalled the tribulation of Sarah Mancer. "The cloud was heavy over her, and it passed so slowly that her life never more escaped from it. She died in a madhouse," [22] "driven mad," said *The Examiner*, "by the sufferings and terrors," "[t]he persecutions . . . the harassing interrogations to which she was subjected preceding the providential discovery of the guilt of Courvoisier . . ." [23] Of the lawyers in the courtroom at the time who now came to Phillips' defense, they were oblivious to the suffering of Sarah Mancer " 'while the advocate was thundering forth denunciations against her.' . . . They were busy admiring the ingenuity of the rack, and had no leisure to notice the victim quivering beneath it." [24] The paper thought this carried Lord Brougham's bombast beyond limits. "Destroying the character of a maid servant, we are simple enough to think, implies a higher stretch of moral recklessness than the confronting of a King . . ." It was, said *The Examiner*, "revolting aggression upon the innocent . . ." [25]

For Phillips, an anonymous Middle Templar had maintained right from the start that he had done what the advocate is bound to do—

". . . to point out to the jury any contradictions, inaccuracies, or omissions that may appear to

20. *Id.*, No. 2,182, pages 737, 738, Nov. 24, 1849.

21. *Id.*, No. 2,184, pages 769, 771, Dec. 8, 1849.

22. *Id.*, 770.

23. *Id.*, No. 2,182, pages 737–738, Nov. 24, 1849.

24. *Id.*, No. 2,184, pages 769, 770, Dec. 8, 1849.

25. *Id.*, No. 2,182, pages 737, 738, Nov. 24, 1849.

him in the evidence produced by the prosecutors; and, if through any maudlin sentimentality, or through any fear of inculpating others, he should neglect to do so, he would be guilty of gross violation of duty, and would deserve to have his gown stripped off his back." [26]

Most of Phillips' defenders did not go that far. They, like Phillips, accepted the premise of the accusation, that to carry devotion to the client and his confidence to the point of accusing the innocent would have been shameful. They insisted with Phillips that he had not done it.[27] It remained for barrister William Digby Seymour, seven years after *Courvoisier's Case*, to push the cause of devotion to client to the absolute position Phillips and his friends had shrunk from. It came as an aftermath of the cases known in the annals of English crime as the Mirfield Murders.

In May, 1847, police arrested two itinerant peddlers Michael M'Cabe and Patrick Reid, suspected of murdering James Wraith, 76, his wife, 65, and their servant Caroline Ellis, age 20. The family had all been killed while eating their noonday meal, the discovery made at 1:30 in the afternoon when a neighbor saw blood oozing from under the front door of the shuttered and curtained Wraith home, Wateroyd Hall. The body of the servant girl was found "quite dead, though warm," the throat cut, the skull fractured. One garter was missing, reportedly later found in M'Cabe's possession.[28]

M'Cabe was the first arrested, and at Reid's trial for the murder of Wraith, M'Cabe turned state's evidence. He testified for the prosecution that about the time of the murder he had come to the door of the Wraith house selling pots. A man opened the door about six inches, said he didn't want anything, and shut the door. That had been time enough, said M'Cabe, for him to notice blood on the floor, and to identify the man who answered his knock as the defendant Patrick Reid.

Except for M'Cabe, who had claimed a government reward of £100.0.0 and a pardon, no one placed Reid at the scene of the

26. Chronicle (London), "License of Counsel," June 25, 1840.

27. Warren-Phillips, *supra* ch. III, note 75, at 22–28; S. Warren, *The*

Mystery of Murder, and its Defence, supra note 14, at 47–51.

28. The Times (London), May 15, 18, 27, June 7, 12, 21, July 9, 1847.

crime. His counsel Mr. Serjeant Wilkins (assisted by William Seymour) spoke to the jury for three hours, and Reid was acquitted.[29]

Five months later, Reid and M'Cabe were brought to trial for the murder of Caroline Ellis. A new witness appeared for the prosecution. Thirteen year old Mary Hallas had been caught in a thunderstorm, took shelter at the Wraith wall on the day of the murder; as the church clock struck one, she saw both M'Cabe and Reid in the yard of Wateroyd Hall, and saw them leave.

William Seymour argued for Reid that "M'Cabe was really the murderer," that the new evidence did not "substantiate the case against" Reid but left things exactly as they were at the first trial when Reid had been acquitted. M'Cabe's assigned counsel told the jury M'Cabe's presence at the Wraith house was consistent with his innocence.

In a three hour summing up, the judge viewed the evidence as to time "very favorable to M'Cabe." He told the jury there was nothing to show the prisoners had known each other, and thought it would be remarkable if two strangers had killed in concert. The evidence about Miss Ellis' garter the judge found "quite ridiculous."

Two hours later, the jury found both men guilty. As the black-capped judge sentenced both to death, "Reid maintained his firmness till the last, but M'Cabe fainted . . . and was obliged to be supported." Back in his cell Reid confessed that he alone had committed all three murders; M'Cabe, as M'Cabe had always insisted, was innocent.[30]

Rumor said that there had been an earlier confession, and that his counsel had Reid's full confession and the exculpation of M'Cabe before the trial started. This William Seymour publicly denied. He acknowledged that from statements Reid had given him "I had reason strongly to presume Reid's guilt," but nothing "irreconcilable   with   the   supposition   of   M'Cabe's   guilt . . ." He had found Reid's replies to questions he had posed "so contradictory in themselves, and so totally opposed to the evidence for the prosecution, that I did not believe them, and in no single point did I vary the line of defence I had already resolved to follow."

---

29. *Id.*, July 21, 22, 1847.   **30.** *Id.*, Dec. 22, 23, 24, 1847.

Seymour explained his attack on M'Cabe:

> "The evidence offered on the trial as to time and other matters pressed with about equal weight on the two prisoners; but M'Cabe's stories and conduct, and equivocation strengthened the case against him. No concert whatever was proved between them; both prisoners admitted they were at Wraith's about the time of the murders. M'Cabe at the last trial swore that the man he saw at Wraith's was Reid. What course was open to me? If M'Cabe was innocent and spoke truth, the man he saw was my client. If M'Cabe was guilty, and no concert was made out,   .   .   . was it not clear my client was innocent—clear, I mean, as a reasonable argument, drawn from the evidence before the jury? "

Whether it was conscience or conviction that led him to say more, Seymour went the last step; he continued, in a letter to *The Times*:

> "And now, Sir, assuming that to be true which I deny, and admitting for a moment that a 'full confession' was made to me 'previous to the trial which wholly exculpated M'Cabe,' I am yet to learn that I would be deserving of blame for endeavouring to throw the whole guilt upon M'Cabe if the evidence warranted such a course. I am yet to learn that this would be either morally or professionally wrong. When a counsel accepts a brief for a prisoner he becomes, in my opinion, bound by a twofold obligation. I esteem it in the first place to be his strict and solemn duty to keep faithful to his client during the trial, and to hold his secrets as a religious trust. They are *commissa fidei*— they must not be violated—they must not be exposed.

> "And in the next place, it is equally his bounden duty to frame the best defence in his power from the evidence at the trial. If a prisoner confesses his guilt, or makes admissions which tend to criminate him while they acquit his fellow prisoner, is his counsel to hurry into the witness-box to ruin and betray him? If not, then his confession is not in evidence; and does a counsel overstep his duty who adopts a line of defence whol-

ly irrespective of that confession, but which is founded on the evidence before the jury, borne out, and justified by it? When a veto is put upon this exercise of a counsel's discretion—when, instead of his argument being weighed and measured by the nature of the evidence, his motives and private opinions are publicly submitted to a rigid moral test—the relation of client and counsel will be deranged, and their mutual confidence interrupted; the independence of the bar will be violated, and the principle of advocacy will be abolished altogether." [31]

That did it for *The Times*. "If the principles laid down by Mr. William Digby Seymour . . . were true," it editorialized, "it would be very desirable that the office of advocate should be abolished altogether . . . We cannot yield our minds up to such sophistry as that an advocate, being fully conscious of the guilt of one of two persons, and the innocence of the other, is justified in saving a guilty client at the expense of his innocent companion . . . [I]f successful, he brings an innocent man to the gallows . . .

"The last remarkable instance we remember of unscrupulous advocacy of the sort attributed to Mr. Seymour," continued the paper, "was in *Courvoisier's* case, where the counsel for the defence attempted to throw the guilt on one of the prisoner's fellow servants . . . To recur to the Mirfield Murders and the case of Mr. Seymour, actually before us, what would have been his line of conduct had this gentleman succeeded in his defence, and procured an acquittal for Reid, and an adverse verdict against M'Cabe? Would he, knowing M'Cabe to be innocent, have allowed him to die upon the scaffold? We presume not. Mr. Seymour, we suppose, would have stated the fact, or written an account of Reid's confession, to the proper authorities in order to save M'Cabe's life. Even so, however, the relation between client and counsel, as it is understood by Mr. Seymour must have received a certain shock. If the robes of the barrister are to afford as sacred a pledge of confidence as the confessional of

31. *Id.*, Dec. 30, 1847, page 6.

the Roman Catholic priest, Mr. Seymour would have been no more justified in disclosing the sacred confidence to him after, than before acquittal. If the question of discretion is to be allowed at any moment to creep in, it is the discretion of an honest man, and must be judged by the common rules of honesty and morality. This does not, however, appear to be Mr. Seymour's notion   .   .   . We have, however, not one shadow of doubt that to save a client by the sacrifice of an innocent man, whom counsel know to be innocent, is a direct violation of honour, of morality, and of the laws of God and man. If such were—as it is not—the general feeling of the bar, no man of common honesty —not to say, no gentleman—would submit to the degradation of being enrolled in its ranks." [32]

The Law Magazine agreed. "The fact is," wrote their commentator, "that it is alike improper and unprofessional for counsel to do that for a prisoner which it would be unjustifiable in the prisoner to do for himself: and we apprehend there can be small doubt that it would be unjustifiable in a prisoner to get an innocent man hanged in order to save his own neck from a halter. We have been several years at the bar without once hearing such a course countenanced, and we believe Lord Brougham, Mr. Phillips and Mr. Seymour must divide between them the enviable distinction of giving it sanction." [33]

Fairly or not, this committed Lord Brougham and Charles Phillips to Seymour's rationalization for a knowing attack on the innocent, a logical, too logical, extreme that neither Brougham nor Phillips acknowledged. As we have seen, it was an extreme that Phillips was to expressly repudiate two years later; and it has since been condemned by the organized barristers [34] and separately by the organized solicitors of England.[35] Yet to the popular mind, the sting of the attack on Seymour and Brougham and Phillips was not merely that their immoral logic led inexorably to connivance in the death of the innocent. The

---

32. *Id.* 4.

33. "Licence of Counsel," The Law Magazine, vol. 39 Old Series, vol. 8 New Series, pages 53, 59 (1848).

34. Boulton, *supra* ch. IX, note 49, at 71; see also, Code of Trial Conduct § 4(b) (1963, 1972).

35. Lund, *supra* ch. IX, note 50, at 106.

code itself was damnable: by Brougham-Phillips-Seymour standards the advocate was to approach the task of defending any client with a singleminded and ruthless devotion.

The no-holds-barred theory of the lawyer's duty to his client, as proposed by barrister Seymour, was again brought to the notice of the English public two years later, in the joint trial of the Mannings, husband and wife, for the murder of Mrs. Manning's paramour Patrick O'Connor. While here there was no question of a confession to counsel, the defendants were separately represented, and the same Mr. Serjeant Wilkins who had won an acquittal for Reid opened the defense of Mr. Manning with a violent and personal attack on Mrs. Manning.

> "My hypothesis," Serjeant Wilkins told the jury, "is one which at first sight may appear shocking and unmanly, but we must not allow the usual urbanities of life to interfere with our judgment on questions like the present. We are all in the habit of associating the female character with the idea of mildness and obedience, and that of the man with the idea of power and strength. It is not necessary, however, to come to the conclusion that this rule is an universal one. History teaches us that the female is capable of reaching higher in point of virtue than the male, but that when once she gives way to vice she sinks far lower than our sex. My hypothesis, then, is that the female prisoner Manning premeditated, planned, and concocted the murder, and that she made her husband her dupe and instrument for that purpose .   .   .   It might be said, as it has been said, that Mr. Manning is crowning himself with infamy by throwing the blame upon his wife. That is easily said; but if the blame is justly due to his wife—if it is she alone who committed the murder, has not the husband suffered enough from her already, without standing cooly and allowing himself to be sacrified by the wicked woman who entrapped him?

Serjeant Wilkins proceeded to recount how on a Wednesday Mrs. Manning had invited O'Connor to Thursday dinner. The body was later found buried in the kitchen. He recalled to the

jury a Friday conversation between Mrs. Manning and a Mr.
Keating:

".   .   .   observe her hypocrisy—her falsehood—
her consummate wickedness. Keating asked Mrs. Manning if she had seen O'Connor. She replied that she
had not seen him since Wednesday night. Keating said
it was a very strange thing. 'Very strange,' repeated
the female prisoner, 'for I invited him to dinner on
the Thursday, and Mr. Manning thought it a most un-
gentlemanly thing that he did not come at the appointed time. I went to his lodgings to ascertain the reason
why he did not come.'

"On that occasion," the Serjeant continued, "the only
time when her lip was noticed to quiver and her cheek
to blanch—she made use of an expression which struck
me, as I saw it did some of you. She said,—'Poor Mr.
O'Connor! he was the best friend I had in the world.' "

The Serjeant echoed it, "Poor Mr. O'Connor! "
"Why poor Mr. O'Connor? " And then, as the reporter saw it, "apparently addressing the prisoner,"

"You   .   .   .   knew his body was mouldering in
your kitchen. You knew you were at that moment in
possession of his property. You knew his voice would
never be heard again. You knew that he had been hurried out of time into eternity. Well might you say,
'Poor Mr. O'Connor,' thrown off your guard at the moment. If you believed merely that he had gone out of
town in some freak or fancy,—for you describe him as
a fitful and fanciful person—why exclaim 'Poor Mr.
O'Connor? ' "

Serjeant Wilkins had prefaced this spitting confrontation
with a statement of his notions of the role of the advocate:

"I don't dictate to you," he said, "what your verdict
shall be. It would be arrogant in me to do so, it is no
part of my duty. My duty is to watch my adversary,
to see that he takes no unfair advantage of my client,
to see that whatever is attempted to be proved against
him, if proved at all, is proved in a proper manner, and
to urge upon you every topic which I may think enti-

At another point, he had tried to steel the jurors against the inevitable rebuttal:

" . . . I have to urge upon you a line of defence which at first sight appears very odious, and, in the next place, I am to be followed—strange as it may appear—by another defending counsel, whose duty it will be to neutralize, as far as in him lies, all that I may urge, and to destroy, if he can, the man whom I wish to save."

Mr. Ballantine, for Mrs. Manning, declined to follow suit.

"I would have been glad," he told the jury, "to avoid certain observations which I feel bound to make—but which I shall endeavour to make temperately—upon the course pursued by my learned friend Serjeant Wilkins. I would have been glad if you could have escaped the spectacle, unparalleled in a criminal court, of finding an advocate, either for the prosecution or for the defence, in the presence of a person who is undergoing a trial for her life, denouncing her in terms that, to say the least, were utterly unnecessary,—terms which I can hardly help calling somewhat coarse. I consider that the presence of the person against whom these observations were made ought, at all events, to have prevented my learned friend from using them, whatever might be the necessities of his case. Far be it from me to say that my learned friend did not exercise the best judgment that he could apply to this matter,—that he did not conscientiously follow the instructions he had received; for I will do my learned friend the credit of believing that he acted contrary to his own taste and feeling in performing what he believed to be his duty to his client.

"My learned friend appeared to anticipate that I would follow his example, and endeavour to throw upon the male prisoner the burden of this miserable, this unhappy transaction. God forbid that I should pursue that course! I would far rather never enter this court, or any other, than in the presence of a fellow-creature awaiting his doom—who might be led from this court to the scaffold, and might soon have to appear before his Creator—I would use such terms as were applied by my learned friend to the female prisoner.

"I will do that which is my duty as an advocate; but if my duty as an advocate requires that I should cast upon the male prisoner the sort of observations and accusations which have been made against the woman, I would feel that my profession was a disgrace, and that the sooner I abandoned it for one somewhat more creditable, the sooner I would be a respected, an honest, an honourable, and an upright man, and placed in a position better to respect myself.

"Every advocate who is called upon to defend a cause must take the evidence that has been submitted to the jury; he must show how that evidence weighs, and, as far as his humble abilities enable him, to point out to the jury the mode in which he desires them to view it. If that evidence inculpates others it might be necessary to apply some observations to the subject, but when this painful duty is cast upon an advocate it ought to be performed in a calm and temperate manner."

Having given a lesson in manners to Serjeant Wilkins, Mr. Ballantine proceeded to demonstrate what he thought were "proper observations" in the performance of a "painful duty." Less strident, but hardly less pointed than Wilkins, Ballantine observed:

"Taking the most innocent and virtuous woman in the world, or the most profligate and abandoned, the course which they would adopt on finding that a husband had murdered their friend would depend very much on the temper and temperament of the parties. In the present instance the woman resolved to get away from her husband, and while doing so she possessed herself of a considerable amount of property."

The jury adopted the dim view each counsel took of the other's client, and found both of the Mannings guilty. [36]   *The Examiner*, implacable critic of Phillips (who had now become Mr. Commissioner Phillips of the Insolvent Debtor's Court), joined in the public condemnation of Serjeant Wilkins, and praised Mr. Ballantine for having the courage to denounce the Serjeant's courtroom conduct, noting that public opinion had begun to have some influence "even on the bar."   It also seized upon the occasion to dredge up the sins of Charles Phillips:

> "How much worse," said *The Examiner*, "was Mr. Phillips' attempt to throw the suspicion of the murder of Lord William Russell on the innocent female servants, in order to procure the acquittal of his client Courvoisier, of whose guilt he was cognizant!   But so little was he prejudiced in the highest places of legal authority and patronage by this horrible endeavour, that he was soon afterwards advanced to a seat of judicature, about the same time that one of the unfortunate women whose characters and lives he would have placed in jeopardy was lodged in a lunatic asylum, driven mad by the terrors that had successively beset her.   But public opinion has, since then, had its effect even upon the licentiousness of the Bar;   and though there may now be unscrupulous advocates capable of re-enacting the part of Mr. Phillips, and Mr. Serjeant Wilkins approaches it, yet we are very certain that both the judgment of the profession and the public would put a perpetual veto on their promotion, and they would remain, what is significantly called, marked men." [37]

This was the editorial that provoked Phillips into a public defense of his conduct, nine years after the trial of Courvoisier. Phillips' response in turn spread the controversy throughout the English press and the Anglo-American legal world.[38]   In the bur-

---

36. The Times (London), Oct. 27, 1849, pages 5, 6, 7, with corrections of person and tense.

37. Examiner (London), No. 2,179, page 691, Nov. 3, 1849.

38. The Times (London), Nov. 20, 1849, page 5; Warren-Phillips *supra* ch. III, note 75; and see e. g. "The Defence of Courvoisier, And the Plea for It," The Law Magazine, vol. 43 Old Series, vol. 12 New Series, page 26 (1850); "On

geoning discussion more was at issue than Phillips' attack upon the "female servants."

3. DISCREDITING THE TRUTHFUL WITNESS

One of the routine duties of the trial lawyer is to probe and test the evidence that is offered by the other side, exposing weakness, innocent mistake, prejudice, sometimes perjury. In this jousting, by cross-examination and argument, it is believed there is a better opportunity for jury or judge to arrive at a whole picture and a just decision. The lawyer's penetration below the layer of words into what is not obvious—motivation for lying, a disposition to shield someone, a pattern of persistent bias, physical or psychological bases for inadequate observation —is sharpened by his own bias in favor of a client. In turn, the lawyer's trained suspicion stimulates the thinking of judge and jury, encourages them to be cautious in acting on ready-made conclusions. Through his questioning and argument the lawyer is trying to inform judge and jury, to persuade them to come to a just conclusion "on the evidence." Which is to say, to become convinced in a court of law, rather than beforehand, on the basis of hunch, rumor, and backdoor gossip.

Juries sometimes ignore the evidence. One juror tells another in the wash room, in a case having nothing to do with prostitution, "That woman is a whore; she'll never get my vote." Still, our system of justice rests on its being worth the effort to try to get juries (and judges too) to decide cases according to the law and the evidence.

The lawyer's private knowledge is not part of that evidence. As we have seen, at least insofar as the jury was concerned, what Courvoisier told Phillips in confidence remained confidential throughout the trial. The judge told the lawyer he was bound to continue the defense, "and to use all fair arguments arising on the evidence." Sound enough advice all right, but how do you follow it?

the Principle of Advocacy as Developed in the Practice of the Bar," The Law Magazine, vol. 51 Old Series, vol. 20 New Series, pages 265, 291 (1854); G. Sharswood, A Compend of Lectures on the Aims and Duties of the Profession of Law 40–44, and Appendix No. I, page 107 (1854); "Legal Ethics," 1 The American Lawyer 46, 47 (1893).

Here is a witness for the prosecution—Constable John Baldwin. He testifies there were no marks in the dust on the roofs adjacent to Lord Russell's house, closing off that avenue of entry to the house by someone other than Courvoisier. The constable also testifies that his testimony is not influenced by hope of a reward, because he never heard of any reward. No-marks-in-the-dust is the truth. No-knowledge-of-the-reward is a lie. And Mr. Phillips' persistent cross-examination had exposed the lie, before Courvoisier confessed to his lawyer. But by the time he came to argue to the jury, Phillips had the confession, and with it good reason to believe that even if Baldwin lied about the reward, his testimony bearing directly on Courvoisier's guilt was honest testimony. What does one say about Baldwin? Phillips denounced him to the jury as a "miscreant bloodhound", lying under oath to get the reward money.

In the view of the evidence that Phillips urged upon the jury, Baldwin's perjury was only one facet of a police conspiracy to convict—to convict a man Phillips had good reason to believe guilty. The central fact in the conspiracy was the strange discovery of the bloody gloves, the bloody handkerchiefs, and the torn shirt front among the same clothes that had been repeatedly searched, discovered only after a reward had been announced, and only after Courvoisier was already in jail. Here was a mystery never cleared up, not even at the gallows. At best the police were negligent. But the facts could be persuasive of much worse: planted evidence, coupled with perjury by the police, to bolster up a case they thought might not convince a jury, even if Courvoisier were the murderer. A police conspiracy to convict a guilty man. A police conspiracy to end the public jeering at police incompetence, and also incidentally to claim a reward. There was more here than the ordinary police eagerness to "solve" a crime, which could routinely explain the attempted police intimidation of Courvoisier.

Of the police witnesses whose sometimes reluctant testimony made these unwholesome inferences reasonable, all but Baldwin testified on the second day of the trial. So of them it could not be said as with the testimony of Sarah Mancer and Constable Baldwin, that the damning facts revealed by an innocent and vigorous cross-examination were already laid out to the jury before counsel had the confession. Phillips had now to wrestle out of nowhere a proper etiquette for cross-examining witnesses whose testimony was headed in the right direction, even if there were lesser lies or some rottenness along the way. Cross-examine as he thought proper, and make "all fair arguments arising on the evidence."

Samuel Warren claimed for his friend the best of both worlds. At the same time complimenting Phillips on continuing a vigorous defense of Courvoisier, he professed to find a commendable self-restraint after the "blighting confession . . . had been communicated to the bewildered advocate," with cross-examination by "the crest-fallen questioner" sharply reduced. "From that moment," wrote Warren, "his fire slackened . . . ."[39] If it did, the fire had certainly been re-stoked when Phillips set upon cross-examining Mrs. Piolaine, and it was a full head of steam that propelled his address to the jury.

With Mrs. Piolaine, also testifying after Courvoisier's confession to Phillips, the attack on her credibility seems the most vicious. With her, there was no suggestion from the testimony itself that she had any part in the planting of evidence, or of conspiracy with the police. The worst that could be discovered in her testimony was its unusual timing, so late in the day, an almost casual happening upon the stolen Russell silver, when all of London had been in a dither over murder and theft for many weeks. Could she have been a party to the theft, and only reluctantly through fear of discovery have turned in her accomplice at the 11th hour? The best that may be said for Phillips is what he himself told the jury. He had had no opportunity to check out her story or her character or her motives—before he faced the lady across the courtroom. Yet as he cross-examined her, he did so with the distinct impression from his client that whatever Mrs. Piolaine's character or motive or deviation from precise gospel, her story bore with deadly effect the mark of truth.

Almost joyously, *The Examiner* rushed to the attack on Phillips, characterizing him as "the assailant and accuser of witnesses whose truth he had no reason to suspect after receiving the murderer's confession." Conceding his right to retain the brief for Courvoisier, it said "he should have refrained from any line

---

39. S. Warren, "The Mystery of Murder, and its Defence," *supra* note 14, at 1, 28, 30.

of defence, the effect of which, if successful, would have procured the acquittal of his guilty client by criminating or destroying the character of persons who had borne true evidence
against him." They were inclined to believe Phillips was as interested in saving his already prepared speech as in saving his
client. They pounced in particular on what Phillips had said in
his own defense of his sleepless night of conscience before the final day of trial:

> "Mr. Phillips has favoured us with a description of
> his restless night before he delivered his speech, where-
> by it would seem, such is the effect of that golden link
> which is called the *honorarium*, that a conscientious
> professional man fee'd by a murderer and afflicted with
> nocturnal visions, does not hear the aged and butchered
> victim crying for justice, but the cowardly and quiver-
> ing assassin shrieking for impunity. But supposing Mr.
> Phillips' strenuous efforts to have been rewarded by a
> verdict, would he have dreamt of the fee he had earned,
> or of the innocence he had placed in jeopardy?" [40]

Thoughout *The Examiner's* attack on Phillips runs that more
or less explicitly stated premise that Courvoisier, having confessed to his lawyer, was still entitled to a defense, but it must
not be a successful defense. Under no circumstances may there
be an acquittal. Which indeed is a notion commonly held
among those who have already decided that any man on trial is
guilty. Follow the forms, as long as you nail him. With the
unexpressed premise that if somehow the culprit slips through
the net of justice, the forms should not have been followed.
And were no good in the first place.

Which is a premise that would end our system of justice.

It is to be recalled that at least one of the judges at Courvoisier's trial, Mr. Baron Parke, knew—as Phillips spoke to the
jury, and as Chief Justice Tindal charged the jury, and as the
jury considered its verdict—that Courvoisier had already confessed. Yet presumably Baron Parke kept his peace. For the
sake of the survival of a continuous system of justice, content
with the possibility that a guilty man might be acquitted, yet

40. Examiner (London), No. 2,182,
page 737, Nov. 24, 1849.

the forms of justice maintained. So too with the Chief Justice. Whether or not he knew anything privately about Courvoisier's confession, he—with St. Thomas Aquinas—would judge "according to what is alleged and proved in court . . . and not according to his private opinion." [41] Of the witness Constable Baldwin, no matter how honest his testimony may have been about no-marks-in-the-dust, it was clear to the Chief Justice that Baldwin's no-knowledge-of-the-reward was a lie. The judge shared the common experience of mankind that a man who lies once will lie again, an experience distilled by the law into the rule that a witness false in one part of his testimony is to be distrusted in the rest. The Chief Justice took it all the way. Not with Phillips' flamboyance, but sharply, effectively, he told the jury to ignore all of Baldwin's testimony, "it would be dangerous in such a serious inquiry as this to give any credit to it."

The Chief Justice also reminded the jury there were other credible witnesses who testified to the same effect as Baldwin on the critical no-marks-in-the-dust, so it could be said perhaps he was not throwing away too much when he dumped Baldwin's story lock, stock, and barrel. Yet it could have been that something about the bumbling, simple, ingratiatingly stupid manner of Constable Baldwin's story might have otherwise impressed a jury; it could easily have been that of all the witnesses who testified for the prosecution, the only hope of a conviction lay in the words of a perjurer. Small nuances of style or inflection or bearing carry their own message of persuasion to some of us. Yet if we are to have a rule for all seasons, a rule that people who live by a system of justice are to have confidence in, it must be a rule that pays as much attention to means as to ends. One of those rules that men have found it reassuring to live by, to have their courts and trial runs by, is that perjury must be rejected, even perjury in a good cause. The perjury that today helps make out a convincing case against a man who murdered in the dark, the perjury that may even be the striking bit of glib falsehood persuading a jury to acquit an innocent man, might also on another day serve to acquit the guilty, or worst of all to convict the innocent. In the same manner, the truthful statement from the witness stand cannot always be relied upon to see

41. Aquinas, *supra* ch. IX, note 9, Question 67, Article 2, page 1484; see J. Davis, The Moral Obligations of Catholic Civil Judges 66–75 (1953).

that justice is ultimately done. A truthful word—placing a man at the scene of a crime—may be the undoing of an innocent, as it may also acquit the guilty, convict the guilty, or at its best acquit the innocent. But day in and day out the mutual faith of men rests on our being judged by realities rather than on the sworn fantasies of liars and kooks. Accordingly, when perjury is discovered in court, it is rejected, as did Chief Justice Tindal, even at the risk of weakening the state's hold on a confessed murderer. Rejected, for this case, and the cases to come.

For the same underlying reason, but with the focus on protection of the rights of the man on trial, the defense lawyer probes for perjury, and when he discovers it, denounces it, properly so, even though in the immediate case, revulsion against the perjurer might free a murderer. A practical demonstration to all men, in this case in which they are onlookers, as it will be in their own case when they are at the bar, that a system of continuing justice does not run on perjury.[42]

So too with the planting of evidence against Courvoisier, attempts by the police to intimidate him, attempts by those whose duty is to enforce the law to serve themselves an extra helping of public reward. Again, for the record, it is to be made known here and now, and each time it happens, that crooked means will not be tolerated even to rid us of crooks. This as much a part of a continuous system of justice as the final judgment, policed in the United States by the Supreme Court, guardian against the guardians.[43] So it was that Mr. Baron Parke told Phillips to continue the defense even though Courvoisier had quietly confessed his guilt; "use all fair arguments arising on the evi-

---

42. Cf. M. Freedman, "Professional Responsibility of the Criminal Defense Lawyer: The Three Hardest Questions," 64 Mich.L.Rev. 1469, 1475–1478 (1966).

43. Brown v. Mississippi, 297 U.S. 278, 56 S.Ct. 461, 80 L.Ed. 682 (1936); Chambers v. Florida, 309 U.S. 227, 60 S.Ct. 472, 84 L.Ed. 716 (1940); Ashcraft v. Tennessee, 322 U.S. 143, 64 S.Ct. 921, 88 L. Ed. 1192 (1944); Haley v. Ohio, 332 U.S. 596, 68 S.Ct. 302, 92 L. Ed. 224 (1948); Rochin v. Califor-

nia, 342 U.S. 165, 72 S.Ct. 205, 96 L.Ed. 183 (1952); Payne v. Arkansas, 356 U.S. 560, 78 S.Ct. 844, 2 L.Ed.2d 975 (1958); Spano v. New York, 360 U.S. 315, 79 S.Ct. 1202, 3 L.Ed.2d 1265 (1959); Culombe v. Connecticut, 367 U.S. 568, 81 S.Ct. 1860, 6 L.Ed.2d 1037 (1961); Mapp v. Ohio, 367 U.S. 643, 81 S.Ct. 1684, 6 L.Ed.2d 1081 (1961); reh. denied, 368 U.S. 871, 82 S.Ct. 23, 7 L.Ed.2d 72 (1961); Beecher v. Alabama, 389 U.S. 35, 88 S.Ct. 189, 19 L.Ed.2d 35 (1967).

dence," not only for Courvoisier. "It is to the interest of justice, then," wrote the editors of London's *Law Magazine*, "that the evidence be fully tested before it is relied upon for condemnation." [44]

Phillips tested the evidence, questioning the testimony that came from men encouraged by the hope of special reward to somehow produce evidence that would convict. Questioning all the possibilities of perjury, not good perjury or bad perjury, perjury directed to conviction of the guilty or perjury to convict the innocent or perjury by habit, but all perjury, all misjudgment, all chance of error. In such a process, some mud. Unfair to Charlotte Piolaine. As it turned out, unquestionably. But as she comes to the stand a witness out of nowhere, the defense makes one quick calculation. Regardless of what my man has done, he does not have to submit to conviction by lies or mistakes. How do I know what motivates this woman, or where the police have found her at the 11th hour? If defense counsel weighs too too cautiously the undoubted risks of giving offense, in this and the case of every other witness, he loses all effectiveness. False witness is not packed standard. It comes chic and seedy, horny pawed and manicured, virginal and dissolute, bald, crewcut, and bearded. The lawyer makes his quick decision, and in doubt that decision is weighted for him on the side of his client. He may make mistakes, and those mistakes too must go into the accounting of a system of justice. The need for competent counsel with guts, overawed neither by popular clamor for a victim nor by the majesty and force of official accusation, brushes now lightly, now sharply against other and equally urgent requirements of a system of justice.

A "plain man" of London voiced such concerns. He confessed himself "perhaps unable to balance the advantages of continuing that license which is extended to counsel, against the disadvantage of restricting" it. But he questioned whether Mr. Phillips' duty to a client could justify his treatment of Mrs. Piolaine, "casting disgraceful aspersions on her character; thus seeking to render the discharge of that sacred duty to society which she had come there to perform . . . a most painful and de-

---

44. "The Defence of Courvoisier, and the Plea for It," *supra* note 38, at 29.

grading circumstance . . . " From having followed the course of Courvoisier's Case, he concluded as a "practical" man, "firstly that I never would stretch out my hand to arrest a murderer, with these pains and penalties before me; and secondly, that no earthly consideration should induce me to permit my wife or daughter to give evidence at the Old Bailey, if any effort of mine could shield her from such a trial." [45]

4. ACCOMMODATION

Other men, some less "plain," some more "practical," only some of them lawyers, have also worried over the delicate balance between preserving the rights of an accused and encouraging honest witnesses to perform their essential duties as fearlessly as counsel for the accused.

A few years before Courvoisier's trial, Samuel Taylor Coleridge instructed the readers of his *Table Talk* in the balancing of inconveniences. He was "not disposed to be very strict" in criticizing the treatment of witnesses, having "seen the witness have the best of it as often as his assailant."

> It is of the utmost importance in the administration of justice, [wrote Coleridge] that knowledge and intellectual power should be as far as possible equalised between the Crown and the prisoner, or plaintiff and defendant. Hence especially arises the necessity for an order of advocates,—men whose duty it ought to be to know what the law allows and disallows, but whose interests should be wholly indifferent as to the persons or characters of their clients. If a certain latitude in examining witnesses is, as experience seems to have shown, a necessary means towards the evisceration of the truth of matters of fact, I have no doubt, as a moralist, in saying that such latitude within the bounds now existing is justifiable.[46]

45. Chronicle (London), "The License of Counsel," June 23, 1840; see also, "[T]he Licence of Prisoners' Counsel," 35 Westminster Review, no. 1, Art. I, pages 1–23 (1841).

46. S. T. Coleridge, "Duties and Needs of an Advocate," Oct. 27, 1831, in Table Talk 140, 141 (T. Ashe ed. 1884).

He agreed with Ecclesiastes that there could be an excess even of righteousness.[47]   The sage also had a parting word of advice for lawyers.   He recommended some moral study "to counteract the operation of legal studies and practice, which sharpen, indeed, but like a grinding-stone, narrow whilst they sharpen." [48]

Incisive enough, this was written before prisoner's counsel could address the jury, and it was softer talk than Victorian tempers aroused by the trials of Courvoisier, and the Mannings, and the murders at Mirfield permitted.   In particular, Phillips' conduct in *Courvoisier's Case* remained a point of sensitivity to the English bar.   *The Law Magazine* wanted it understood that Phillips' morals were not that of the whole profession.   His shortcomings in a moment of extreme difficulty were looked upon as an evil flowing from a too literal commitment to the doctrine of Brougham's speech for Queen Caroline.   It was said that Lord Brougham's famous line, "an advocate in the discharge of his duty knows but one person in all the world, and that person is his client," did not have the approval of "the reputable portion of our profession." [49]   Plagued with the taunt through the rest of his life, Phillips was five years in the grave when Lord Brougham, still formidable at 86, told the bench and bar of England to their face that he stood by his words.

It was an occasion.   The most famous of French advocates Antoine Pierre Berryer, in a long career counsel for Marshal Ney, Montalembert, Chateaubriand, Louis Napoleon, was honored guest of the Bar of England.   Four hundred sat down to "a sumptious banquet" in the great hall of the Middle Temple, "this splendid old chamber, so rich in historical and legal traditions." The judges of England were there, the Chancellor of the Exchequer Mr. Gladstone, "[a]ll the leading members of the Bar were present, with scarcely an exception, and there probably has not been such a gathering of the legal profession in the memory of the oldest member of it."   The Attorney General presided.   Lord Brougham, a former Lord Chancellor, but a few years before

---

47.   Eccl. 7:16.

48.   S. T. Coleridge, *supra* note 46, at 141–142.

49.   "Licence of Counsel," *supra* note 33, at 61; see also, "On the Principle of Advocacy as Developed in the Practice of the Bar," *supra* note 38, at 291–292; "The Defence of Courvoisier, And the Plea for It," *supra* note 38, at 34–36; and R. Harris, Hints on Advocacy 148–151 (1879).

honored by Queen Victoria for his efforts at abolition of slavery and Negro emancipation, was Berryer's host on his visit to England and sat next to him at the head table.

Following toasts to the Queen, the Prince and Princess of Wales, and the Emperor of the French, the Attorney General proposed the toast to M. Berryer as one who had "upheld the dignity of the noble profession to which you all belong. (Loud cheers.)"

> "I rejoice," continued the Attorney General, "in seeing around me so many gentlemen of our noble calling—a calling which vulgar minds frequently misrepresent and underestimate, but upon which in no small degree depend the rights and liberties both of individuals and nations. (Cheers.) It is its high privilege and duty to supply the just weights and balances of the scale of justice, by laying before justice all the considerations which ought to weigh on every side of every question, to stand forward for the weak and miserable, and upon great occasions, when public liberties are in question, to stand forward undaunted and assert the public right—a privilege which has been discharged by our ancestors in this country in times past, which we should be ready to discharge again, and which we rejoice to see discharged as it ought to be in every other country. (Cheers.) There are three great, inestimable blessings which we in this country enjoy, and which we should be glad to see all the rest of the world enjoy, and I venture to say that where they exist public liberty cannot be extinguished. They are a free Press, a free Parliament, and a free Bar. (Cheers.) "

The Attorney General hailed Berryer as "the dauntless and fearless advocate of every unfortunate man who needed his services. (Cheers.) " In his reponse to the toast, Berryer singled out Lord Brougham for special tribute, as the propagator of all the progressive and liberal institutions of a free England. ("Loud cheers.") Following a speech by the Bâtonnier, or president, of the organized advocates of Paris, the Attorney General toasted the health of Lord Brougham.

The Law Times reported the response:

"Lord Brougham, who was loudly cheered, in returning thanks, said he had always the greatest pleasure in
meeting the members of the noble profession to which
they all belonged, but especially on the present occasion, when they were assembled to do honour to one of
its greatest ornaments. He should not liken M. Berryer to any of the great orators of classic times, but to
one who was greater than them all—our own Erskine
—one of the greatest advocates, perhaps the world ever
saw—and with whom M. Berryer might fairly be put in
rivalry. In both of them he had remarked that faculty
of conducting cases with perfect skill and matchless
eloquence; and in both, above all, he had noted that
indomitable courage which in the interests of their
clients quailed neither before Kings, nor Courts, nor
Judges. *In both was observed the first great quality of
an advocate, to reckon everything subordinate to the
interests of his client.* (Hear, hear.) In this country
the administration of justice depended principally on
the purity of the judges; but next on the prudence, the
discretion, and the courage of the advocate (hear,
hear), and no greater misfortune could befall the administration of justice than an infringment of the independence of the bar or the failure of courage in our advocates. (Cheers.) As one of the most distinguished
orators of the Senate, M. Berryer had always set himself against any infringment of the rights of the people,
and on every question the powers of his eloquence and
learning had been fearlessly employed in defence of the
liberties of his fellow-citizens. (Cheers.) " [50]

Independence of the bar was a major theme of the evening's
addresses, including Gladstone's. But the sentence here italicized was an extra fillip, harking back almost 50 years to the
trial of Queen Caroline; it was a "proud recollection," [51] and a
blunt rejection of the criticism since directed at Brougham's

---

50. "The Bar Dinner to M. Berryer," in 40 The Law Times 16–18
(Nov. 12, 1864); see also The
Times (London) Nov. 9, 1864, page
9, and see too pages 7 and 8.

51. "The Moral Code of the Bar,"
in 40 The Law Times 574 (Sept.
30, 1865).

touchstone of the advocate. It had met with a dignified "hear, hear," but not "loudly cheered" as was his own presentation to the audience, nor with the "Cheers" for his salute to M. Berryer.

Responding to the very next toast, to "The Judges of England," the Lord Chief Justice Cockburn picked up Brougham's challenge. His opening remarks were careful, proper, undistinguished. As the last "Hear, hear" faded, Lord Cockburn added this:

> "Much as I admire the great abilities of M. Berryer, to my mind his crowning virtue—as it ought to be that of every advocate—is, that he has throughout his career conducted his cases with untarnished honour. (Loud cheers.) The arms which an advocate wields he ought to use as a warrior, not as an assassin. (Cheers.) He ought to uphold the interests of his clients *per fas* [through what is lawful], but not *per nefas* [through what is criminal]. (Cheers.) He ought to know how to reconcile the interests of his client with the eternal interests of truth and justice. In all the great interests which he has upheld, M. Berryer has never forgotten the honour of the advocate, and for this I respect him as much as for the eminent talents which have cast so much lustre on his name and profession. (Loud cheers.)" [52]

As Mr. Serjeant Robinson recalled it years later, the Chief Justice had said that the advocate "is entitled to use the weapons of a warrior, but not those of an assassin." He thought the "[r]eiterated cheers" "from all parts of the hall" that greeted this phrase "was especially intended as a protest against the doctrine that Lord Brougham, had, years before, laid down, and which seems never before to have been so openly challenged." [53]

The Law Times came to Brougham's defense:

> "When Lord Brougham uses the words 'everything subordinate,' he uses them in the presence of brave and honourable men, whom he knows, will apply them with

---

52. "The Bar Dinner to M. Berryer," *supra* note 50, at 17; see also The Times (London), Nov. 9, 1864, page 9.

53. Robinson, *supra* ch. III, note 7, at 194; see also S. Rogers, "The Ethics of Advocacy," 15 L.Q.Rev. 259, 270–271 (1899).

bravery and honour, not as lurkers and outlaws. It is
the quailing, or the 'glozing' before kings, before
courts, or before judges, above which Lord Brougham
would lift the advocate. If you have any doubt, inter-
pret his words by his own great career. His client was
his first consideration, yet no assassin stroke, no *nefas*,
is ever discoverable there." [54]

It was a nice interpretation, one of many that have been made
attempting to reconcile Brougham's paramount devotion to client with Cockburn's strictures as to honor. The difficulty of the
reconciliation is observable even in the slight variation between
the reports of Serjeant Robinson and *The Law Times*. The Serjeant reports two sets of weapons, the warrior's and the assassin's. But *The Law Times* has Lord Cockburn speaking of but
one set of arms that can be used honorably or dishonorably, a
more accurate statement of the fineness of the separation between what is proper and improper for the conscientious lawyer.
It is not a matter of deliberate substitution of corrupt skills for
correct ones, which would make the choice clear and simple, but
rather of using the same skills within unmarked bounds that
others, not in the fray, will later consider not merely legal but
decent.

The English bar and the English solicitors have set out a few
guideposts through this shadowland. Both groups agree that
when the quiet confession comes to counsel in mid-trial, the defense must continue, putting the prosecution to its proof of guilt.
But the defense is now limited: counsel may not set about prov-
ing "facts" he knows to be inconsistent with the confession—
such as the defense of alibi, "My man wasn't even there."
Above all (shades of *Courvoisier's Case*) counsel must not try to
place the guilt on someone else. These are clearly compromises,
implying as they do that counsel must be influenced to a degree
by something his client has told him privately, acting as though
it were true, even though not proved by the prosecution. Counsel limits his defense based on something not in evidence, yet in-
consistently continues the defense, because he cannot permit his
client to be convicted against his will, except on the evidence
proved in a court of law. The "more difficult question" of ex-

---

54. "The Moral Code of the Bar,"
supra note 51, at 575.

actly how a lawyer "tests" the evidence of prosecution witnesses under such circumstances is left without specific resolution.[55]

Until recently the rules of the American College of Trial Lawyers were in one important respect similar to the English rules. Through the 1963 edition, its *Code of Trial Conduct* said:

> A confidential disclosure of guilt alone does not require a withdrawal from the case. *However, after a confidential disclosure of facts clearly and credibly showing guilt, a lawyer should not present any evidence inconsistent with such facts.* He should never offer testimony which he knows to be false.[56]

The 1972 revision of that *Code* deleted the italicized words, so that the parallel provision now reads:

> A confidential disclosure of guilt alone does not require a withdrawal from the case, but he should never offer testimony which he knows to be false,[57]

thus giving freer rein to the lawyer's own judgment.

On shifting the guilt to someone else, the rule of the American College of Trial Lawyers, unchanged in the 1972 revision, reads:

> The crime charge should never be attributed to another identifiable person unless evidence introduced or inferences warranted therefrom raise at least a reasonable suspicion of such person's probable guilt.[58]

This provision is presumably of general application, i. e. whether or not there has been a confidential confession. It is not clear here whether "reasonable suspicion" refers to suspicion in the mind of jury or counsel. If the former, then despite a confidential confession to counsel, there may be (as in *Courvoisier's Case*) evidence and inferences which point to guilt of someone other than the confessing defendant; and the rule of this group of American trial lawyers would be substantially different from the rule of the English bar, and closer to the path of Charles Phillips.

55. Boulton, *supra* ch. IX, note 49, at 71–72; Lund, *supra* ch. IX, note 50, at 106–107.

56. Code of Trial Conduct, § 4(a) (1963).

57. *Id.* (1972).

58. *Id.,* § 4(b) (1963, 1972).

The rules of the American Bar Association are even less instructive. Beyond having a general legal as well as ethical duty not to act illegally nor perpetrate a fraud upon the court,[59] lawyers are advised by the new Code of Professional Responsibility that they "should not ask a witness a question solely for the purpose of harassing or embarrassing him." [60] And the old Canons of Professional Ethics said that "A lawyer should always treat adverse witnesses and suitors with fairness and due consideration . . ." [61] It was a Canon agreeably soft, yet paid more heed by competent lawyers than any witness would ever believe.

The specifics of authoritative guidance fall far short of the endless variety the lawyer meets every day in the courtroom. Each time he is on his own, called upon for immediate decision, for his client and for himself. The sticky ones are not matched by the few specific rules. Still less are they soluble by the recollection of prayerful hopes that lawyers should be God's noblemen, paragons—fearless, devoted, honorable.

The anguish of the lawyers and their critics and friends points at least to some principle of accommodation, that the lawyer has no absolute duty to client inexorably separating him from the human race. The duty to client exists as a part of a system of justice; and while that duty calls upon the lawyer to perform more than one task that purses some pious lips and gives some faint hearts the trembles, it does not ask him to forget that many generations of lawyers have practiced this profession and lived in honor among their neighbors.

To say, as Phillips said, in his own twisted version of Brougham on the duty of the advocate, "The moment he accepts his brief, every faculty he possesses becomes his client's property," justifies the worst that has been said of the profession. Granted the difficulty of Phillips' position, there is still space for some moral leavening of the supposed professional absolutism he called up as a rationalization of his own uneven performance under fire. As in *Courvoisier's Case*, there are for every lawyer moral crises without precedent; no code section; no case; no

---

59. ABA CPR, *supra* ch. VIII, note 12, DR 1–102(3) and (4), Canon 7, EC 7–1, EC 7–26, DR 7–102.

60. *Id.*, EC 7–25.

61. ABA Old Canons, *supra* Intro. note 29, Canon 18.

rule of thumb. But some feel for an appropriate response is to be had from what others in and out of the profession have said and have refrained from saying; some help from the experience of lawyers who have deserted clients, or conscience, or both, as well as from those who have managed to live with conscience and still give a client the last ounce of professionalism the moment called for.

Baron Parke told Phillips only that he was bound to continue the defense, and "use all fair arguments arising on the evidence." He might have added, as another English judge did some years later, "There is an honourable way of defending the worst of cases." [62]

62. Hannen, President, in Smith v. Smith, 7 P.D. 84, 89 (1882).

Chapter XI

BELIEF IN A CLIENT'S CAUSE

1. PROFESSIONAL WORDS AND PUBLIC EFFECT

It was not the crime of Courvoisier that made it "the worst of cases," though it was revolting enough to put him in wax in the Separate Room at Madame Tussaud's.[1] Killing by the knife, by stealth, has a considerably longer pedigree than more refined, scientific, or efficient forms of murder. Even the killing of a nobleman did not make it uniquely evil. As cases go, it rested on incomplete and circumstantial evidence, the police had bungled their job of investigation, one at least had perjured himself, and another had tried to intimidate an uncharged man; it was an easier case to defend than most criminal lawyers dare hope for. *Courvoisier's Case* was nonetheless "the worst of cases" precisely because the quiet confession made it almost impossible to chart any "honourable way" of defense. It was a special involvement of "honor" in his speech to the jury that held a particular fascinating horror for Victorians, became a leading part in history's judgment of Phillips, and remains a source of concern to 20th century lawyers.

The pontifical *Dictionary of National Biography* has let stand unmodified its damnation of Charles Phillips:

> " . . . [H]is conduct of the defence of Courvoisier, a valet charged with the murder of his master, Lord William Russell, in 1840, was generally condemned. It was said that, though fully aware of his client's guilt, he pledged his word that he was innocent, and sought to fasten the crime on another." [2]

What was really being said at the time was a substantial shade worse, that he had appealed to God to witness "his belief in Courvoisier's innocence." [3] It was a charge that no lawyer, no man, certainly no Victorian, could live with in honor. And

---

1. L. Cottrell, Madame Tussaud 133 (1951).

2. 15 Dictionary of National Biography 1082 (L. Stephen & S. Lee ed. 1917).

3. Warren-Phillips, *supra* ch. III, note 75, at 12; Examiner (London), No. 1,691, pages 401, 402, June 28, 1840.

Phillips did something about it at once. As he later recalled, on the very Monday after the Saturday verdict [4] (certainly within the week) [5], Phillips brought a published report of the charge into the alderman's room at the Old Bailey and read it aloud to the judges and lawyers, adding:

> " 'I take the very first opportunity which offers, my lords, of most respectfully inquiring of you whether I ever used any such expression?'
>
> " 'You certainly did not, Phillips,' was the reply of the late lamented Lord Chief Justice, [this is still Phillips' report] 'and I will be your vouchee whenever you choose to call me.'
>
> " 'And I,' said Mr. Baron Parke, happily still spared to us, 'had a reason which the Lord Chief Justice did not know for watching you narrowly, and he will remember my saying to him when you sat down, "Brother Tindal, did you observe how carefully Phillips abstained from giving any personal opinion in the case?" To this the learned Chief Justice instantly assented.' " [6]

Phillips never called upon the Lord Chief Justice to vouch for him, though after Tindal's death two lawyers reported he had found the attacks on Phillips without foundation.[7] Mr. Baron Parke also gave indirect confirmation of Phillips' account.[8] In his own statement nine years after the trial, Phillips labeled the charge "false as it is foul," "an utter impossibility under the circumstances," continuing in a polished medium-high dudgeon that alternately shrieks and coos even in print:

> "What! appeal to Heaven for its testimony to a lie, and not expect to be answered by its lightning? What! make such an appeal, conscious that an honourable colleague sat beside me, whose valued friendship I must for ever have forfeited? But above all, and beyond

4. Warren-Phillips, *supra* ch. III, note 75, at 13.

5. Examiner (London), No. 1,691, pages 401, 402, June 28, 1840.

6. Warren-Phillips, *supra* ch. III, note 75, at 13–14.

7. *Id.* 25 and 28.

8. *Id.* 8; S. Warren, *The Mystery of Murder, and its Defence, supra* ch. X, note 14, at 1, 61–62, and 61n.; Sir Edward Ridley, J., quoted in G. W. Kingston, A Gallery of Rogues 23 [1924?].

all, and too monstrous for belief,—what!—would I
have dared to utter falsehood in the very presence of
the judge to whom, but the day before, I had confided
the reality?   There, upon the bench above me, sat
that time-honoured man—that upright magistrate, pure
as his ermine, 'narrowly watching' every word I said.
Had I dared to make an appeal so horrible and so im-
pius—had I dared so to outrage his nature and my own
conscience, he would have started from his seat, and
withered me with a glance." [9]

This was pretty strong tonic. It convinced *The Times*, accustomed to accept as good authority the opinions of respected
judges.[10]   Doubters remained.   They turned to Phillips' own
words, widely, if not officially, reported.   Phillips himself acknowledged the accuracy of *The Times* version of his speech to
the Courvoisier jury.[11]

He had reminded the jurors of the burden the prosecution had
"undertaken":

"They must prove that the murder has been committed by Courvoisier, and unless they do so, he must be
acquitted. Unless that is proved, I beseech you to be
cautious how you imbrue your hands in this man's
blood. [One account, not generally accepted, made this
"innocent blood."] The Omniscient God alone knows
who did this crime."

A similar juxtaposition of doubt, innocence, and God was
worked in towards the close:

"And, even supposing him guilty of the murder, which
indeed is known to the Almighty God alone, and of
which for the sake of his eternal soul, I hope he is innocent . . ."

There were those who thought that God had company. "God
alone knows . . ."   "This," remarked *The Examiner*,

9. Warren-Phillips, *supra* ch. III,   11. Warren-Phillips, *supra* ch. III,
   note 75, at 12–13.   note 75, at 16.

10. The Times (London), Nov. 20,
    1849, pages 4, 5; Warren-Phillips,
    supra ch. III, note 75, at 29–30.

"was said by the man who himself knew who did the crime, and who profaned the name of the Diety by thrusting it into a solemn assertion, of the untruth of which he was cognizant." [12] Some time later the paper editorialized that Mr. Baron Parke "must have been somewhat wanting in attention to what passed from Mr. Phillips, if he detected no deliberate falsehood, very strongly involving 'personal opinion' in Mr. Phillips' reiterated solemn asseverations that the Omniscient God alone knew who did the crime . . . " [13]

Old Serjeant Ballantine was only a slight degree less emphatic. "Such expressions," he said, "from the mouth of an advocate possessing the knowledge that Phillips did at the time he used them, were not only offensive to good taste, but scarcely escaped conveying a positive falsehood." [14]

Phillips' concluding pitch had served to firm up the impression that he and God and Courvoisier were all on the same side. It was a final small thought-for-the-day to take into the jury room:

> "I speak to you in no spirit of hostile admonition.
> Heaven knows I do not. I speak to you in the spirit of
> a friend and fellow Christian. And in that spirit I tell
> you that if you pronounce the word lightly, its memory
> will never die within you. It will accompany you in
> your walks. It will follow you in your solitary retire-
> ments like a shadow. It will haunt you in your sleep
> and hover round your beds. It will take the shape of
> an accusing spirit, and confront and condemn you be-
> fore the judgment seat of your God. So beware what
> you do."

As *The Scotsman* saw it those words were but a token of Phillips' "Old-Bailey morality":

> "In brief he told the jury 'Heaven knew'—is that not
> 'an appeal to Heaven'?—that he spoke only as 'a
> friend and fellow-Christian' when he warned them that
> they would be '*condemned* before the judgment seat of

---

12. Examiner (London), No. 1,691, pages 401, 402, June 28, 1840; see also Examiner (London), No. 2,182, page 737, Nov. 24, 1849.

13. Examiner (London), No. 2,182, page 737, Nov. 24, 1849.

14. Ballantine, *supra* ch. III, note 7, at 63.

their God' if they pronounced the word guilty against a
man whom he *knew* to be guilty." [15]

A reader of the *Chronicle* left it to Phillips "and his own conscience" to find justification for "appealing so frequently and
solemnly to his God in behalf of a man whose hands he knew
were reeking with venerable blood, most savagely, barbarously,
and inhumanly shed   .   .   .   and in plainly stating that
the jury, in finding him guilty, endangered their eternal salvation   .   .   ." [16]

Phillips, his friends replied, had not expressed his own opinion
about Courvoisier's guilt or innocence. "God only knows," may
have been a trifle irreverent, but it was nothing more than a figure of speech, not to be taken literally; listeners would certainly
have understood that not only God but at the least the prisoner
himself must know whether or not he was guilty. Further, it is
literally true that a juror must carefully consider his verdict; if
not, if he pronounces "lightly" the irrevocable "Guilty," he will
never forget it.[17]

"It was contended," Serjeant Robinson later wrote, broadening
somewhat the scope of Phillips' defense,

> "that he had called God to witness that *he believed* the
> prisoner to be innocent. What he did say was, that
> *God only knew* whether or not he was guilty. Perhaps
> there was a little surplusage of assertion here, consider-
> ing the circumstances; but it was very different from
> the other version. There was a bare possibility, al-
> though it was to last degree improbable, that the pris-
> oner uttered a falsehood when he confessed his guilt.
> But Phillips must have uttered an atrocious one, if he
> solemnly asserted that he did not believe him." [18]

In short, the difference between calling God to witness Phillips'
belief in Courvoisier's innocence and saying that God alone knew

---

15. Quoted in Examiner (London),
No. 2,183, pages 755, 756–757, Dec.
1, 1849.

16. "The License of Counsel,"
Chronicle (London), June 23, 1840.

17. S. Warren, *The Mystery of
Murder and its Defence, supra*, ch.

X, note 14, at 1, 60–66; see also
Standard, quoted in Examiner
(London), No. 2,184, pages 769,
770, Dec. 8, 1849.

18. Robinson, *supra* ch. III, note 7,
at 61–62.

if he was guilty, was the important difference between vouching for a lie, and urging caution, merely calling attention to the fallibility of human judgment.

The two sides thus crossed swords, thrust, feinted, and parried, but never met in full force, for they never came to agreement on the objective.

Phillips' critics struck at fundamental immorality in the profession. Liars! Here was a lawyer engaged in "passionate and profane" [19] deception. Enough that he defends a man he knows to be guilty, now compounding evil with implications that he himself has confidence in Courvoisier's innocence and that anyone who finds him guilty will have to answer to God for a bad day's job. If Phillips had not lied in so many words, he had acted a lie, with his "solemnly *acted* belief in the murderer's innocence." [20] That from an old enemy *The Examiner*. But *The Jurist* too took up the cry, denouncing Phillips' "vehement adjurations and appeals, which, so far from not involving the expression of personal opinion, had no other purpose or significancy than to intimate that the speaker's belief in his client's innocence was so earnest as to have aroused his sympathies on his behalf." It continued:

> "A man may argue for any conclusion without asserting his belief; but when he adds to his argument gesticulations and expressions of emotion, he tells us of a conviction so pervading as to have extended from the region of the intellect to that of the affections. We know no difference between a lie acted and a lie spoken." [21]

This was a distant echo of Aquinas, embellished in the 17th century by Jeremy Taylor's *Rule of Conscience* warning that "A man may look a lie, and nod a lie, and smile a lie." [22] In the view of his critics, Phillips had done all of this, and for a fee.

What should he have done? "What," asked Samuel Warren, "is the meaning of an advocate's acting a belief of his client's innocence? Would the *Examiner* have him do the reverse, and

19. Examiner (London), No. 2,184, page 769, Dec. 8, 1849.

20. *Id.*, No. 2,182, page 737, Nov. 24, 1849.

21. 13 The Jurist 497, 498 (Dec. 15, 1849, No. 675).

22. 13 J. Taylor, Works 384 (3d ed. Reginald Heber ed. 1839).

act a belief of his client's guilt? Would they have an advocate go through a 'solemn' and cruel mockery, only of defense? Would they have his looks, his gestures, his topics, 'solemnly' belie the purpose for which he had professedly risen? It is a matter which does not bear an instant's arguing." [23]

Warren took for granted that "the purpose for which" any lawyer professedly rises is to say the best that can be said for his client, to win for him if possible, in the case even of Courvoisier—to see him acquitted if the jury were not convinced of his guilt. It was the lawyer's job to present a case, to argue a case, to argue the law, and the application of the law to particular facts. This was the role of the professional, to take the grist that comes to him, and make the best of it, whatever the result. The limitation was that he must carry through as a professional, with professional correctness, presenting a case and not his personal beliefs. It would have been wrong in this view if Phillips had expressed his personal belief in Courvoisier's innocence— whether Courvoisier had been innocent or guilty, whether he had quietly confessed or not. It would have been wrong for Phillips to have expressed his personal belief in Courvoisier's innocence, even if he actually thought him innocent; if, in addition, he misrepresented his belief, that would have been adding a gentleman's to a lawyer's sin. Even Serjeant Ballantine, who disapproved of Phillips' language, agreed on the principle. "It is the essence of advocacy," he said, "that counsel should under no circumstances convey his own belief, or use expressions calculated to do so   ." [24]

Phillips and the judges and Warren and the other lawyers who defended Phillips' conduct were counting words, carefully chosen words of a prepared jury speech, meticulously chosen to avoid the very charge that had been made. They were satisfied that Phillips had argued well, had made his points well, but they were the points of a case, and not his personal belief.

For such nicety the public could not have cared less. Phillips, they thought, had expressed a dishonest opinion. They would not have been outraged for an instant if Phillips had openly expressed his belief in Courvoisier's innocence, if only Courvoisier

23. S. Warren, *The Mystery of Murder and its Defence, supra* ch. X, note 14, at 1, 63.

24. Ballantine, *supra* ch. III, note 7, at 63.

had been innocent. They would have been only mildly critical if Phillips had expressed that belief honestly, though it turned out he had been mistaken. But for the punctilio of professional aloofness—indifferent alike to good and evil—interested only that the lawyer's own opinion not be interjected, the public were not concerned; or if concerned, could only think it something unnatural and wrong. In this was something of the moralist's view that a man really guilty was not fit to be defended, combined with a basic unsophisticated notion that decent people ought to be able to rely on the appearance of things: that in rising to the defense, a lawyer represents not merely a client's position, but stands committed, personally and professionally, to his client and his client's cause.

To keep the record straight Phillips' friends felt called upon to reaffirm the old right of every man, even a guilty one, to be defended. Beyond that, they made a double denial: Phillips had not misrepresented his personal belief; he had not expressed any personal opinion at all.[25] He had followed the strict line of the professional—committed only as a professional, to see to it that his client got what the law allows. In this professional commitment the man inside the lawyer is not involved, even if the casual listener might think otherwise—of Mr. Phillips' colored remarks, as of Mr. Adolphus' calmer "　.　.　.　the conclusion to which I have come is that the prisoner at the bar is the guilty person."

2.　BELIEF OR COMMENT?

Despite talk of professional dispassion,[26] adherence to such a doctrine, even among proper Victorian barristers, was another matter. Had it been otherwise, it is unlikely Mr. Baron Parke would have found it worth a whisper to "Brother Tindal" that Phillips had "abstained from giving any personal opinion."

On the date of that revealing whisper, Tindal had for a decade been Chief Justice of Common Pleas, attentive to a full measure

25. S. Warren, *The Mystery of Murder, and its Defence, supra* ch. X, note 14, at 1–68.

26. See, "Privileges of the Bar," 22 The Law Magazine, No. XLVI, Art. I, page 259 (1839), and "Mr. Brougham's Speech for Ambrose Williams," 2 The Law Magazine, Art. V, pages 102, 121 (1829); and cf. 13 The Jurist, No. 672, pages 469, 470 (1849).

of the personal opinions of eminent counsel. Four years earlier, the year before Victoria's accession, he had presided uncritically as leaders of the bar addressed the jury in the great criminal conversation (i. e. civil action for adultery) trial of the age. It was the case of *George Norton v. William Lamb, Lord Viscount Melbourne*, prime minister and soon to be Queen Victoria's favorite, charged with a protracted and adulterous liaison with Mrs. Norton.

Opening for the offended husband was Sir William Follett, his repeated expressions of personal opinion reflecting then as now a distinction the profession makes between permissible and impermissible expression of opinion. It is a tenuous line we lawyers draw; few jurors would recognize it; Follett did; and he made some attempt to keep to leeward of a line that separates comment on the evidence from forbidden expression of counsel's belief in the merit of his client's cause. Sir William, for example, told the jurors:

"Now I think the evidence I am about to disclose to you will satisfy your minds that very shortly after the first acquaintance between Lord Melbourne and Mrs. Norton a criminal intercourse commenced between them, and was continued for a very considerable time afterwards . . .   In this, as in all other cases of crime—for crime it is—you convict the parties by circumstantial evidence, which will lead your minds to the inference and conclusion, that the guilty act has taken place . . .   There is still other evidence . . .   I allude to those marks which are the consequence of intercourse between the sexes. We shall show those marks existed on the day linen; they will be shown to have existed on her gown; from which, and the other facts I have stated, there can, I apprehend, be no doubt of the guilty connection of the parties . . .   If you are satisfied, as satisfied I think you must be, upon the evidence, from the facts I have stated, of the mode of Lord Melbourne's visits . . .   that this guilty intercourse has taken place, it will remain for you to consider what damages the plaintiff is entitled to . . .   I never will believe that the absence of Mr. Norton, affording the opportunities which Lord Melbourne took in consequence of that absence, can be brought as a charge against him at all . . . I think no man can look at these visits . . . and not feel satisfied that for a considerable space of time Lord Melbourne had been carrying on an illicit intercourse with this unfortunate lady." [27]

It is difficult to imagine that any juror could have listened to those remarks without being convinced that Sir William Follett at least believed that Melbourne was guilty. The lawyer must certainly have included himself in the closing sentence, "I think no man can look at these visits . . . and not feel satisfied" of the defendant's guilt.

By tying his opinions to the evidence, Sir William was at least making a colorable compliance with the professional ban on personal indorsement of a client's case. His adversary, the Attorney General of England—John (later Lord) Campbell—dropped even the pretense of dispassionate professionalism. He not only gave his personal opinion that Melbourne was innocent, but went so far afield as to suggest that Follett thought so too.

The day after the trial, *The Times* reported that Melbourne's counsel had "asserted his innocence," [28] this at a time when under the English rules of evidence even the party accused was not permitted to testify to his own innocence; Melbourne could (and did) plead "Not guilty," but that was all. Yet his counsel's argument was full of John Campbell's personal views, and Lord Melbourne was acquitted without presenting any evidence and without the jury leaving the box. Here are a few excerpts from the speech to the jury:

"I confess, Gentlemen, I think it would have been more graceful if my friend, Sir William Follett, instead of opposing, had seconded my application [for a continuance]; but such is the nature of the case he has today to advocate, that upon this occasion he cannot permit himself to be candid or courteous. From the com-

27. The Times (London), June 23, 1836, page 2.

28. *Id.* 4; see S. Rogers, "The Ethics of Advocacy," 15 L.Q.Rev. 259, 268 n. 2 (1899).

mencement of the trial till his resistance to the indul-
gence craved he has pretty distinctly shown that he has
no confidence in his case;—and I am firmly persuaded
that if his opinion had been asked by the Plaintiff before this action was brought, he would strongly have
dissuaded him from bringing it, and would earnestly
have counselled him to dismiss from his mind the un-
founded suspicions instilled into it, and to place undoubting confidence in the purity and affection of his
wife   .   .   .[29]

"In this case, the observation I am now going to
make is immaterial, as there never was any criminal
design or impropriety of conduct on either side; but as
a general principle, it is the duty of Juries to bear in
mind, that an action like the present cannot be supported, unless the crime has been consummated, whatever
familiarities short of this may have passed.[30]

* * *

"But the evidence when examined is of the most flimsy
description; and I must express my unfeigned astonishment, that, assuming as I do the entire innocence of the
parties,—witnesses so picked up and so disciplined,
have not made out a more plausible or I should rather
say, a less preposterous and less ridiculous case against
them.[31]

* * *

"The evidence of Elizabeth Gibson the next witness
[that adultery occurred six times a week], I denounce
as false, incredible, and impossible.

"I do not know if my friend will allow me to refer to
Debrett's Peerage for the age of the noble Defendant
without claiming a reply.

"Sir William Follett.   Certainly not.

"Sir John Campbell.   Then gentlemen, I will not say
that my noble client was born in the year 1779 [mak-
ing him 57 years old], or how nearly he approaches his
grand climacteric.   But you may be guided by our own

---

29. Campbell, Speeches 3 (1842).   **31.** *Id.* 13.

30. *Id.* 5.

observation, and you may know that instead of being now a gay and gallant young man, he is somewhat 'declined into the vale of years'. With him 'the heyday in the blood is tame'. But were he still in flaming youth, —is no allowance to be made for satiety—for palled appetite,—for occasional indifference,—for the ebbs and as well as the flows of passion—for the interruptions of business? I have never heard any imputation upon the present premier, that he has neglected his official duties for his private gratifications;—and surely these daily interviews must some times have been prevented by cabinet councils; by attendance at Court; by preparation for debate in the House of Lords; by receiving deputations in Downing street; by applications for favours from vacillating opponents; by the thrice told grievances of disappointed friends.[32]

*   *   *

"Gentlemen, I confess that when I entered the court, I had upon this subject [the letters] some anxiety. Never doubting the innocence of the parties, I was afraid from the rumours confidently circulated of the discovery of letters, that from the intimacy subsisting between them, he might in writing have unguardedly used some expression liable to be misconstrued   .   .   ." [33]

Finally came the Attorney General's peroration, and flouting rules of evidence and of professional aloofness, he told the jury:

"I read in your countenances, Gentlemen, your undoubting opinion of her [Mrs. Norton's] spotless innocence, and your desire now to publish this opinion to the world.

"But before I conclude, I am bound according to the express instructions I have received from Lord Melbourne, to declare in his name, and in the most solemn and emphatic manner, that he is not guilty of the charge brought against him, and that neither by word or deed has he ever abused the confidence reposed in him by Mr. Norton.

32. *Id.* 17–18.   **33.** *Id.* 23.

"I know well, Gentlemen, that you cannot act upon this assertion, and I do not seek to influence by it that verdict which you have sworn to find according to the evidence.—Look to the evidence, and if it supports this charge, I desire you, regardless of the consequences, to find a verdict for the Plaintiff with exemplary damages. But the evidence, instead of bringing home guilt to the accused, only reflects disgrace on the accuser

.   .   .

"Gentlemen, I sit down in the calm conviction that you will without a moment's hesitation free my client from the groundless charges brought against him

.   .   ." [34]

Twenty years after getting that verdict for Lord Melbourne by becoming his partisan as well as his lawyer, the former Attorney General now Lord Campbell presided over the trial of Mr. William Palmer, accused of murdering John Cook with a dose of strychnine. Long before the trial the evidence had been so publicly digested that, as Palmer's counsel Serjeant Shee put it, "an opinion has universally prevailed that the voice of the blood of John Parsons Cook was crying unto us from the ground, and that that cry was met by the whole population under an impression and conviction of the prisoner's guilt in a delerium of horror and indignation by another cry of 'blood for blood!'   .   .   ." [35]

Shee considered how "to breast a storm of public prejudice such," he thought "as has never before imperilled the calm administration of justice!" [36] Whatever had been required in the case of a prime minister charged merely with adultery (and in a civil suit) was at least as urgently needed in the defense of this surgeon charged with murder.

He said to the jury:

"[T]hough of course, like everybody else, I knew generally and loosely, very loosely indeed, the history of these transactions at Rugely, I had formed, when the papers came into my hands, no opinion upon them, no opinion upon the guilt or innocence of the prisoner at

---

34. *Id.* 30–31.   **36.** *Id.*

35. The Queen v. Palmer 174 (London: J. Allen, 1856).

the bar, and my mind was perfectly free to form what I trust will be declared by you a right judgment in this case. I commence his defence, I say it in all sincerity, with an entire conviction of his innocence. I believe that there never was a truer word pronounced than the words which he pronounced when he said 'Not guilty' to this charge. If I fail in establishing this to your satisfaction I shall be under a great misgiving that my failure was more attributable to my own inability to do justice to this case than to any weakness in the case itself; and I will give you this proof of the sincerity with which I declare upon this evidence my conviction of his innocence, that I will meet the case of the prosecution foot to foot at every stage . . .[37]

After analyzing the evidence, Shee concluded:

"Such, gentlemen, is the man whom it is my duty to defend. Upon the evidence which is before you I cannot believe him guilty . . . I call upon you to expand your minds to a capacity for estimating the high duty that you have to perform. You have to stem the torrent of prejudice; you have to vindicate the honour and character of your country; you have with firmness and courage to do your duty, and find a verdict for the Crown, if you believe that guilt is proved; but if you have a doubt upon the point, and depend upon it the time will come when the innocence of this man will be made apparent, and when you will deeply regret any want of due and calm consideration of the case which it will be my duty to lay before you."[38]

After Serjeant Shee had presented his evidence, the Attorney General (Sir Alexander James Edmund Cockburn, who as Lord Chief Justice of England was later to lecture Brougham on the morality of lawyers) replied, saying in part:

"Gentlemen, you have had introduced into this case one other element which I own I think would have been better omitted. You have had from my learned friend the unusual, and I think I may say unprecedented, assurance of his conviction of his client's innocence."[39]

37. *Id.* 174–175.   39. *Id.* 306.
38. *Id.* 214.

Shee, with an eye to Lord Campbell on the bench, and a longer memory than the Attorney General, contented himself with a curt interruption: "Not unprecedented."

"I can only say," replied the unflustered prosecutor, "I think it would have been better if my learned friend had abstained from so strange a declaration." [40]

Sir Alexander continued with some strange declarations of his own, with somewhat more subtlety than Shee, yet he too implicitly denying the basic tenet of the advocate's profession, that it is possible for a lawyer to separate advocacy from belief, that he stands for his client but not with him. The Attorney General asked:

> "What would he think of me if, imitating his example, I at this moment stated to you, upon my 'honour', as he did, what is my internal conviction from a conscientious consideration of this case? The best reproof which I can administer to my learned friend is to abstain from imitating so dangerous an example.
>
> "My learned friend in that address, of which we all admired the power and ability, also adopted a course sometimes resorted to by advocates, but which I cannot help thinking is more or less an insult to a jury, the endeavouring to intimidate them by the fear of their own consciences, and the fear of the country's opinion from discharging firmly and honestly the great and solemn duty which you have to perform upon this occasion. My learned friend told you that if your verdict should be Guilty, one day or other the innocence of the prisoner would be made manifest, and you would never cease to repent the verdict you had given. If my learned friend was sincere in that—and I know he was—there is no man in whom the spirit of truth and honour is more keenly alive—he said what he believed; but all I can say in answer is that it shows how when a man enters with a bias upon his mind upon the consideration of a subject he is led into error; and when my learned friend said that he had entered upon this case with an unbiassed and an unprejudiced mind, who could have

failed to feel that never in anything could he have been more deceived in thinking that? For who that has to give his best energies to a defence upon such a charge as this would not shrink in his own mind from the conclusion that he was to advocate the cause of one who he believed to have been guilty of the foulest of all imaginable crimes? I say, therefore, I think my learned friend had better have abstained from making any observations which involved the assurance of his own conviction . . ." [41]

On the bench, Lord Campbell, while interrupting neither Shee's nor the Attorney General's observations on this point, had time to think back over his defense of Lord Melbourne, and perhaps of the public and professional comment since *Courvoisier's Case*, the Mirfield Murders, and the trial of the Mannings. In his charge to the jury, he administered a polite rebuke to Serjeant Shee, prefaced by the inevitable compliment which is a danger signal to any lawyer. The defendant, said the Judge, "has had the advantage of having his case conducted by one of the most distinguished advocates at the English bar."

"Gentlemen," continued Lord Campbell, "I most strongly recommend to you to attend to everything that fell so eloquently, so ably, and so impressively from that advocate, with the exception of his own personal opinion. It is my duty to tell you that that ought to be no ingredient in your verdict. You are to try the prisoner upon the evidence before you, according as that evidence may be laid before you upon the one side and on the other, and by that alone, and not by any opinion of his advocate. I feel also bound to say that it would have been better if his advocate had abstained from some of the observations which he made in his address to you, in which he laid great stress upon his own conviction of the prisoner's innocence of the crime imputed to him, and of his apprehension that if you returned a verdict of Guilty, you one day would have to regret your verdict. The fact of the prisoner saying 'Not guilty' is a mere form; it goes for nothing, and it may lead to the most disastrous consequences if that

41. *Id.*

formal answer is to be dwelt upon with too much importance, as it may lead a jury to believe that a prisoner is not guilty, because his advocate expresses his perfect conviction of his innocency. And, upon the other hand, if the advocate withholds an opinion, the jury may suppose that he is conscious of his client's guilt, whereas it is the duty of the advocate to press his argument upon the jury, and not his opinion." [42]

Palmer was convicted, and is known to history as "the Rugely Poisoner."

The point of professional etiquette in the *Queen v. Palmer* arose a decade later in *Ryves and Ryves v. The Attorney General*. This was the case of the self-styled "Princess Olive," trying to establish heirship to the throne through proof, among other things, of her own bastardy. (She ended up disappointed but legitimate.) In what might possibly have been considered a personal opinion, the Attorney General described the "Princess'" story as "ridiculous," [43] one "of such rank and audacious imposture [that it] could not be too thoroughly exposed." [44] Her case rested on some documents.

> "The internal evidence proved," the Attorney General told the jury, "that they are the most ridiculous, absurd, preposterous, series of forgeries that the perverted ingenuity of man ever invented. If every expert that ever lived in the world swore to the genuineness of every one of these documents, you could not possibly believe them to be genuine." [45]

It would not be stretching the matter too far to conclude that counsel for the "Princess" sensed in this language something of a personal attack; he had just managed to say,

> "[I] believe, on my word and honour as a gentleman, that the documents which the petitioner has produced —" [46]

---

42. *Id.* 307–308.

43. Ryves and Ryves v. The Attorney General (1866), in The Annual Register, vol. 108, pt. II, pages 223, 253 (1867).

44. *Id.* 249.

45. *Id.* 255, tense corrected.

46. *Id.*, person and tense corrected.

when the erstwhile Attorney General of the *Queen v. Palmer*, now Lord Chief Justice Cockburn, with less restraint than Lord Campbell, interrupted:

> "I insist on your not finishing that sentence. It is a violation of a fundamental rule of conduct, which every advocate ought to observe, to give the jury your personal opinion." [47]

Unintimidated, counsel J. Walter Smith quickly located the first cousin of a personal opinion once removed, and gave that instead:

> "I will not intentionally trespass beyond my proper limits," he said, "but I am entitled to say that the eminent genealogical lawyer who took up the petitioner's case in 1821 believed her documents to be genuine on his word of honour as a gentleman." [48]

3. THE OLDER TRADITION

In the argument of counsel in *Norton v. Lamb* (1836), *Queen v. Palmer* (1856), and *Ryves and Ryves v. The Attorney General* (1866) it is a very thin line, if any, that separates proper comment on the legal effect of evidence from forbidden personal opinion. Yet there can be little doubt that the views of Lord Campbell in *Queen v. Palmer* and of Lord Cockburn in *Ryves and Ryves v. The Attorney General* represented a gradual tightening of the restraint on expression of counsel's opinion in argument. Opinion (used here interchangeably with "belief"), in these cases, is taken to mean an attempt to add the weight of a lawyer's repute to the merits of his client's cause. And, though frequently misunderstood, the older tradition did not find the practice objectionable. It was quite proper that the lawyer voice his own opinion, doing what the layman thinks the lawyer does anyhow, i. e. personally vouch for the client and cause he represents.

Henry Brougham had done just that in defense of Queen Caroline. Brougham, who had drawn the wrath of Lord Cockburn at the Berryer banquet for reiterating in old age his earlier credo of the advocate's complete dedication to the client's cause, in

---

47. *Id.*   48. *Id.*, person and tense corrected.

the very same case had assured the House of Lords in unequivocal terms of his personal belief in the Queen's innocence. In the first minutes of his opening statement, as part of the barrister's formulary expression of humility in the face of heavy responsibility, Brougham said:

> ". . . I am borne up in my task with that conviction of its justice, and of the innocence of my illustrious client, which I share in common with all mankind . . . While, however, other counsel have trembled for fear of guilt in a client, or have been chilled by indifference, or have had to dread the weight of public opinion against them, I have none of these disadvantages to apprehend. Public opinion has already decided on the case, and I have nothing to fear but the consequences of perjury." [49]

In his own summing up, the Attorney General disapproved Brougham's extreme statement of the advocate's devotion to client [50] but did not criticize the expression of personal belief in the Queen's innocence. He himself refrained from anything quite so bald, tying to the effect of the evidence his personal "I think" that a verdict of guilty is inevitable.[51] He was, however, followed by the Solicitor General who said that the prosecution had anticipated conflicts in the evidence; then, as though from personal knowledge, added that he and the Attorney General, "Knowing, however, the truth of the story . . ." were "perfectly satisfied" that guilt would be established.[52]

Thomas Denman, one of Brougham's co-counsel and later Lord Chief Justice of England, also dwelt in closing on the "imperative" effect of the evidence. But he coupled it with a note that can only be classed as an expression of personal belief. The evidence "I say it boldly, has satisfied my mind, has satisfied the minds of the learned friends with whom I act . . ." as well as the public at large, that the Queen must be acquitted.[53]

Moreover, in that same speech, Denman cast doubt on the very notion of the uninvolved advocate. Conceiving the prose-

---

49. 2 Trial of Queen Caroline 6, person and tense corrected (1821).

50. 3 Trial of Queen Caroline 437 (1821).

51. Id. 438.

52. Id. 438–439.

53. Id. 178, person and tense corrected.

cution of the Queen to be fraudulent, he excuses his own lack of dispassion and denies that another advocate could decently act in support of the King's cause. Apologizing for an unintended attack on the veracity of the Attorney General, Denman said:

> "I have no intention of giving uneasiness in any quarter; but I must say that I have felt it deeply, and often, in the course of this proceeding. It is therefore impossible for a man not to ask indulgence for any warmth into which he might have been betrayed; because the illustrious individual who is our client has been from the first moment in which she set foot in this country, the victim of the most cruel oppression, and the most dreadful and irreparable wrong. That galling recollection has attended us through the whole of these proceedings; it must be our excuse for any undue warmth with which we might have expressed ourselves; and having said that, I shall proceed, without further apology, to our case itself.
>
> "But whilst I disclaim all personal imputation on my learned friends, I claim the right of adverting, with the utmost freedom, on his conduct as advocate, inasmuch as from the conduct of an advocate not only the impressions of his mind might be collected, but also much of the nature of the instructions under which he acts, and of the spirit in which the prosecution has been commenced and conducted to its close. To have to conduct a case in such a spirit I conceive to be a misfortune for which no rewards, no honours, could afford an equivalent—a misfortune which has weighed down my learned friend throughout the whole of these proceedings—a misfortune to which I declare before God, that nothing within the scope of human ambition could have tempted me to have submitted for a single moment—I mean the office of prosecuting this bill of pains and penalties to divorce and degrade the wife of the King of England." [54]

As Brougham and Denman thus warmly committed themselves personally and professionally to the vindication of Queen Caro-

---

54. *Id.* 178–179, person and tense corrected.

line, they were supported from the floor by the vote and the still persuasive voice of a 70 year old former Lord Chancellor,[55] whose career at the bar had set these younger men a pattern. This was the famous Thomas Erskine, known to lawyers everywhere as *Erskine*, Lord Erskine, generally acknowledged the greatest advocate of the English bar, by whose stature others are measured even today.[56]

Erskine is remembered for more than the undoubted power of his advocacy. He stands as a symbol of the independence of the lawyer and of the press, both aspects of a reputation stemming from his defense of clients charged with political offenses—treason and especially criminal libel. Prosecution for libel—scandalous libel, seditious libel, impious and blasphemous libel—was a powerful weapon of the times, used politically to silence critics of the status quo; the radical Thomas Paine was a logical target for such weaponry, and one of Erskine's most widely known cases is his defense of Paine (1792) for publication of the *Rights of Man, Part the Second*.[57]

As with other symbols, the figure of Erskine has been draped with sufficient worshipful nonsense to distort the image of a great lawyer. Laymen hail Erskine's devotion to freedom of the press in his resounding (but unsuccessful) defense of Paine, overlooking his gloryless (but successful) appearance five years later as private prosecutor of the publisher of Paine's *Age of Reason*;[58] in the second trial Erskine was counsel for The Proclamation Society, also known as The Society for the Suppression of Vice and Immorality, counsel and client denouncing the book as a blasphemous libel. In each instance, Erskine argued from personal conviction and said so. He did not believe the *Rights of Man* was seditious, and in the spirit of Milton's *Areopagitica* urged upon the jurors that "Constraint is the natural parent of resistance, and a pregnant proof that reason is not on the side of those who use it."[59] But the *Age of Reason* collided with Erskine's intense devotion to established religion. ". . .

---

55. e. g. *id.* 620–631, 757.

56. 13 Holdsworth, A History of English Law 580 (1952); Birkett, Six Great Advocates 82 (1961); 8 Encyclopaedia Britannica 697 (1948).

57. Rex v. Paine (1792), 22 How.St. Tr. 358 (1816–1826).

58. Rex v. Williams (1797), 26 *Id.* 653.

59. Rex v. Paine (1792), 22 *Id.* 358, 471.

I rose from the reading of [it] with astonishment and disgust; " [60] he reminded the jury that the press' freedom, ". . . like every other, must be limited to be enjoyed . . ." [61] All of this in keeping with his own view of the lawyer's role, expressed in the trial of Captain Baillie (1778) that first brought him to public notice, where Erskine had said, "I speak not as an advocate alone.—I speak to you as a man . . ." [62]

It is paradoxical then that some of his words in the Paine trial have been taken out of context to set up Erskine as an exemplar of the bar's rule forbidding counsel to speak to his own belief. Erskine, it is said, ". . . complained that the Attorney General had thought fit 'to add the just weight of his private character to his public duty.' He went on to deal in a fine passage, with the impersonality which should attach to the advocate." [63]

What happened at the Paine trial was this: In opening the case against Paine's *Rights of Man*, the Attorney General said he must ". . . obviate a rumour . . . that this prosecution does not correspond with my private judgment . . ." Untrue, said the Attorney General, ". . . I should think I deserved to be with disgrace expelled from the situation with which his Majesty has honoured me in his service, and that of all my fellow-subjects, had I, as far as my private judgment goes, hesitated for one instant to bring this enormous offender, as I consider him, before a jury of his country." [64]

"Enormous offender" showed a little something for almost two centuries of civiliz'ı ; since an earlier Attorney General (Coke) had given his personal opinion of the defendant Sir Walter Raleigh, addressing him as "a monster," with "an English face, but a Spanish heart," "the absolutest Traitor that ever

60. Rex v. Williams (1797), 26 *Id.* 653, 661; cf. 1 Erskine, Speeches 574 (J. High ed. 1876).

61. Rex v. Williams (1792), 26 How.St.Tr. 653, 661 (1816–1826).

62. Rex v. Baillie (1778), 21 *Id.* 1, 44; cf. Herschell, The Rights and Duties of An Advocate 13 (1890);

and see also 2 J. F. Stephen, History of the Criminal Law of England 342 n. 2 (1883).

63. S. Rogers, "The Ethics of Advocacy," 15 L.Q.Rev. 259, 267 (1899).

64. Rex v. Paine (1792), 22 How.St. Tr. 358, 381 (1816–1826).

was." [65] Yet it was still a personal opinion of counsel, and of the supposedly impartial prosecutor to boot. Unlike Raleigh though, Paine had counsel.

Erskine took note of the Attorney-General's "rumour," which he thought a very puny one. But rather than complaining, Erskine meant exactly what he said when he spoke of the Attorney-General adding "the *just* weight of his private character to his public duty." Erskine went on to add "the just weight of his" own "private character" to the defense of Paine.

He said that "the whole people of England have been witnesses to the calumnious clamour that, by every art, has been raised and kept up against ME. In every place where business or pleasure collects the public together, day after day my name and character have been the topics of injurious reflection.—And for what?—only for not having shrunk from the discharge of a duty which no personal advantage recommended, and which a thousand difficulties repelled." [66] (At the time of the trial Erskine was Attorney-General for the Prince of Wales, and lost the position for representing Paine.) [67]

He forgave those who attacked him. "Little indeed did they know me," he said, "who thought that such calumnies would influence my conduct." And then Erskine added, in words that Howell's *State Trials* (ed. 1817) records in solid capitals:

> "I WILL FOREVER, AT ALL HAZARDS, ASSERT THE DIGNITY, INDEPENDENCE, AND INTEGRITY OF THE ENGLISH BAR; WITHOUT WHICH, IMPARTIAL JUSTICE, THE MOST VALUABLE PART OF THE ENGLISH CONSTITUTION, CAN HAVE NO EXISTENCE." [68]

Erskine took the practical view that a jury would of course be influenced by the reputation of counsel, whether for prosecution or defense, even by the reputations of lawyers who were conspicuously absent from a case. That was one reason why it was wrong for counsel to refuse a case because of his own personal views; if he refuses he prejudges the case. "[A]nd," said Er-

---

65. Rex v. Raleigh (1603), 2 *Id*. 1, 7–9.

66. Rex v. Paine (1792), 22 *Id*. 358, 411–412.

67. 13 Holdsworth, A History of English Law 585 (1952).

68. Rex v. Paine (1792), 22 How.St. Tr. 358, 412 (1816–1826).

skine, "in proportion to his rank and reputation, puts the heavy influence of perhaps a mistaken opinion into the scale against the accused . . ." [69] Taking the case, as it was his duty to do, counsel must do what he can for his client. And here, in defense of Thomas Paine, Erskine made counsel's personal involvement explicit.

> "[B]efore I enter upon it," he said, referring to the central question of freedom of the press, "I wish to fulfill a duty to the defendant, which, if I do not deceive myself, is at this moment peculiarly necessary to his impartial trial.—If an advocate entertain sentiments injurious to the defence he is engaged in, he is not only justified, but bound in duty, to conceal them; so, on the other hand, if his own genuine sentiments, or anything connected with his character or situation, can add strength to his professional assistance, he is bound to throw them into the scale.—In addressing myself, therefore, to gentlemen not only zealous for the honour of English government, but visibly indignant at any attack upon its principles, and who would, perhaps, be impatient of arguments from a suspected quarter, I give my client the benefit of declaring, that I am, and ever have been, attached to the genuine principles of the British government; and that, however the court or you may reject the application, I defend him upon principles not only consistent with its permanence and security, but without the establishment of which it never could have had an existence." [70]

What if Paine's views were "adverse to our system"? The burden of Erskine's defense, repeated many times since, was ". . . that opinion is free, and that conduct alone is amenable to the law." [71] Accordingly, he said, even if Paine's opinions were wrong, ". . . still I am not removed from the principle of his defense.—My defence has nothing to do with the rectitude of his doctrines." [72] He nonetheless went out of his way "to express my own admiration of the real principles of our constitution," [73] and to insist that it was only because he

69. *Id.*

70. *Id.* 414.

71. *Id.* 419.

72. *Id.* 424.

73. *Id.*

personally considered Paine's opinions constitutionally proper that he defended him.

After quoting the Preface to the *Rights of Man*, Erskine continued:

> "Mr. Paine expressly says, I obey a law until it is repealed;—obedience is not only my principle but my practice, since my disobedience of a law thinking it *bad*, might apply to justify another man in the disobedience of a *good one*; and thus individuals would give the rule for themselves, and not society for all.— You will presently see that the same principle pervades the whole work; and I am the more anxious to call your attention to it, however the repetition may tire you, because it unfolds the whole principle of my argument; for, if you find a sentence in the whole book that invests any individual, or any number of individuals, or any community short of the WHOLE NATION, with a power of changing any part of the law or constitution, I abandon the cause—YES, I freely abandon it, because I will not affront the majesty of a court of justice by maintaining propositions which, even upon the surface of them, are false.[74]

Erskine made no attempt to reconcile this rhetorical gesture of abandonment of Paine with his previous assertion of the duty of counsel never to reject a client's cause. Before this hostile jury was not the time and place to do so. But he clearly placed his personal indorsement, his personal belief before the jury for what good it would do his client, even as the Attorney General had added his own "*just* weight" to the prosecution.

In an earlier case, Erskine openly placed himself in even closer personal alliance with a client and his cause. His opening speech in *The King v. Shipley, Dean of St. Asaph* (1784)[75] gives a taste of that complete absence of professional aloofness so cheering to a beleaguered client. It approaches the quality the Chicago conspiracy trial defendant Jerry Rubin (1970) found in what he calls "movement attorneys." These lawyers, says Rub-

---

74. *Id.* 421.

75. Rex v. Shipley (1783–1784), 21 How.St.Tr. 847 (1816–1826).

in, so identified themselves with their clients that (in some of his admiring words):

> When we are on trial, they are on trial. When we go to jail, they go to jail. They cannot afford to be cynical like everyone else in the courthouse. *They are defending their brothers.*[76]

Erskine's client was indicted for seditious libel for having published *The Precepts of Government, in a Dialogue between a Gentleman and a Farmer*, which, said counsel for the private prosecutor, "I declare upon my honour . . . that I not only think it a libel, but I think it a most enormous, and a most mischievous libel." [77]

In reply Erskine said that if this book were "seditious or libellous, the Bill of Rights . . . was a seditious libel;—the Revolution was a wicked rebellion;—the existing government is a traitorous conspiracy . . ." These absurdities, he said, would follow inevitably from the view that upon the evidence presented the *Dialogue* was a libel,[78] and this:

> ". . . following the example of my learned friend, who has pledged *his* personal veracity in support of his sentiments, I assert, upon *my* honour, to be my unaltered, and I believe I may say, unalterable opinion, formed upon the most mature deliberation; and I choose to place that opinion in the very front of my address to you, that you may not, in the course of it, mistake the energies of truth and freedom for the zeal of professional duty.
>
> "This declaration of my own sentiments, even if my friend had not set me the example by giving you his, I should have considered to be my duty in this cause; for although in ordinary cases, where the private right of the party accused is alone in discussion, and no general consequences can follow from the decision, the advocate and the private man ought in sound discretion to be kept asunder; yet there are occasions, when such sepa-

---

76. J. Rubin, Do It! 160 (1970).   **78.** *Id.* 899.

77. Rex v. Shipley (1784), 21 How. St.Tr. 847, 889 (1816–1826).

ration would be treachery and meanness.—In a case where the dearest rights of society are involved in the resistance of a prosecution,—where the party accused is (as in this instance) but a mere name,—where the whole community is wounded through his sides,— and where the conviction of the private individual is the subversion or surrender of public privileges, the advocate has a more extensive charge: the duty of the patriot citizen then mixes itself with his obligation to his client, and he disgraces himself, dishonours his profession, and betrays his country, if he does not step forth in his personal character, and vindicate the rights of all his fellow citizens, which are attacked through the medium of the man he is defending.

"Gentlemen, I do not mean to shrink from that responsibility upon this occasion; I desire to be considered the fellow criminal of the defendant, if by your verdict he should be found one, by publishing in advised speaking (which is substantially equal in guilt to the publication he is accused of before you), my hearty approbation of every sentiment contained in this little book; promising here, in the face of the world, to publish them on every suitable occasion, amongst that part of the community within the reach of my precept, influence, and example. If there be any more prosecutors of this denomination abroad among us, they know how to take advantage of these declarations." [79]

Erskine closed this speech on another personal note, warning against a verdict of guilty:

"As the friend of my client, and the friend of my country, I shall feel much sorrow, and you yourselves will probably hereafter regret it, when the season of reparation is fled." [80]

Erskine's injection of the lawyer's personal opinion into his arguments was the passing style of the day. His distinction between "ordinary cases" when a lawyer ought not to argue his personal opinion, and cases affecting public right when it "would be treachery and meanness" for the lawyer to cling to his dis-

79. *Id.* 899–900.   **80**. *Id.* 929.

crete role as lawyer, was Erskine's own rationalization, not accepted by common lawyers. There was a special vigor firing all of Erskine's eloquence that bespoke a self-righteousness rooted in intense religious zeal rather than the law book learning of the lawyer. As he himself said in prosecuting the publisher of Paine's *Age of Reason*, "The people of England are a religious people, and, with the blessing of God, so far as it is in my power, I will lend my aid to keep them so." [81]

As we have seen, the church much earlier had strongly condemned the lawyer who knowingly undertook the defense of the guilty or even continued to defend a man after becoming convinced of his guilt. As a moral agent, a lawyer no less than ordinary laymen was forbidden to speak up for sin. By this standard, constantly reinforced by special injunctions to lawyers to use their God-given gifts for moral ends, when a lawyer speaks —properly, he speaks only for the righteous. So, for Erskine or any lawyer to add in argument that personally he believes in his client's cause was no more than the sin of redundancy. Of course he believes in his client's cause. He must, or he is a scoundrel.

4. ON LYING

a. THE THREATENED MORAL POSITION

The trouble with the religious and moralist insistence that a "good" lawyer speak only for the causes he believes in (by definition the "good" causes) is that it collides head on with the anciently recognized English right of every man to have what the law allows him. Unless a lawyer convinces himself of the rightness of every cause offered (which happens only with lawyers of limited practice or limited conscience) rejection of causes for lack of a lawyer's believing in them results in some laymen facing the unequal terrors of the law alone.

In the earliest English days of the profession, courtroom lawyers primarily argued only points of law, and in such a legal setting the collision of desirables (speak for right v. speak for all) was minimal. Given the uncertainties of common law, a lawyer's conscientious belief could (and does) easily embrace adver-

81. Rex v. Williams (1797), 26 How.St.Tr. 653, 668 (1816–1826).

sary interpretations of law. But late in the 16th century, changes were introduced in the legal procedures of proof; English lawyers became examiners of witnesses, and cross-examiners, in addition to being pleaders of law; [82] and the ideal of a lawyer's conscientious belief in his case was severely strained. Credibility and weight of frequently contradictory testimony of witnesses became critical to decision, and inevitably the character of the counsel who introduced these sharply opposing testimonies became associated more intimately than ever before with the character of the witnesses. Whether or not this association existed in the mind of counsel, it would exist in the minds of those who watched the judicial drama unfold.

That association troubled the religious. Reminiscing, after the death of Sir Matthew Hale, his friend Richard Baxter recalled: "And indeed Judge Hale would tell me, that Bishop Usher was much prejudiced against Lawyers, because the worst causes find their Advocates; but that he and Mr. Selden had convinced him of the Reasons for it, to his satisfaction: And that he did by acquaintance with them, believe that there were as many honest men among Lawyers, proportionally, as among any Profession of men in England (not excepting Bishops or Divines)." [83] Baxter does not tell us exactly what convinced Bishop Usher; it could have been that a lawyer might with moral safety have something good to say for even a bad man—something in extenuation, something to induce compassion for a sinner, as long as the "law" was not used to stand in the way of "justice." If Hale, as he said, reserved his powers of advocacy for good causes, a contemporary in the profession still noted approvingly: "As great a Lawyer as he was he would never suffer the strictness of Law to prevail against Conscience, as great a Chancellor as he was, he would make use of all the Niceties and Subtilities in Law, when it tended to support Right and Equity." [84]

This thought that even for "the good advocate" there is a difference between the permissible in a good cause and in one not

82. D. Mellinkoff, Language of the Law 138–139 (1963).

83. R. Baxter, Additional Notes on the Life and Death of Sir Matthew Hale 26 (1682).

84. G. Burnet, Life and Death of Sir Matthew Hale, Kt., 176–177 (2d ed. 1682).

so good is a pervasive one. The season for eloquence, "all the Niceties and Subtilities in Law" (let us not call it chicane) to support Right, but not otherwise. The distinction was supported by that most rigid of Churchmen the right Reverend Jeremy Taylor in his *Ductor Dubitantium, or the Rule of Conscience* (1660). Dr. Taylor held that lying was an unmitigated sin, that the advocate even "in a good cause, must not use evil arts." [85] But short of that, in a good cause, though not in a bad one, "artifices and crafty intercourses" even if not strictly proper might "have very much to excuse them." [86] Thin ice.

As law business increased, and the numbers of lawyers of all sorts increased, complaints of chicanery increased. And with the passage of the Prisoners' Counsel Bill (1836), giving every man indicted for felony right to counsel, the instances were greatly multiplied when lawyers must argue to the jury on behalf of those many still regard—even before conviction—as "the criminal element." Association of client and counsel, especially in the minds of the public, became ever closer; as in the centuries before the Prisoners' Counsel Bill, the cynical of the lay public needed no convincing that a lawyer's expression of belief in the cause for which he pleaded was only a barker's pitch, induced by a fee.

b. THE PALEYAN HERESY

Whatever the marketplace opinion of lawyers, it nonetheless came as something of a jolt to the community of respectables, lay as well as professional, when a respected 18th century minister began telling his university students there was nothing immoral about a lawyer expressing his belief in any cause that came down the pike.

In his popular Cambridge lectures, published as *The Principles of Moral and Political Philosophy* (1785), William Paley said that the evil of lying lay in the breaking of a tacit promise to speak the truth, and in the possibility that someone might suffer from a lie. But, he continued, "There are falsehoods which are not lies . . .," because ". . . no one is deceived." This was the case not only with jokes and fairy tales, but with "a prisoner's pleading not guilty, an advocate asserting the

---

85.   13 J. Taylor, Works 362 (3d ed.   **86.**   *Id.* 364, and see also 382.
R. Heber ed. 1839).

justice, or his belief of the justice of his client's cause. In such instances," Paley concluded, "no confidence is destroyed, because none was reposed; no promise to speak the truth violated, because none was given, or understood to be given." [87]

In the torrent of denunciation that has greeted Paley, it is his rationalization of lying, not his appraisal of practice at the bar that has been disputed. The bluntest answer to Paley came from a young Quaker. Why, asked Jonathan Dymond, "if no one ever believes what advocates say, [do] they continue to speak[?]" To Dymond the answer was as simple as the advocate was corrupt. "He intends and indeavours to mislead. His untruths therefore are lies to him, whether they are believed or not; just as, in vulgar life, a man whose falsehoods are so notorious that no one gives him credit, is not the less a liar than if he were believed." [88] Dymond's condemnation of the lawyer's expression of a false belief was of a parcel with his acceptance of the religious position that the lawyer must speak only for good causes; the only exception he recognized to this general position was that the lawyer might "assist a client even with a bad cause . . . to prevent the client from suffering too far." [89] But as for bad causes indifferently undertaken by lawyers, this—to Dymond—was "intellectual and moral prostitution." [90] If anyone thought it impracticable for a lawyer to practice with complete moral integrity, Dymond doubted that it had ever been tried, but his solution was equally direct: "A man is not compelled to be a lawyer . . ." [91]

For those not prepared to take Dymond's quick way out, trying to reconcile a general availability of advocacy with strict morality produced sharp cornering and fine slicing.

Thomas Gisborne denounced Paley's cynical preachments as absurd and vicious counsel of expedience, destructive of basic notions of right, and of the role of man as a moral agent.[92] A

---

87. W. Paley, The Principles of Moral and Political Philosophy 117–118 (New ed. 1821; 1st ed. 1785); cf. 2 Boswell's Life of Johnson 47 (G.B.Hill ed. 1887).

88. J. Dymond, Essays on the Principles of Morality 130–131 (1834; [1st ed. 1829]).

89. *Id.* 138.

90. *Id.* 136.

91. *Id.* 137–139.

92. T. Gisborne, The Principles of Moral Philosophy Investigated v–vi; 1–14; and especially 122–123 (1789).

lawyer addressing a jury, he wrote, "is not at liberty to assert any false propositions . . .," [93] though it was proper "to place his claim before them in the most attractive garb with which sincerity will permit him to invest it . . ." [94] A lawyer was "bound in the sight of God to refuse all connection" with causes so evil they contributed "to the encouragement of fraud, rapine, and of violence; to the subversion of the very ends for which law is established . . ." and to drop them "if he finds himself inadvertently entangled . . ." [95] At the same time, nothing wrong with a lawyer's insisting on what the law entitles men to, regardless of the lawyer's personal opinion.[96] And—to Dymond's disgust—[97] Gisborne warned that if principled lawyers were too squeamish, rejecting "causes on insufficient grounds," litigants would be driven "into the hands of needy and unprincipled chicaners . . ." [98] In a further passage Gisborne touches the general impropriety of a lawyer injecting himself into his case: "He will not strive to impose on the ignorance of the Jury, nor entrap them into the service of his Client, by practicing on their partiality for himself . . . He will not represent those who come forward in support of his Client as entitled to be believed, when he discovers that they are unworthy of confidence . . ." [99] But this was rather a warning against fraud than any general brief against personal expression of opinion.

English lawyers too railed against what one Queen's Counsel called "the wretched sophistry of Paley." That from William Forsyth (1849), who wrote that "Every man is under an obligation to speak the truth if he speaks at all . . ." [1] He went so far along the moralist path as to deny the basic tenet of the English bar, that advocates were obliged to take all cases regardless of merit. But; there was a but. He also thought that the general uncertainty of most litigated matters made it possible that ". . . an advocate may in most cases, with a

---

93. T. Gisborne, An Enquiry Into the Duties of Men in the Higher and Middle Classes of Society in Great Britain 357 (2d ed. 1795).

94. Id. 361.

95. Id. 320–321.

96. Id. 320.

97. J. Dymond, *supra* note 88, at 133.

98. T. Gisborne, *supra* note 93, at 348–349.

99. Id. 360–361.

1. W. Forsyth, Hortensius 406–407 (2d ed. 1874; 1st ed. 1849).

safe conscience, take either side on which he happens first to be retained." [2]

While conceding that substantial opinion of the bar opposed him, barrister Edward O'Brien (1842) said that no lawyer could escape "a law of the moral world that the character of an individual may be known from his companions." "Dishonesty," he concluded, "naturally seeks out the dishonest—infamy the infamous . . . miserably adding crime to crime, and filling to the full that cup of wrath which, if they repent not, advocate and client must one day drink together to the very dregs." [3] He also reverted to the religious theme that in effect recommended first or second class advocacy, as the lawyer's conscience and morality dictated. "How they will lead him to act; whether altogether to reject a case or to lend it only a lukewarm and hesitating support, or to prosecute it with all his powers and energies; these are questions that can be determined only by the character of each individual case that comes before him." [4]

The celebrated barrister James Scarlett, then Lord Abinger, in his somewhat equivocal speech favoring passage of the Prisoners' Counsel Bill (1836), without naming Paley rejected his carte blanche to lawyers for indiscriminate expressions of belief. "[I]n cases where the prisoner's guilt was clearly proved," he said, "no counsel of the least discretion would think of addressing the jury to assert his innocence." [5] Implicit here is an acknowledgement of the propriety of a lawyer's expressing an honest opinion of his client's innocence, but whether such expression would arise by express declaration or merely from the act of speaking in the client's behalf is not entirely clear.

The closest approach to support for the Paleyan heresy came from a well known barrister Basil Montagu (1837). He rejected religious and moralist views on the duty of counsel; this in the interest of making certain that all men, not some, might be represented by counsel.

In his most controversial passage, Montagu wrote:

> The statement by opposite advocates may not be
> most beneficial to the practitioner; and, as the advo-

2. *Id.* 405.

3. E. O'Brien, The Lawyer 46–50 (1842).

4. *Id.* 29.

5. The Times (London), July 15, 1836.

cate may profess feelings which he does not feel, and
may support a cause which he knows wrong; as it is a
species of acting without an avowal that it is acting, it
may appear at variance with some of our best feelings.
It is, however, nothing but appearance. The advocate
is in reality an officer assisting in the administration of
justice, and acting under the impression that truth is
elicited and difficulties disentangled by the opposite
statements of able men. He is only troubling the waters, that they may exert their virtues.[6]

Montagu apparently felt that even if a lawyer "profess feelings which he does not feel," it was yet not lying. Not as Paley
asserted because no one believed him; but because it could be
readily understood that the feelings he gave expression to were
not his own but his client's. Thus the lawyer's personal integrity remained intact, and he himself continued—as he must—personally uninvolved.

Speaking from personal experience in the practice, with possibly an in jab at the style of some of the greats of the bar, including Erskine, and Brougham, and especially the then recent
defense of Lord Melbourne by John Campbell, Montagu wrote of
the advocate:

> *He does not mix himself with the client or the cause,*
> with the slanderer, the adulterer, the murderer, or the
> traitor, whom it may be his duty to defend. He lends
> his exertions to all; himself to none.
>
> .   .   . *The result of the cause,* except as far as
> he has an opinion of right, independent of the parties,
> *is to him a matter of indifference.* It is for the court
> to decide; it is for him to argue.
>
> .   .   . *In general he does not exercise any dis-
> cretion as to the suitor for whom he is to plead.*—If a
> barrister were permitted to exercise any discretion as
> to the client for whom he will plead, the course of jus-
> tice would be interrupted by prejudice to the suitor,
> and the exclusion of integrity from the profession. The
> suitor would be prejudiced in proportion to the respect-

6. B. Montagu, Essays and Selec-   well's Life of Johnson, *supra* note
tions 266–267 (1837); cf. 2 Bos-   87.

ability of the advocate who had shrunk from his defence, and the weight of character of the counsel would
be evidence in the cause. Integrity would be excluded
from the profession, as the counsel would necessarily be
associated with the cause of his client.

Here, Montagu referred to Erskine's views on the imperative
duty to defend, and continued:

Our advocate, therefore does not exercise any discretion; to him it is a matter of indifference, whether he
appears for the most unfortunate, or the most prosper-
ous member of the community; for the poorest bank-
rupt, or the noblest peer of the realm; for a traitor, or
for the King.

. . . *In some extreme cases he declines to act
as advocate when the appearance of opposition is in violation of some of our best feelings.*—He will not, like
Lucius, proceed in judgment against his own sons

. . .

. . . *He does not exercise any discretion, from
his opinion of the goodness or badness of the cause.*[7]

Montagu, like others, was groping his way to a resolution of
the lawyer's dilemma, towards some means of rationalizing the
delicate moral position of the advocate in a legal system increasingly committed to equality before the law. The more literally
the judicial system took the old thought that all men were entitled to their law, the more the system called for lawyers, decent
lawyers, ready to represent those who asked for representation.
The only way, it seemed to men like Montagu, that there could
be complete involvement of the lawyers in the legal system as a
whole, was that he be completely uninvolved in the merits of the
individual cases he appeared in. The moment that lawyer and
client became identified in the public eye, representation of anyone inevitably meant the indiscriminate sharing of anyone's
morals, and an end of personal and professional honor.

7. *Id.* 267–269.

Montagu's tract for professional survival, even with its sophisticated revision of Paley, did not satisfy the moral opposition. Barrister O'Brien pecked at it.[8] And a few years later it drew heavier fire from a treatise that was to have a lasting influence on the conduct of the whole Anglo-American community of law. For many lawyers, philosopher William Whewell's *Elements of Morality* (1845) was a final demonstration of the ethical impossibility of expressing belief in a cause not believed in.

Without the threat of damnation implicit in O'Brien, Whewell undertook a careful destruction of Paley and (without naming him) Montagu, at least the portion of Paley justifying a lawyer's false statement of belief in his cause, and the portion of Montagu similarly permitting an advocate to "profess feelings which he does not feel, and   .   .   .   support a cause which he knows to be wrong."

To Paley's assertion that everyone knows lawyers make "no promise to speak the truth," Whewell gave a politer version of Dymond's answer: "If there is no mutual understanding that he shall speak truly, to what purpose does he speak, or to what purpose do the judges hear?" [9]

To Montagu's position that the Advocate "is not the Judge;— that it is not his office to determine on which side Justice is; and that therefore his duty, in his office, is not affected by his belief on this subject," Whewell was prepared to "grant that it is likely to answer the ends of Justice in a community, that there should exist a Profession of Advocates; ready to urge, with full force, the arguments on each side in doubtful cases." Well and good, said Whewell:

> And if the Advocate, in his mode of pleading and exercising his profession, allows it to be understood that this is all that he undertakes to do, he does not transgress his Duties of Truth and Justice, even in pleading for a bad cause; since even for a bad cause, there may be arguments, and even good arguments. But if, in pleading, he assert his belief that his cause is just, when he believes it unjust, he offends against Truth; as any other man would do who, in like manner, made a like assertion. Nor is it conducive to the ends of jus-

8. E. O'Brien, *supra* note 3, at 15–16.

9. 1 W. Whewell, The Elements of Morality 257 (1845).

tice, that every man however palpably unjust his cause be, should have such support to it.

To the argument, that the Advocate is not the Judge, and therefore, that he is not responsible for his judgment on the merits of the case; the Moralist will reply, that every man is, in an unofficial sense, by being a moral agent, a Judge of right and wrong, and an Advocate of what is right; and is, so far, bound to be just in his judgments, and sincere in his exhortations. This general character of a moral agent, he cannot put off, by putting on any professional character. Every man, when he advocates a case in which morality is concerned, has an influence upon his hearers, which arises from the belief that he shares the moral sentiments of all mankind. This influence of his supposed morality, is one of his possessions; which, like all his possessions, he is bound to use for moral ends. If he mix up his character as an Advocate, with his character as a Moral Agent, using his moral influence for the Advocate's purpose, he acts immorally. He makes the Moral Rule subordinate to the Professional Rule. He sells to his Client, not only his skill and learning, but himself. He makes it the Supreme Object of his life to be, not a good man, but a successful Lawyer.

If it be alleged, that by allowing the difference of his professional and unprofessional character to be seen in his pleading, the Advocate will lose his influence with his hearers; the Moralist will reply, that he ought not to have an influence which arises from a false representation of himself; and that if he employ the influence of his unprofessional character, he is bound, in the use of it, to unprofessional Rules of Duty.[10]

It is to be noted that Whewell, like Dymond, concerns himself with how a lawyer may remain moral as distinguished from how a lawyer may continue to practice law. He does not worry himself with what the barrister Montagu was striving after—a complete dispassion in the role of the advocate. Whewell is not a discouragement to the lawyer's taking a personal moral position in his argument; only that once he does that, he is the ordinary

---

10. *Id.* 257–259.

involved moral man, not the uninvolved lawyer, and must come down on the right side. Neither does Whewell give too much encouragement to a profession wondering whether it is humanly possible for the advocate to live thus fine split between Advocate and Moral Man; there is an undercurrent in Whewell that perhaps any advocacy is necessarily an expression of morality.

5. AMERICAN VARIATIONS

a. NO FALSE EXPRESSION OF BELIEF

The American David Hoffman set down his views of the permissible scope of the lawyer's personal involvement, in 1836, i. e. after Paley but before either Montagu or Whewell. He lacks the boldness of Paley, the subtlety of Montagu, or the purity of Whewell, but offered some domestic guidance where none existed before. If defending a man "charged with crimes of the deepest dye, and the evidence   .   .   .   legal, or moral, be such as to leave no just doubt of   .   .   .   guilt," a lawyer could not use his "own personal weight of character." In cases not that bad and not that clear, the choice was more pragmatic than moral, but weighted in favor of the worthy cause:

> Whatever personal influence I may be so fortunate as to possess, shall be used by me only as the most valuable of my possessions, and not be cheapened, or rendered questionable by a too frequent appeal to its influence. There is nothing more fatal to *weight of character* than its common use; and especially that unworthy one, often indulged in by eminent counsel, of solemn assurances to eke out a sickly and doubtful cause. If the case be a good one, it needs no such appliance; and if bad, the artifice ought to be too shallow to mislead any one. Whether one or the other, such *personal pledges* should be *very sparingly* used, and only on occasions which obviously demand them; for if more liberally resorted to, they beget doubts where none may have existed, or strengthen those which before were only feebly felt.[11]

11. 2 D. Hoffman, A Course of Legal Study 755–757 (2d ed. 1836).

This was a crackerbarrel guide to success rather than anxious straining over principle.

Hoffman's successor, the influential Judge Sharswood (1854), welcomed Whewell's teachings to America. He told his law students, and the American bar generally:

> Moreover, no counsel can with propriety and a good conscience express to court or jury his belief in the justice of his client's cause, contrary to the fact. Indeed, the occasions are very rare in which he ought to throw the weight of his own private opinion into the scales in favor of the side he has espoused. If that opinion has been formed on a statement of facts not in evidence, it ought not to be heard,—it would be illegal and improper in the tribunal to allow any force whatever to it; if on the evidence only, it is enough to show from that the legal and moral grounds on which such opinion rests.[12]

After quoting Whewell,[13] Judge Sharswood then pictures the unfair position of the young lawyer faced by a veteran's expression of his personal opinion:

> In proportion, then, to the age, experience, maturity of judgment, and professional character of the man, who falsely endeavors to impress the court and jury with the opinion of his confidence in the justice of his case, in that porportion is there danger that injury will be done and wrong inflicted—in that proportion is there moral delinquency in him who resorts to it.[14]

Again, in his discussion of *Courvoisier's Case*, while approving the conduct of Phillips on the facts as he understood them, Sharswood says it would have been wrong for him " . . . even to stand up and falsely pretend a confidence in the truth and justice of his cause, which he did not feel." [15] And finally, as we have seen, approving Baron Parke's advice to Phillips "to use ALL FAIR ARGUMENTS ARISING ON THE EVIDENCE," Sharswood added his own carefully constructed

---

12. G. Sharswood, A Compend 37–38 (1854).

13. *Id.* 38–40.

14. *Id.* 40.

15. *Id.* 42.

comment, "Beyond that, he is not bound to go in any case; in a case in which he is satisfied in his own mind of the guilt of the accused, he is not justified in going." [16]   George Warvelle agreed.[17]

In all of this, there is the suggestion by Judge Sharswood (as by Hoffman, Whewell, and Warvelle) that in a good cause the lawyer is justified in greater efforts, in laying everything on the line, including himself, involving himself as personally as Erskine ever did, giving his personal, honest belief in the cause he advocates. This is a legacy of the religious, the moralist background of the profession of law, though it is to be observed that Sharswood says the occasions for expressions of personal belief are "very rare," a step more restrictive than Hoffman's "very sparingly."

b. NO EXPRESSION OF BELIEF

Despite the fact that the first American code of ethics leaned heavily on the teachings of Judge Sharswood, that Code (Alabama State Bar Association, 1887) did not follow Sharswood (or Hoffman or Whewell) in distinguishing between permissible and impermissible expressions of counsel's belief in his client's cause. All expressions of belief were disapproved. This followed from the Code's preliminary advice to lawyers not to testify for a client except as to "formal matters" or in exceptional cases "when essential to the ends of justice   .   .   ." [18] a rule still of general application today.[19]   The Code continued:

> The same reasons which make it improper in general for an attorney to testify for his client, apply with greater force to assertions, sometimes made by counsel in argument, of personal belief of the client's innocence or the justice of his cause. If such assertions are habitually made they lose all force and subject the attor-

---

16. *Id.* 44.

17. G. Warvelle, Essays in Legal Ethics 136–137, 215–216 (1902).

18. Code of Ethics (Ala.) § 18, in Proceedings of the 18th Annual Meeting of the Ala. State Bar Assn. CXII, at CXVII–CXVIII (1895), and 35 Report of the Ala. Bar Assn. 145 (1912).

19. ABA Old Canons, *supra* Intro., note 29, Canon 19; ABA CPR, *supra* ch. VIII, note 12, EC 5–9, EC 5–10, DR 5–102.

ney to falsehoods; while the failure to make them in
particular cases will often be esteemed a tacit admission of belief of the client's guilt, or the weakness of
his cause. [20]

Even that fleeting nod to Judge Sharswood's distinction, in the
reference to "falsehoods," was omitted in the American Bar Association's version of the rule adopted as a part of Canon 15 in
1908. Like the current rule in England the prohibition is unequivocal:

> It is improper for a lawyer to assert in argument his
> personal belief in his client's innocence or in the justice
> of his cause.

American judges have repeatedly reaffirmed the principle of
Canon 15: no-personal-belief, whether that belief be dishonest or
honest, in a "bad" cause or a "good" cause.[21] But the widest
latitude is permitted lawyers in expressing beliefs based on the
evidence; [22] even sharp criticism for disregard of the canon does
not necessarily bring a reversal for misconduct; [23] and the reports do not show that counsel have been disciplined for such in-
fractions. Personal experience indicates that American lawyers
have continued to express personal opinions when they are so
moved; lawyers in civil as well as criminal cases; lawyers for
defense and for prosecution. An informed guess would be that
Canon 15 has been the most violated of all the old Canons of
Professional Ethics.

---

20. Code of Ethics (Ala.) § 19, *supra* note 18, at CXVIII, and 35 Report of the Ala.Bar Assn. 145
(1912).

21. People v. Bain, 5 Cal.3d 839,
848–849, 97 Cal.Rptr. 684, 688–689,
489 P.2d 564, 568–569 (1971); Adams v. State, 280 Ala. 678, 680–
681, 198 So.2d 255, 257 (1967).

22. State v. Hipplewith, 33 N.J. 300,
310–312, 164 A.2d 481, 486–487
(1960); Henderson v. United
States, 218 F.2d 14, 19 and *dissent*
at 20–23 (6th Cir. 1955); *cert. denied*, 349 U.S. 920, 75 S.Ct. 660, 99

L.Ed. 1253; *reh. denied*, 349 U.S.
969, 75 S.Ct. 879, 99 L.Ed. 1290
(1955). 50 ALR 2d 754, ann. at
766, ALR Supp. pages 150–158
(1967), 49–55 LCS Supp. pages
39–42 (1971); and see Code of
Trial Conduct, § 20(h) (1963 ed.)
and § 19(a) (4) (1972 Rev.).

23. Sabella v. So. Pac. Ry., 70 Cal.
2d 311, 318, 74 Cal.Rptr. 534, 538,
449 P.2d 750, 754, and *dissent* by
Traynor, C.J., 70 Cal.2d at 321, 74
Cal.Rptr. at 540, 449 P.2d at 756
(1969), *cert. denied*, 395 U.S. 960,
89 S.Ct. 2100, 23 L.Ed.2d 746.

Even so, old Canon 15 was recognized and expanded in the new Code of Professional Responsibility, as one of the limits to a lawyer's zeal in representing his client: [24]

> In appearing in his professional capacity before a tribunal, a lawyer shall not: . . . (4) Assert his personal opinion as to the justness of a cause, as to the credibility of a witness, as to the culpability of a civil litigant, or as to the guilt or innocence of an accused; but he may argue, on his analysis of the evidence, for any position or conclusion with respect to the matters stated herein.[25]

Further, the new Code goes beyond reaffirming the no-personal-belief rule as a general guide to proper professional conduct. Nominally, it has become a prohibition enforcible as a disciplinary rule, conjuring up the unlikely spectacle of hordes of American lawyers facing discipline at the hands of their fellow lawyers for what has become too much of a commonplace.

c. RATIONALE

Ethical Considerations for the no-personal-belief rule are stated in the Code:

> In order to bring about just and informed decisions, evidentiary and procedural rules have been established by tribunals to permit the inclusion of relevant evidence and argument and the exclusion of all other considerations. The expression by a lawyer of his personal opinion as to the justness of a cause, as to the credibility of a witness, as to the culpability of a civil litigant, or as to the guilt or innocence of an accused is not a proper subject for argument to the trier of fact. It is improper as to factual matters because admissible evidence possessed by a lawyer should be presented only as sworn testimony. It is improper as to all other matters because, were the rule otherwise, the silence of a lawyer on a given occasion could be construed unfavorably to his client. However, a lawyer may argue, on

---

24. ABA CPR, *supra* ch. VIII, note 12, Canon 7.   **25.** *Id.,* DR 7–106(C) (4).

his analysis of the evidence, for any position or conclusion with respect to any of the foregoing matters.[26]

This statement of reasons for the no-personal-belief rule—violation of a rule of evidence, and potential harm to a client if his lawyer did not say he believed in the client's cause—is not new.[27] Curiously, it leaves largely ignored the fundamental reason for the rule, i. e. an attempt to resolve the ancient and continuing ethical problem of the profession: how to give counsel to clients without sharing their morals. And it may be worth a moment to speculate on the omission.

As we have seen, for centuries many men were denied even the right to counsel, and for a variety of reasons, not the least being the moral objection that "bad" men and "evil" causes did not deserve to be defended. With the passage of the Prisoners' Counsel Bill in 1836, England became firmly committed to the proposition that all men are entitled to have someone trained in the law speak for them in a court of law; otherwise there could be no reality to the ancient promise that every Englishman "have that the law giveth him."

The 1836 extension of the right to counsel only sharpened the long-standing ethical embarrassment of lawyers. The clergy and others were still insisting first, that it was every man's duty (lawyers included) to speak out for righteousness, and second, that if a cause were bad enough no decent lawyer could participate. Question: Who would speak out for the cause that was obviously evil, even though somehow it turned out not to be? Answer: No decent lawyer. Question: Was the lawyer really honest who professed to speak in a good cause, when the verdict has proved very clearly the cause was rotten from the start? Answer: Not bloody likely.

With such prods and such restraints, lawyers considered the implications of a professional rule that would permit expression of belief "in the honesty or validity of his client's case." A former Lord Chancellor Lord Herschell gave his views (1889):

It is obvious that, if such a course were sanctioned, the absence of any expression of opinion would be viewed

---

26. *Id.*, EC 7–24; and see Code of Trial Conduct, § 19(a) (4) (1972 Rev.)

27. Drinker, *supra* ch. VIII, note 17, at 147; Code of Ethics (Ala.), § 19, *supra* note 20; Herschell, The Rights and Duties of An Advocate 10–11 (1890); see also ABA CPR, *supra* ch. VIII, note 12, Canon 7, n. 83; etc.

as an indication that the client's case was ill-regarded by his own advocate, and an unfavourable conclusion, in excess of what was justifiable, would be only too likely to be drawn. An unscrupulous advocate, too, would express a belief which he did not entertain, whilst a scrupulous one, from the very desire to avoid exaggeration in the indication of his views, would probably do his client less than justice.

But this is the least part of the evil which would ensue. The mischief calculated to flow from the appearance of an advocate of position and character in support of a case which proves to be without merit, can only be obviated if it be distinctly understood that he is an advocate only, and that it is his client's case, and not his personal views or opinions to which he is giving expression. It is only by keeping this rule .   .   . constantly in mind, and by a strict adherence to it in practice, that the risk of injury to the moral character of the advocate from his seeking to convince others by arguments which have not brought conviction to his own mind can be avoided.[28]

Accordingly, both in England and America lawyers profess to reject the option given us by Whewell, i. e. to express personal opinion in a good cause, and opt for a moral and professional alternative—to express no personal opinion in any cause. For while the individual lawyer may convince himself that he believes in his cause, when the smoke of battle has cleared and the cause is lost, who is to say that the lawyer was an innocent misled or a participant in fraud? It is too fine a thread for the reputation of a profession or of a single decent practitioner to hang by. The only rule that can assure representation to all and integrity to the profession is to have it distinctly understood that a lawyer speaks only for the client, not for himself.

The object of the "whole system of professional morality .   .   ." as Sir James Fitzjames Stephens generalized it in 1861, "is to maintain rigidly the representative character of the advocate. It forbids every expression and every form, either of statement or of interrogation, which would involve a surrender of that character, and make the advocate a partisan, instead of a professional agent." [29]

---

28. Herschell, The Rights and Duties of An Advocate 10–11 (1890).

29. J. F. Stephens, "The Morality of Advocacy," 3 The Cornhill Maga-

For the English barrister the position of the independent professional agent expressing no personal opinion becomes a necessity, because he is bound to take the cases that come to him. He serves the man who needs his case presented in court. He provides what the client cannot provide—professionalism at law; the client already has a personal opinion.

A similar note of professionalism was present in the Alabama Code of 1887: the no-personal-belief rule was coupled with a duty to represent—not in all cases, but in the most critical of all. If a lawyer believed an accused innocent, he was not to appear as a private prosecutor, nor "press for a conviction" as a public prosecutor.[30] If a lawyer believed a civil suit was instituted "merely to harass or injure," he was to decline service.[31] But even though "he knows or believes" an accused guilty of crime, he *can not reject the defense.*[32]

Contrariwise, the canons of the American Bar Association (whether the old *Canons of Professional Ethics* or the new *Code of Professional Responsibility*) have never placed American lawyers under a general duty to render their services to all comers. There is no American "taxi-cab" rule. As we have noted, even an expression of "the right of the lawyer to undertake the defense of a person accused of crime, regardless of his personal opinion as to the guilt of the accused"[33] has been omitted from the *Code of Professional Responsibility.* At present, such an opinion is simply not a "compelling reason" for the lawyer seeking to beg off when a court orders him to serve or a bar association requests him to.[34] Not burdened with the

zine 447, 453 (1861); accord: S. Rogers, "The Ethics of Advocacy," 15 L.Q.Rev. 259, 267 (1899); see, Shawcross, The Functions and Responsibilities of an Advocate 26 (1958).

30. Code of Ethics (Ala.), § 12, *supra* note 18, at CXVI; cf. ABA Old Canons, *supra* Intro. note 29, Canon 5, and see ABA CPR, *supra* ch. VIII, note 12, EC 7–13, and DR 7–103(A) and (B).

31. Code of Ethics (Ala.), § 14, *supra* note 18, at CXVII; accord: ABA Old Canons, *supra* Intro., note 29, Canon 30, and ABA CPR,

supra ch. VIII, note 12, EC 2–3 and EC 2–30, and DR 2–109(A) (1) and DR 7–102(A) (1).

32. Code of Ethics (Ala.), § 13, *supra* note 18, at CXVII; cf. ABA Old Canons, *supra* Intro., note 29, Canons 5 and 31; and cf. ABA CPR, *supra* ch. VIII, note 12, EC 2–29 and EC 2–26, and see EC 2–27 and EC 2–28.

33. ABA Old Canons, *supra* Intro., note 29, Canon 5.

34. ABA CPR, *supra* ch. VIII, note 12, EC 2–29.

duty to serve imposed by the Alabama Code of 1887 nor with the duty to serve that is the rule and pride of the British bar, should we end up with the same insistence on no-personal-belief that characterizes the British bar and was the rule of the old Alabama Code?

If the American lawyer is free to pick his own clients, free to follow conscience, and need not represent "bad" clients and causes, should it still be considered unprofessional for the lawyer to express his personal belief (as he often does) in the justice of the cause he speaks for? Should we revert to the older religious and moralist position that the only evil opinion is one that supports evil or is itself a dishonest opinion? Against the value to a client of the righteous zeal of his lawyer expressing an honest belief in the cause he speaks for, it seems almost a trivial cause for complaint that such plain speaking might violate a rule of evidence (which could be changed) or occasionally prejudice a client whose cause was not so warmly supported (perhaps because it did not merit such warmth). Why should we adhere to a rule that is neither honored in practice by the bar nor believed by the American public. At least while serving as jurors, under the lawyer's spell, most laymen I think are led to feel that the very appearance of a lawyer in a case means that his heart as well as his talent and his purse are riding on the issue. Further, it cannot be ignored that identification of a lawyer with the cause and client he represents is the more common in America than in England even when the American lawyer refrains from expressing personal belief; for we have here no split profession, no solicitor to screen clients for the courtroom lawyer; the public knows (or thinks it knows) that the lawyer has taken the case because he wants it.

It seems to me that the no-personal-belief (no-personal-opinion) rule is still worthwhile,[35] imperatively so, despite these objections to it. It is still the only satisfactory approach yet found to maintain the existence of the lawyer as an independent professional, enabling him to counsel those who need counseling without qualms over personal, moral delinquency. To the extent that the rule works against the identification of counsel with client and cause, it represents an essential element of our system of justice.

---

35. See H. Taft, Ethics of the Law 13, 19 (1914); C. Wolverton, "The Ethics of Advocacy," 8 The American Lawyer 62, 66 (1900).

In one important respect, the no-personal-belief rule has the same compelling professional necessity in the United States that it does in England. Even in the watered down form in which *duty to counsel* emerges in the new *Code of Professional Responsibility*, many American lawyers *are* duty bound to represent clients they believe guilty or otherwise undesirable, duty bound because a court has appointed them, or a bar association requested them to serve. Moreover, the expanded recognition of a Constitutional *right to counsel* in the second half of this century means that lawyers in vastly increasing numbers become "appointed counsel," with a *duty to counsel* imposed by court and bar.[36] The word ought to be spread to the lay public that these duty bound lawyers act in the tradition of our calling, that they speak not for themselves but for the sake of right guaranteed by law.

A more general understanding of this unique representative function of the lawyer will also have a consequence beyond the group of lawyers who are strictly duty bound to serve. The rule that counsel, appointed or otherwise, need not, indeed must not, express his personal belief in the forlorn cause or the pariah he represents gives less reason, less excuse, for any lawyer, whether from timidity, prejudice, or venality, to back off from service to those who need it. It may be expected that more and better lawyers will volunteer their services in unpopular causes, lawyers who otherwise might stand aloof lest they be tainted.

Finally, even apart from the cases which now draw public attention and the attention of the courts to expanding areas of right to counsel, it remains today as it has been for centuries that the law to ordinary men and women is a vast complexity, urgently calling for expert explanation, guidance, representation. The need of such counsel increases daily, and argues as urgently for the freedom (even if there be no duty) of lawyers to take cases, whether or not they are morally committed to a client's views. If the notion of the lawyer's dispassion expressed in the no-personal-belief rule becomes the well established norm, understood alike by profession and the public, there is a greater possibility that every man will find counsel, and every man receive what the law allows him. Certainly no claim is made here that

---

36. See Argersinger v. Hamlin, 407 U.S. 25, 92 S.Ct. 2006, 2012, 32 L. Ed.2d 530 (1972); Criminal Justice Act of 1964, 18 U.S.C.A. § 3006A (amended 1968, 1970).

this will end the problems of the unfilled needs for legal services, nor of the proper bounds of the lawyer's *duty to counsel* without regard to the size of fee or of any fee; those are subjects for more than one more book.[37] But a whole-hearted acceptance by bar and public of the no-personal-belief rule will remove at least one substantial obstacle in the way of making legal services available to all.

Those who argue most vehemently for the complete commitment of the lawyer, mind and soul, to his client's causes,[38] are often those who suffer most from the too well accepted notion that a lawyer takes only those cases he believes in. The unpopular defendant may have no choice but to take his lawyer where he finds him, from among those of similar views. But education of the bar to the desirability of dispassion as the best assurance of the independence of the profession will ultimately make available to the unpopular litigant a wider choice of the best of legal talent. Disciplining lawyers for violation of the no-personal-belief rule ought to follow not precede a mass conversion of American lawyers to the conviction that the rule of no-personal-belief lies at the heart of the independence and integrity of the bar.

This argument for the no-personal-belief rule, as a rule of professional independence, does not deny a lawyer his personal beliefs, only the expression of them in argument to judge or jury in a deliberate attempt to add personal support to a cause entitled only to professional support. Even with the rule well established, there will remain predilection, belief, urgings conscious and otherwise, pecking at the lawyer, affecting his fervor, his eagerness or reluctance to undertake one cause and reject another, to make one legal move rather than another. A lawyer's belief in the cause of oppressed minorities draws him irresistibly to their defense.[39] His intense affections and hates for one or another political party, for a particular politician or union leader, a corporation, or life style, draw him irresistibly into associations where those affections and hates can be converted into legal action. No rule of the bar can eliminate the thousand more

---

37. See Marks, Leswing, and Fortinsky, The Lawyer, The Public and Professional Responsibility (1972).

38. See J. Rubin, Do It! 160 (1970), Marks, Leswing, and Fortinsky, The Lawyer, The Public, And Professional Responsibility 201 (1972).

39. Marks, Leswing and Fortinsky, The Lawyer, The Public and Professional Responsibility, 182–183 (1972).

or less subtle influences that press upon us all our lives. The rule can minimize the effect of those influences in court, to the end that juries will not be charmed or enraged into confusing or fusing lawyer and client.

With or without his expression of personal opinion, no judge or jury that came under the spell of Clarence Darrow could be oblivious of his lifelong abhorrence of any capital punishment.[40] What of Charles Phillips and the Courvoisier jury?

At this date it is hazardous to speculate on the thoughts in the mind of that jury or of Phillips when he spoke of the youth of Courvoisier:

> "[E]ven supposing him guilty of the murder　.　.　.
> it is better far that in the dreadful solitude of exile
> he should, though not in the sight of man, yet before
> the presence of God, atone by lingering repentance for
> the deed, than that he should now be sent in the dawn-
> ing of his manhood to an ignominious death in a case
> where the truth is not clear."

It might only have been rhetoric, that solemn caution:

> "To violate the living temple which the Lord hath
> made, to quench the fire that His breath [hath] given,
> is an awful and tremendous responsibility. And the
> word 'Guilty' once pronounced, let me remind you, is ir-
> revocable."

We do know that some seventeen years after Courvoisier was hanged, Phillips then "One of Her Majesty's Commissioners of the Court for the Relief of Insolvent Debtors" published a small and remarkable pamphlet entitled *Vacation Thoughts on Capital Punishments*. He said there were uncertainties and inequities and errors in the administration and review of death sentences; many sentenced to death never hanged; others did, later found to be innocent. "What deduction do we draw from this?" he asked. "The obvious and the righteous one, that erring man should not inflict punishment fatal and irreparable." [41]

---

40. See C. Darrow, The Story of My Life, 180, 232, 336, 359–375 (1932), and [C. Darrow], Attorney for the Damned 460 (A. Weinberg ed. 1957).

41. C. Phillips, Vacation Thoughts on Capital Punishments 65 (1857); cf. J. F. Stephen, "Mr. Phillips on Capital Punishment," 2 The Satur-day Review 635 (1856).

As evidence of the lack of uniformity in the administration of capital punishment, Phillips reproduced ". . . a list from 1840 to the present year, of capital convictions, with their several results, confining ourselves to those involving violence." It was a long list, including the names of 45 murderers, only 24 of them hanged. Heading the list, the capital convictions for 1840, were three names: James Dodd, in March, "burglary with violence;" Samuel Bailey, in May, "wounding, intent to murder; " Constantine Sullivan, in July, "rape;" all "transported for life." [42] Where was Courvoisier, convicted of murder in June, 1840, hanged July, 1840? Inadvertence? Modesty? Forgotten? Too painful to be set down?

Whatever the reason for the omission, the bitterness of the aftermath of the confessions of Courvoisier and of the personal attacks on Charles Phillips could not be forgotten. In the pamphlet, Phillips recounted the cases of the Perrys, the mother reputed a witch, and her two sons, one half-witted, executed for murdering a man who reappeared three years later. "From the grave of the Perrys, a monitory voice should have arisen," wrote Phillips, "repealing forever capital punishments in England." Fifty-six years later, he continued, Mary Hicks and her 11 year old daughter were executed for witchcraft.[43]

"We have made mistakes enough," Phillips argued, "and for a time we even fostered them by the promise of reward upon conviction[.]" [44] A flame was rekindled; suddenly he seemed back before Courvoisier's jury denouncing the police conspiracy. "[M]iscreants," the pamphlet continued, "tempted by the 'pieces of silver,' counted their blood-money upon the coffins of their victims. The foulest accusations supported by the perjury as foul, often proved fatally successful, bewildering the juries into the most terrible injustices." [45] The fire was gone. Charles Phillips died two years later, age 70.

42. C. Phillips, Vacation Thoughts on Capital Punishments 62–64 (1857).

43. *Id.* 68–71.

44. *Id.* 71.

45. *Id.*

THE MAN-IN-TROUBLE—A CONCLUSION

The cynic, even having come this far, may yet answer with malicious enthusiasm, "Yes, now I know. Now I know who it is that loves a lawyer." Who? Besides God, the lawyer's present wife, the relatives who still say "Hello," and an under-strength squad of tolerant friends? "Murderers! Murderers! who tell their lawyers they are guilty, and are still defended!"

Well *The Queen v. Courvoisier* is an unusual case. It forced self-examination upon the profession for the very reason that it deals in ultimates that common lawyers are schooled to avoid; yet even *Courvoisier's Case* does not stand entirely alone. Other lawyers have met extreme ethical challenges similar to the one that never ceased to trouble Charles Phillips.[1] Most lawyers never encounter anything quite so stark to test their stomachs. Yet every lawyer in active practice finds the golden absolutes he grew up with daily becoming less absolute, as he lends an ear and some help to the man-in-trouble.

The young lawyer is shocked at much of what he hears from clients in confidence. Embittered accounts of human depravity (and occasionally also of incredible generosity) that ought to exist only in storybook tales.

The shock wears off. The variety continues, but misfortune seems more usual than any innocent or even a law professor could ever have imagined. Cruelty, oppression, deception, unhappiness, worry, strain, incomprehension, frustration, bewilderment—a sorcerer's bag of misery. These become the expected. Then the saddest of all human cries: "Who will help me?" Try God, and politics, and medicine, and a soft shoulder, sooner or later a lawyer. Too many do.

The lawyer, as lawyer, is no sweet kind loving moralizer. He assumes he is needed, and that no one comes to see him to pass the time of day. He is a prober, an analyzer, a planner, a decision maker, a compromiser, eventually a scrapper, a man with a strange devotion to his client. Beautifully strange, or so it seems to the man-in-trouble; ugly strange to the untroubled onlooker.

1. *See* The King-Emperor v. Barendra Kumar Ghose, 22 Calcutta W. N. 170, 178–184 (1923); Scott v. The State, 114 Tex.Cr.R. 631, 26 S.W.2d 263 (1930), *explained* in J. York, "ABA President-Elect Jaworski-Defender of Unpopular Causes," 51 Harvard Law Record, No. 4, page 6 (1970); Tukiar and The King, 52 Commw. L.R. 335 (Austl. 1934).

It is a devotion that cannot be dismissed as the natural product of a fee. Money has never assured loyalty in combat, not when someone might get hurt—him that gives and him that receives. The man-in-trouble finds in the lawyer the informed fortitude he himself lacks, the sturdy professionalism that lasts through reverses that long since exhausted both the client and his money.

This man-in-trouble is not always, nor even usually, a Courvoisier. He is you, and I, and our neighbor, at the right moment. The lawyer, some lawyer, is there for each of us, with a lack of discrimination among clients and causes so disgusting to authoritarians of every stripe and stature. Some lawyers, as individual lawyers, become the favorites of power. But as a profession, the independent lawyer like the free press is unpopular with those who consider democracy only an inefficiency and other people's liberties an inconvenience. This is not only the lesson of our English legal heritage. It is the story of our own times—smudged on police blotters and written in the records of courts,[2] not the least our highest.[3] Even headlines from distant lands bear their negative tribute to the profession:

ATHENS EXILES

4 LAWYERS IN

COURT DISPUTE [4]

* * *

3 TOP BRAZIL LAWYERS

TELL OF 3 DAYS OF FEAR

Say They Were Seized, Blindfolded, Held in Jail Without Knowing Where or Why.[5]

2. Cooper v. Superior Court, 55 Cal.2d 291, 10 Cal.Rptr. 842, 359 P.2d 274 (1961); Sobol v. Perez, 289 F.Supp. 392 (E.D.La., 1968); Sanders v. Russell, 401 F.2d 241 (5th Cir. 1968).

3. Holt v. Virginia, 381 U.S. 131, 85 S.Ct. 1375, 14 L.Ed.2d 290 (1965); Escobedo v. Illinois, 378 U.S. 478, 84 S.Ct. 1758, 12 L.Ed.2d 977 (1964); Miranda v. Arizona, 384 U.S. 436, 86 S.Ct. 1602, 16 L.Ed.2d 694 (1966); reh. denied, California v. Stewart, 385 U.S. 890, 87 S.Ct.

11, 17 L.Ed.2d 121; Johnson v. Avery, 393 U.S. 483, 89 S.Ct. 747, 21 L.Ed.2d 718 (1969); In re Anastaplo, 366 U.S. 82, 114–116, 81 S. Ct. 978, 995–997, 6 L.Ed.2d 135, 154–155 (1960) (dissenting opinion, Black, J.); reh. denied, 368 U.S. 869, 82 S.Ct. 21, 7 L.Ed.2d 69 and see cases, supra ch. X, note 43.

4. International Herald Tribune (Paris), July 4, 1969, page 2 (Reuters).

5. Los Angeles Times, Nov. 8, 1970, Sec. A, page 4.

Of course there are unsavory lawyers. They were people before they were lawyers, and becoming lawyers has not reformed them. Most of them would have become disreputable for the solid old vices of lying and stealing if they had never gotten into the profession; and benefit-of-the-doubt makes getting rid of them at times difficult. Some of them are not "gentlemen," a term increasingly difficult to define, and in this context dangerous to define too thinly lest it confuse decency with meekness, and so emasculate the profession. The profession itself also has its weaknesses; some stubborn vices that yield only slowly to change; some really defects in the law itself, inevitably laid to the administrators who are putting the law to work.

But a substantial part of the major criticism of the lawyer—his presumed indifference to truth—is rooted in fundamental misconception of the lawyer's mission. The lawyer does not exist to spread the word of truth and goodness to the ends of the earth. Somewhat more limited, the lawyer's mission is the nonetheless awesome task of trying to make a reality of equality before the law. If your "truth" or mine gets dented some in the process, it is only because we deal here with something less than the Kingdom of God, and something more than one Truth.

While we work at improving the profession and the whole system of law, its fairness, efficiency, and availability, we need remind ourselves and non-lawyers who will listen that our lawyer's mission is vital to any democratic society that hopes to stay that way. Old history and current history tell us, and the increasing complexity of just getting through 24 hours in today's world tells us again, that only through the mediation of the lawyer can rights of person and property be vindicated. The horrible old rule that men indicted for felony could have no counsel resisted change so long, because it served the purposes of unlimited power that anyone in the way should be denied the means of making his opposition effective. Every government (or at least the temporary occupants of rooms in buildings built by government) fancies itself more secure if the voices of opposition are muted. And the first steps toward such "security" are encroachments on freedom of the press and on the lawyer-client relationship.

In recent years English solicitors have been advised by their governing Law Society that:

> There appears to be one case, and one case only, in
> which, despite the existence of privilege, a solicitor is

at liberty to disclose confidential information, and that
is where in a National Emergency the national interest
demands disclosure.[6]

Unless the lawyer has been consulted for advice as to how to
commit a crime, that advice of The Law Society, it seems to me,
is one of greatest potential danger that has confronted the Anglo-American profession since abolition of the rack. Only the
most absent-minded bunglers would neglect to justify suppression
of liberty in the name of "the national interest." The law, and
access to the law through lawyers are for all men—black and
white, rich and poor, the orthodox and the heretic, murderer
and saint, the "good guys" and the "bad guys," patriot and traitor, or they are for no man.

Some years back, the High Court of Australia considered the
appeal of an aborigine convicted of murdering a policeman, the
case of *Tukiar and The King*.[7] Tukiar had confessed in confidence to his lawyer. After that, in the presence of the jury, the
lawyer ". . . said that he had a specially important matter
which he desired to discuss with the Judge. He was in a predicament," he said, "the worst predicament that he had encoun-
tered in all his legal career." [8] In chambers, Tukiar's lawyer reported the confession to the judge,[9] who so charged the jury as
to raise a more than ordinary suspicion that Tukiar's failure to
testify meant that he was guilty.[10] In reversing the conviction,
the court said that Tukiar's lawyer "was not entitled to divulge
what he had learned from the prisoner as his counsel." Moreover, it added:

> "Our system of administering justice necessarily impos-
> es upon those who practice advocacy duties which have
> no analogies, and the system cannot dispense with their
> strict observance." [11]

The profession of law is unlike any other at times indeed
without "analogies." There are rules, but there are hard questions of propriety to which moral absolutes give no ready answers. Deciding to become a lawyer is a decision to wrack not

---

6. Lund, *supra* ch. IX, note 50, at 98–99.

7. 52 Commw.L.R. 335 (Austl. 1934).

8. *Id.* 341.

9. *Id.* 344.

10. *Id.* 343.

11. *Id.* 347.

only brain but conscience, a turbulence that others avoid—by staying out. The lawyer's choice is the choice of the man who is "not prepared to creep into a corner." [12] His is a learned profession, even a great profession, but it is a learned profession that has deliberately walked down from the tower to mingle with the people. The lawyer shares with the people their best moments and their worst.

12. J. F. Stephen, "The Morality of Advocacy," 3 The Cornhill Magazine 447, 452 (1861).

BIBLIOGRAPHY

I. MANUSCRIPTS

Commissioners of Metropolitan Police: Miscellaneous papers re murder of Lord William Russell, 1840. Public Record Office, London ....VI, 131–132

Coroner's inquest, death of Lord William Russell, 1840: Depositions. Public Record Office, London. Summons, jury list, report and verdict. Library of Westminster Abbey, London ......VI, 17, 22

Preliminary Examination of Francois Benjamin Courvoisier, 1840: Depositions. Public Record Office, London ..VI, 19–22, 33–34, 37–38

II. PRINTED WORKS

Adams, John. *Diary and Autobiography of John Adams.* 4 vols. L. H. Butterfield, ed. Cambridge, Mass.: Belknap Press of Harvard University Press, 1961 171

——. *Legal Papers of John Adams.* 3 vols. L. Kinvin Wroth and Hiller B. Zobel, ed. Cambridge, Mass.: Belknap Press of Harvard University Press, 1965 ....166, 169–170, 171

The Advisory Opinions of the Board of Governors. vol. 1. Henry M. Gray, compil. State Bar of Oklahoma, [1936] 180

Ainsworth, W. Harrison. *Jack Sheppard.* A Romance. With illustrations on steel by George Cruikshank. London: George Routledge & Sons, Limited, [1839] 127–128

Aiyar, K. V. Krishnaswami. *Professional Conduct and Advocacy* being a series of lectures delivered to apprentices-at-law. 3d ed. 1953. Oxford: University Press, Indian Branch, 1960, reprinted with corrections. [1st ed., 1940].

Alabama State Bar Association. See *Proceedings; Report.*

Alexander, James. *A Brief Narrative of the Case and Trial of John Peter Zenger.* Stanley Nider Katz, ed. Cambridge, Mass.: Harvard University Press, 1963 5

American Bar Association. See: *American Bar News; Canons of Ethics; Canons of Professional Ethics; Code of Professional Ethics; Code of Professional Responsibility; Coordinator and Public Relations Bulletin; Opinions of the Committee on Professional Ethics; Reports of the American Bar Association.*

American Bar News. Chicago: American Bar Association, 1972 ..183

American College of Trial Lawyers. See *Code of Trial Conduct.*

American Jurisprudence. And 1971 Cumulative Supplement, vols. 39–58, 1942–1948; 2d Series, vols. 1–57, 1962–1971. San Francisco: Bancroft-Whitney Company, 1971 ....43, 137

Andrews, William, ed. *The Lawyer, in History, Literature, and Humour.* London: William Andrews & Co., 1896 ----------1, 2

The Annals of Our Times. A Diurnal of Events, Social and Political, Home and Foreign, From the Accession of Queen Victoria . . . by Joseph Irving. 2d ed. 1871. London: Macmillan and Co., 1890. [1st ed., 1869] --------------------------------------VI

The Annual Register. Or a view of the History, and Politics of the year 1840. London: J. G. F. & J. Rivington, and others, 1841 --162

The Annual Register. A Review of Public Events At Home And Abroad, For the Year 1866. New Series. Part II. London: Rivingtons, 1867 -------------------------------------- 236–237

Annual Statement, 1915. See *General Council of the Bar.* Aquinas. See: St. Thomas Aquinas. Arnould, Joseph. See Campbell [Lord], *The Lives of the Chief Justices of England.*

Atlay, J. [James] B. [Beresford]. *Famous Trials of the Century.* London: Grant Richards, 1899 ----------------------VI, 26, 129

——. *The Victorian Chancellors.* 2 vols. London: Smith, Elder, & Co., 1906–1908 --47

Attenborough, F. L., ed. and tr. *The Laws of the Earliest English Kings.* Cambridge: University Press, 1922 ------------------50

Attorney for the Damned. See: [Darrow, Clarence].

Bacon, Francis. "A Preparation toward the Union of the Laws of England and Scotland," 5 *Works* 83. See: Bacon, Francis, *The Works* . . . ---56

——. *The Works of Francis Bacon, Lord Chancellor of England.* 17 vols. Basil Montagu, ed. London: William Pickering, 1825–1834 ---56

Bacon's Essays. See: Whately, Richard.

Ballantine, William. *Some Experiences of a Barrister's Life.* 8th ed. London: Richard Bentley & Son, 1883 [1st ed., 1882] --43, 44, 65, 66, 88, 131, 132, 136, 160, 185, 223, 226

"The Bar Dinner to M. Berryer," 40 *The Law Times* 16 [Nov. 12, 1864]. London: Law Times, 1865 --------------------213–216

Baring-Gould, S. *The Lives of the Saints,* rev. ed. 16 vols. Edinburgh: John Grant, 1914 ---------------------------------------13

Baxter, Richard. *Additional Notes on the Life and Death of Sir Matthew Hale.* The Late Universally Honoured and Loved Lord Chief Justice of the King's Bench. London: Richard Janeway, 1682 ---248

——. *Cain And Abel.* London: Thomas Parkhurst, 1689 --------146

Benét, Stephen Vincent. "The Devil and Daniel Webster," 2 *Selected Works* 32–46 [q.v.] --1

——. *Selected Works of Stephen Vincent Benét.* 2 vols. New York: Farrar & Rinehart, Inc., 1942 ----------------------------1

Bentham, Jeremy. *The Works of Jeremy Bentham.* 10 vols. John Bowring, ed. Edinburgh: William Tait, 1843 ----------------12

Bible. See: *The New English Bible: The Apocrypha; The Scofield Reference Bible.*

Biographical and Descriptive Sketches of the Distinguished Characters which compose the Unrivalled Exhibition of Madame Tussaud and Sons. London: Mandame Tussaud and Sons, 1840 ---------VI

Birkett [Lord]. *Six Great Advocates.* Harmondsworth: Penguin Books, 1961 ---240

Biron, [Henry] Chartres. *Without Prejudice.* Impressions of Life and Law. London: Faber and Faber Limited, 1936 --26, 129, 136

Black's Law Dictionary. rev. 4th ed. St. Paul: West Publishing Co., 1968 ---4

Blackstone, William. *Commentaries on the Laws of England.* 2 vols. William Carey Jones, ed. San Francisco: Bancroft-Whitney Company, 1916. [1st ed., 1765–1769] -----------50, 52, 145, 149, 153

Blaustein, Albert P. and Charles O. Porter. *The American Lawyer.* Chicago: The University of Chicago Press, 1954 --------------9

Bleackley, Horace William. *The Hangmen of England.* London: Chapman & Hall, 1929 ---VI

———. *Jack Sheppard.* With an Epilogue on Jack Sheppard in Literature and Drama, A Bibliography, A Note on Jonathan Wild, and a Memoir of Horace Bleackley by S. M. Ellis . . . Edinburgh: William Hodge & Company, Limited, 1933 ---64, 128–129

Bloom, Murray Teigh. *The Trouble With Lawyers.* New York: Simon & Schuster, 1968 -----------------------------------14

Bollandistes. See: *Vies Des Saints.*

Borchard, Edwin M. *Convicting The Innocent.* Hamden, Conn.: Archon Books, 1961. [1st ed., 1932] ----------------------------5–6

Boswell, James. *Boswell's Life of Johnson.* Including Boswell's Journal of a Tour to the Hebrides And Johnson's Diary of a Journey into North Wales. 6 vols. George Birkbeck Hill, ed. Oxford: Clarendon Press, 1887 -----------------------164, 250, 253

Boulton, W. W. *A Guide to Conduct and Etiquette at the Bar of England and Wales.* 4th ed. London: Butterworths, 1965 --164, 165, 198, 216–217

Bracton, *De Legibus et Consuetudinibus Angliae.* George E. Woodbine, ed. And, *sub. nom. Bracton on the Laws and Customs of England.* 2 vols. Transl., rev., and notes by Samuel E. Thorne. Cambridge, Mass.: The Selden Society and The Belknap Press of Harvard University Press, 1968 ------------------14, 145, 159

Brampton [Baron]. *The Reminiscences of Sir Henry Hawkins Baron Brampton.* 2 vols. Richard Harris, ed. London: Edward Arnold, 1904 --VI

Braun, Richard L. "Ethics in Criminal Cases: A Response," 55 *Georgetown Law Journal* 1048 (1967).----------------------7

Brice, A. [Arthur] H. M. [Montefiore]. *Look Upon the Prisoner.* Studies in Crime. Alexander Cairns, ed. London: Hutchinson & Co. (Publishers) Ltd., [1928] ------------------------------------VI

Bridges, Yseult. *Two Studies in Crime.* London: Hutchinson & Co. (Publishers) Ltd., 1959 --------------------26, 129, 131, 132

Brock, Alan. *A Casebook of Crime* . . . . London: Rockliff, 1948 --26, 129

Brougham [Lord]. *The Life and Times of Henry Lord Brougham.* Written by Himself. 3 vols. New York: Harper & Bros., 1871–1872 --188–189

——. *The Works of Henry Lord Brougham* . . . . Revised and corrected by himself. 11 vols. Edinburgh: A. & C. Black, 1872 --189

Broughton [Lord]. *Recollections of a Long Life.* With Additional Extracts from His Private Diaries. 6 vols. Lady Dorchester, ed. London: John Murray, 1911 --------------------162–163, 187

Burke, Peter. *Celebrated Trials Connected With the Aristocracy in the Relations of Private Life.* London: William Benning & Co., 1849 --VI

Burke's Peerage. 105th ed. Peter Townend, ed. London: Burke's Peerage Limited, 1970 ------------------------------------VI

Burnet, Gilbert. *The Life and Death of Sir Matthew Hale, Kt.* Sometime Lord Chief Justice of His Majesties' Court of King's Bench. 2d ed. London: William Shrowsbery, 1682 --147–148, 248

Butler, Alban. *The Lives of the Saints.* 5 vols. Herbert Thurston and Norah Lesson, rev. New York: P. J. Kennedy & Sons, 1936 --13

Campbell [Lord]. *The Lives of the Chief Justices of England.* 6 vols. and index vol., incl. vols. 5 and 6, continued by Sir Joseph Arnould. Jersey City: Fred D. Linn & Company, 1881 ------------------54

——. *Lives of the Lord Chancellors and Keepers of the Great Seal of England, from the Earliest Times Till the Reign of King George IV.* 10 vols. 5th ed. London: John Murray, 1868 --------------1

——. *Speeches of Lord Campbell.* At the Bar, And In the House of Commons; with An Address to the Irish Bar as Lord Chancellor of Ireland. Edinburgh: Adams and Charles Black, 1842 --229–232

"Canons of Ethics of the American Bar Association." See: "Canons of Professional Ethics of the American Bar Association".

"Canons of Professional Ethics of the American Bar Association." [also known as "Canons of Ethics of the American Bar Association," and "Code of Professional Ethics of the American Bar Association]. Amended to 1963. In pamphlet, *The California State Bar Act and Rules of Professional Conduct* . . ., pp. 45–60. San Francisco: The State Bar of California, 1967. [As originally adopted, Aug. 27, 1908, 33 *Reports of the American Bar Association* 575–584, 1908.] --9, 137, 138, 139, 149, 177–178, 179, 180, 218, 259, 260–261, 264

Carter, Dan T. *Scottsboro. A Tragedy of the American South.* Baton Rouge: Louisiana State University Press, 1969 _____167

Central Criminal Court Sessions Papers. vol. XII, Session VII to Session XII. Eighth Session . . . Minutes of Evidence Taken in Shorthand by Henry Buckler. Case No. 1629, pp. 216–271. London: George Hebert, 1840 _____VI, 15, 132, 135

Chevalier, Ulysse. *Reportorium Hymnologicum.* Catalogue des Chants, Hymnes, Proses, Séquences, Tropes en usage dans L'Église Latine Depuis Lee Origines Jusqu'a Nos Jours. Extrait des *Analecta Bollandiana.* 6 vols. Louvain: Polleunis and Ceuterick, and others, 1892–1920 _____13

Cobb, [Geoffrey] Belton. *The First Detectives.* And the Early Career of Richard Mayne Commissioner of Police. London: Faber and Faber Ltd., 1957 _____VI

"Code of Ethics," [Alabama State Bar Association]. *Proceedings of the 18th Annual Meeting of the Alabama State Bar Association.* pp. CXII–CXXV. [q. v.] _____176–177, 259, 260, 264

———. 35 *Report of the Alabama State Bar Association* 139–152. [q. v.] _____259, 260

"Code of Legal Ethics of the California Bar Association." *Code of Professional Ethics of the American Bar Association* [*1908*] . . . *and of the California Bar Association.* pp. 33–45. [q. v.] _____180

"Code of Professional Ethics of the American Bar Association." See: "Canons of Professional Ethics of the American Bar Association."

Code of Professional Ethics of the American Bar Association [*1908*] . . . *and of the California Bar Association* . . . . San Francisco: Bancroft-Whitney Company, [1910] _____180

Code of Professional Responsibility. [Adopted August 12, 1969; amended February 24, 1970]. Printed by Martindale-Hubbell, Inc. Chicago: American Bar Association, 1970 _____137, 138, 139, 181–183, 218, 259, 261–262, 264, 265, 266

Code of Trial Conduct. Los Angeles: American College of Trial Lawyers, 1963, [Adopted 1956]; and 1972 Revision _____178, 180, 182, 198, 217, 260, 262

Cohen, Felix S. *The Legal Conscience, Selected Papers of Felix S. Cohen.* Lucy Kramer Cohen, ed. copr. Yale University Press, 1960. Archon Books, 1970 _____15

———. "Modern Ethics and the Law," 4 *Brooklyn Law Review* 33 (1934) _____15

———. ———, reprinted in Cohen, Felix S. *The Legal Conscience* . . ., p. 17. [q. v.] _____15

Coke, Edward. *The Third Part of the Institutes of the Laws of England.* Concerning High Treason, and other Pleas of the Crown and Criminal Cases. London: E. and R. Brooke, 1797. [1st publ. 1644] _____48, 53

Coleridge, Samuel Taylor. "Duties and Needs of an Advocate." Oct. 27, 1831. *Table Talk,* pp. 140, 141. [q. v.] --------------211–212

——. *The Table Talk and Omniana of Samuel Taylor Coleridge.* T. Ashe, ed. London: George Bell and Sons, 1884 ----------211–212

A Complete Collection of State Trials. 2d ed. London: J. Walthoe Sr. et al, 1730. See Table of Cases page 295.

——. See: Howell, T. B.

The Complete Newgate Calendar. vol. 5. G. T. Crook, ed. London: Privately Printed for the Navarre Society Limited, 1926 ------VI

"Constitution of the United States." *The Constitution of the United States of America Analysis and Interpretation.* Annotations of Cases Decided by the Supreme Court of the United States to June 22, 1964. Prepared by Legislative Reference Service, Library of Congress. Edward S. Corwin, ed. 1952; Norman J. Small, ed. 1964, Lester S. Jayson, superv. ed. Washington: U. S. Government Printing Office, 1964 -----------------------4, 157

Cooke, John. *The Vindication of the Professors & Profession of the Law.* London: Matthew Walbancke, 1646 --------------4, 12, 147

Cooley, Thomas M. *A Treatise on the Constitutional Limitations which Rest Upon the Legislative Power of the States of the American Union.* Boston: Little, Brown, and Company, 1868 -----175

Coordinator and Public Relations Bulletin. Chicago: American Bar Association, 1971

Correspondence Between Samuel Warren, Esq., Barrister-at-Law, and Charles Phillips, Esq., Relative to the Trial of Courvoisier. With a Preface and Appendix. London: L. King, 1849 ----62, 132–133, 134, 135, 139–140, 159–160, 188, 192, 194, 203, 220, 221–222

Cottrell, Leonard. *Madame Tussaud.* London: Evans Brothers Limited, 1951 ---------------------------------------220

The Court Journal. London, 1840 ---------------------------101

Dacey, Norman F. *How to Avoid Probate!* New York: Crown Publishers, Inc., 1965 ---------------------------------2, 14

[Darrow, Clarence]. *Attorney for the Damned.* Arthur Weinberg, ed. Foreword by Justice William O. Douglas. New York: Simon and Schuster, 1957 ------------------------149, 179, 268

Darrow, Clarence. *The Story of My Life.* New York: Charles Scribner's Sons, 1932 ------------------------------149, 268

Davies, John. *A Report of Cases and Matters Resolved and Adjudged in the King's Courts in Ireland . . .* Now First translated into English. [With "A Preface Dedicatory"]. Dublin: Sarah Cotter, 1762. [1st publ. in Fr., 1615] ------------------52, 146

Davis, John Denis. *The Moral Obligations of Catholic Civil Judges.* Washington, D. C.: The Catholic University of America Press, 1953 ---208

Deans, R. [Richard] Storry. *Notable Trials.* Romances of the Law Courts. London: Cassell and Company, Limited, 1906 --------VI

"The Declaration of Independence—1776." *Documents Illustrative of the Formation of the Union of the American States.* pp. 22–25. [q. v.] --157, 166

"The Defence of Courvoisier, And the Plea for It." *The Law Magazine*, vol. 43 Old Series, vol. 12 New Series, page 26 (1850). London: Henry Butterworth, 1850 ----------------203, 210, 212

Delachenal, Roland. *Histoire des avocats au Parlement de Paris, 1300–1600.* Paris: Librairie Plon. E. Plon, Nourrit et Cie, Imprimeurs-Editeurs, 1885 --13

Dickens, Charles. *The Posthumous Papers of the Pickwick Club.* 2 vols. in 1. Boston: D. Lothrop And Company, [188?] --------47

——. *A Tale of Two Cities.* Boston: D. Lothrop And Company, 188?] --64]

Dictionary of National Biography. 22 vols. Sir Leslie Stephen and Sir Sidney Lee, ed. Oxford: University Press, 1917 --44, 47, 220

Documents Illustrative of the Formation of the Union of the American States. Charles C. Tansill, ed. Washington: Government Printing Office, 1927 -------------------------------------157, 166

Drinker, Henry S. *Legal Ethics.* The William Nelson Cromwell Foundation. New York: Columbia University Press, 1953 --139, 149, 177, 180, 262

Dymond, Jonathan. *Essays on the Principles of Morality, and on the Private and Political Rights and Obligations of Mankind.* New York: Harper & Bros., 1834. [1st ed., 1829] --------12, 250, 251

Elliotson, John. "Courvoisier," being No. I of *Illustrations of Phrenology* . . . by George R. Lewis. London: S. Highley, 1841 --VI

"Eloquence of the Irish Bar." 3 *The Law Magazine* 303–340 (1830) --47

Encyclopaedia Britannica. 24 vols. Chicago: Encyclopaedia Britannica, Inc., 1948 --240

Erskine [Lord]. *Speeches of Lord Erskine, While At the Bar.* 4 vols. James L. High, ed. Chicago: Callaghan & Company, 1876 --156

Ethics Opinions. Opinions of the Committee on Legal Ethics of the Los Angeles County Bar Association with Rules of Professional Conduct and Canons of Professional Ethics Annotated. Los Angeles: Los Angeles County Bar Association and The Los Angeles Daily Journal, 1968; vol. 2 [1972] -----------------180

"Events of the Quarter." *The Law Magazine.* Or Quarterly Review of Jurisprudence, for August, 1840; and November, 1840. vol. 24, p. 238 (August, 1840). London: Saunders and Benning, 1840 --VI

The Examiner. London, 1840, 1849 --12, 128, 187–188, 189, 192–193, 203, 206–207, 221, 222–224, 225

The Execution of Francis Courvoisier for the Murder of Lord William Russell, opposite the debtor's door, this day. [broadsheet]. Pitts, *Seven Dials,* [1840] --129

Foote, Samuel. "The Devil Upon Two Sticks." [1768]. 3 *The Works of Samuel Foote* 1–57. [q. v.] --1

——. *The Works of Samuel Foote.* 3 vols. Jon Bee, ed. London: Sherwood, Gilbert, and Piper, 1830 --1

Forsyth, William. *Hortensius.* An Historical Essay on the Office and Duties of an Advocate. 2d ed. London: John Murray, 1874. [1st ed., 1849] --189, 251–252

Fortescue, John. *De Laudibus Legum Angliae.* S. B. Chrimes, ed. and tr. Cambridge: University Press, 1942. [written c. 1460] --50

Frank, Jerome and Barbara Frank. *Not Guilty.* Garden City, N. Y.: Doubleday & Company, Inc., 1957 --5–6

Freedman, Monroe H. "Professional Responsibility of the Criminal Defense Lawyer: The Three Hardest Questions." 64 *Michigan Law Review* 1469 (1966) --139, 209

——. "The Professional Responsibility of the Prosecuting Attorney." 55 *Georgetown Law Journal* 1030 (1967) --7

Frewen, Moreton. *Melton Mowbray, and Other Memories.* London: Herbert Jenkins, 1924 --26, 129

Froissart, John. *Sir John Froissart's Chronicles.* 2d ed. Thomas Johnes, ed. London: Longman, Hurst, Rees, and Orme, and J. White, 1806 --2

Fuller, Thomas. *The Holy State.* Cambridge: John Williams, 1642 --147

General Council of the Bar, Annual Statement, 1915. London: General Council of the Bar, 1915 --165

Gisborne, Thomas. *An Enquiry Into the Duties of Men in the Higher and Middle Classes of Society in Great Britain.* 2 vols. 2d ed. London: B. and J. White, 1795 --152, 251

——. *The Principles of Moral Philosophy Investigated, and Briefly Applied to the Constitution of Civil Society.* London: E. White & Son, 1789 --250

Glanvill. *Tractatus de legibus et consuetudinibus regni Anglie qui Glanvilla vocatur.* G. D. G. Hall, ed. and tr. *sub nom. The Treatise on the laws and customs of the realm of England commonly called Glanvill.* London: Nelson and Selden Society, 1965 --145

The Golden Legend or Lives of the Saints as Englished by William Caxton. 7 vols. F. S. Ellis, ed. London: J. M. Dent and Co., 1900 --13

Greville, Charles C. F. *The Greville Memoirs.* (Second Part). A Journal of the Reign of Queen Victoria from 1837 to 1852. 2 vols. Henry Reeve, ed. New York: D. Appleton and Company, 1885 --39, 40–41

Griffiths, Arthur [George Frederick]. *Mysteries of Police and Crime.* A General Survey of Wrongdoing And Its Pursuit. 2 vols. London: Cassell and Company, Limited, 1898 ----------------VI

Guillaume de Deguileville. See: Lydgate, John.

[Hale, Matthew]. *Contemplations Moral and Divine.* 2 vols. London: William Shrowsbury & John Leigh, 1676 ------------------148

Hansard's Parliamentary Debates. New Series, 1820–1830, 25 vols.; 3d series, 1831–1891, 356 vols. London: Baldwin and Craddock; and others ----------------------------------57–62, 143–144

The Harleian Miscellany. New ed. 12 vols. London: Robert Dutton, 1808–1811 ---10, 53

[Harris, Richard]. *Harris's Hints on Advocacy.* The Conduct of Cases Civil and Criminal. 18th ed., by George W. Keeton. London: Stevens & Sons, Limited, 1943 --------------------212

——. *Hints on Advocacy.* By A Barrister. London: Waterlow Bros. & Layton, 1879 --------------------------------------212

Harris, Richard. See: Brampton [Baron].

Hawkins, Henry. See: Brampton [Baron].

Hawkins, William. *A Treatise of the Pleas of the Crown.* 2 vols. 6th ed. Thomas Leach, ed. London: 1787. [1st publ. 1716–1721] --56

Hayward, Arthur L. [Laurence]. *The Days of Dickens.* A Glance at Some Aspects of Early Victorian Life in London. London: George Routledge & Sons Ltd., [1926] --------------------VI

Hazard, Geoffrey C. Jr. "Reflections on Four Studies of the Legal Profession." *Law and Society,* p. 48, A Supplement to *Social Problems,* Summer, 1965 -------------------------------------9

Henderson, Emily. *Recollections of the Public Career and Private Life of the Late John Adolphus.* The Eminent Barrister and Historian, With Extracts From His Diaries. London: T. Cautley Newby, 1871 ----------------------------43, 63, 129, 132, 135

Herschell [Lord]. *The Rights and Duties of An Advocate.* Being an Address Delivered to The Glasgow Juridical Society [1889]. Glasgow: The Glasgow Juridical Society and Wm. Hodge & Co., 1890 --241, 262–263

Hilbery, Malcolm. *Duty and Art in Advocacy.* London: Stevens & Sons Limited, 1959. (4th Impr., 1968) --------------------165

Hobhouse, John Cam. See Broughton [Lord].

Hoffman, David. *A Course of Legal Study.* Addressed to Students and the Profession Generally. 2 vols. 2d ed. Baltimore: Joseph Neal, 1836 --------------------------------------7, 171–173, 257

Holdsworth, William. *Charles Dickens as a Legal Historian.* New Haven: Yale University Press, 1928 ----------------------47

——. *A History of English Law.* 9 vols. and Index. Boston: Little, Brown and Company, 1922–1932 ----------------------------V

——. ——. vols. 10–16. London: Methuen & Co., 1938–1966 --V, 1, 2, 136, 240, 242

Holinshed's Chronicles. See: *Shakespeare's Holinshed.*

Holtzoff, Alexander. "Ethics of Advocacy." 16 *Buffalo Law Review* 583 (1967) ---155

House of Commons. See: *Journals of the House of Commons.*

House of Lords. See: *Journals of the House of Lords.*

Howell, T. B. *A Complete Collection of State Trials, and proceedings for high treason and other crimes and misdemeanors from the earliest period to the year 1783.* 33 vols. London: Longman, Hurst, Rees, Orme, and Brown, et al, 1816–1826. See Table of Cases page 295.

Hutchinson, J. [John]. *A Catalogue of notable Middle Templars.* With brief biographical notes. London: The Honourable Society of the Middle Temple, 1902 ---47

Irving, Joseph. See: *The Annals of Our Times.*

Journals of the House of Commons. vol. 91, Session 1836. London: House of Commons, [1836] ---57

Journals of the House of Lords. vol. 68, Session 1836. [London: House of Lords] ---48

The Jurist, editorials, vol. 4, No. 184, pp. 593–594 (July 18, 1840); vol. 13, No. 672, pp. 469–470 (Nov. 24, 1849), No. 675, pp. 497–499 (Dec. 15, 1849) --------------------------------143, 149, 225, 227

Kaplan, John and Jon R. Waltz. *The Trials of Jack Ruby.* New York: The Macmillan Company, 1965 -------------------------5

Keeton, George W. See: [Harris, Richard]. *Harris's Hints on Advocacy.*

Kingston, Charles. *A Gallery of Rogues.* New York: Frederick A. Stokes Company, [1924?] --------------------------------221

Langland, William. *Piers The Ploughman.* [1370]. J. F. Goodridge, tr. and ed. Rev. ed., 1966. Baltimore: Penguin Books, repr. 1968. [1st publ., 1959] ---------------------------------10, 11

Law and Lawyers. See: [Polson, Archer]. *Law and Lawyers* . . . .

The Law Magazine and Review. 55 vols. London: Saunders & Benning, 1828–1856. [vols. 1–31, June, 1828–May, 1844; vols. 32–55, also known as New Series, vols. 1–24, [Dec.], 1844–Feb., 1856] ----------------12, 161, 187, 198, 203–204, 210, 212, 227

The Law's Discovery. Or a brief detection of Sundry notorious errors and abuses contained in our English Laws, whereby thousands are annually stripped of their estates, and some of their lives. By a well-wisher to his country. London, 1653; in 6 *Harleian Miscellany* 322 [q. v.] ---------------------------------------53

"Legal Ethics," 1 *The American Lawyer* 46 (1893) -------------204

Legal Papers of John Adams. See: Adams, John.

The Letters of Queen Victoria. A Selection from Her Majesty's Correspondence Between the Years 1837 and 1861. Published by

Authority of His Majesty the King. 3 vols. Arthur Christopher Benson and Viscount Esher, ed. London: John Murray, 1907 --VI

Letters to Lord G. William Russell from various Writers 1817– 1845. 3 vols. London: Printed for Private Circulation at the Chiswick Press, 1915–1919 ----------------------------------VI

Levot, P. *Biographie Bretonne.* 2 vols. Vannes: Cauderan, 1852– 1857 ---13

Levy, Leonard W. *Origins of the Fifth Amendment.* The Right Against Self-Incrimination. New York: Oxford University Press, 1968 --153, 161

Lewis, George R. *Illustrations of Phrenology.* See: Elliotson, John.

"Licence of Counsel." *The Law Magazine,* vol. 39 Old Series, vol. 8 New Series, p. 53 (1848). London: W. Benning and Co., 1848 --161, 198, 212

". . . [T]he Licence of Prisoners' Counsel . . ." *The West-minster Review.* vol. 35, no. 1, Art. I, pp. 1–23 (Jan.–Apr., 1841). London: Henry Hooper, 1841 ----------------------------------211

Littell's Living Age. vol. 24 and vol. 25. Boston: E. Littell & Company, 1850 ---VI

Lobineau, Gui-Alexis. *Les Vies des Saints de Bretagne* . . . Rennes: Pierre-André Garnier, 1725 ------------------------13

The London Gazette. Numb. 19854, pp. 1149–1176, Friday, May 8, 1840. Published by Authority. London: Printed by Francis Watts, 1840 ---27

Los Angeles County Bar Association. See: *Ethics Opinions.*

Lund, Thomas. *A Guide to the Professional Conduct and Etiquette of Solicitors.* London: The Law Society, 1960. (Repr. 1967) ----------------------------164, 165, 198, 216–217, 273

Lydgate, John. *The Pilgrimage of the Life of Man.* [1426]. transl. from Guillaume de Deguileville [1330, 1355]. F. J. Furnivall, ed. London: Early English Text Society, 1899, 1901, 1904 --------11

Macmillan [Lord]. *Law & Other Things.* Cambridge: University Press, 1937 ---13

Marks, F. Raymond, with Kirk Leswing and Barbara A. Fortinsky. *The Lawyer, The Public, And Professional Responsibility.* Chicago: American Bar Foundation, 1972 -------------267–268

Masseron, Alexandre. *Saint Yves.* ed. L'Art et Les Saints. Paris: Henri Laurens, [1923?] -----------------------------------13

Matheolus. *Les Lamentations de Matheolus.* Et le Livre De Leesce de Jehan Le Fèvre, De Resson. Poèmes Françsais du XIVᵉ Siècle. A.-G Van Hamel, ed. 2 vols. Paris: Émile Bouillon, 1892–1905 --12

Mayer, Martin. *The Lawyers.* New York: Harper & Row, 1967 --7

Megarry, R. E. *Lawyer and Litigant in England.* The Hamlyn Lectures, 14th Series. London: Stevens & Sons Limited, 1962 ------164

Mellinkoff, David. *The Language of the Law.* Boston: Little, Brown and Company, 1963 ------14, 166, 171, 248

——. Review of *The Lawyers* by Martin Mayer [q. v.], in 15 *UCLA Law Review* 1075 (1968) ------VI

Mirror of Justices. [13th c.?]. William Joseph Whittaker, ed. Intro., Frederic William Maitland. vol. 7, *The Publications of the Selden Society,* 1895 [q. v.] ------52

Mitchell, Charles. *The Newspaper Press Directory.* London: C. Mitchell, 1846 ------VI

Mitchell, C. [Charles] Ainsworth. *The Expert Witness.* And the Applications of Science and of Art to Human Identification, Criminal Investigation, Civil Actions & History. Cambridge: W. Heffer & Sons Ltd., 1923 ------VI

——. *The Scientific Detective and The Expert Witness.* Rev. ed. of *The Expert Witness* [q. v.]. Cambridge: W. Heffer & Sons, Ltd., 1931 ------VI

Montagu, Basil. *Essays and Selections.* London: William Pickering, 1837 ------252–254

——. ed. Bacon, Francis. *The Works* . . . . [q. v.]

"The Moral Code of the Bar." 40 *The Law Times* 574 [Sept. 30, 1865]. London: Law Times, 1865 ------214, 215–216

The Morning Chronicle. London, 1840, 1849 ----132, 135, 141, 145, 154, 187, 193–194, 210–211, 224

The Morning Herald. London, 1840, 1849 ------132, 141

The Morning Post. London, 1840, 1849 ------132

"Mr. Brougham's Speech for Ambrose Williams." *The Law Magazine.* Or Quarterly Review of Jurisprudence For April, July, and Oct., 1829. vol. 2, Art. V., pp. 102–129. London: Saunders & Benning. 1829 ------227

"Mr. Charles Phillips." 14 *The Law Times* 193–194 (Nov. 24, 1849) ------VI

"Mr. Charles Phillips and the 'Examiner'." 14 *The Law Times* 215 (Dec. 1, 1849) ------VI

The New English Bible: The Apocrypha. Oxford University Press and Cambridge University Press, 1970 ------175

Newgate Calendar. See: *The Complete Newgate Calendar;* and Pelham, *The Chronicles of Crime; or The New Newgate Calendar.*

[Nicholson, Benjamin]. *The Lawyers Bane, Or the Lawes Reformation and New Modell.* London: George Whittington, 1647 ----2

O'Brien, Edward. *The Lawyer His Character and Rule of Holy Life.* London: William Pickering, 1842 ------11, 252, 255

Pollock, Frederick and Frederic William Maitland. *The History of English Law: Before the Time of Edward I.* 2 vols. 2d ed. Cambridge: University Press, 1898. [1st ed., 1895] ----------V

[Polson, Archer]. *Law and Lawyers; or, Sketches and Illustrations of legal history and biography.* 2 vols. London: Longman, Orme, Brown, Green, and Longmans, 1840 ----------------------13–14

Pound, Roscoe. "The Causes of Popular Dissatisfaction with the Administration of Justice." 29 *Reports of the American Bar Association* 395 (1906) ---------------------------------------43

——. *The Lawyer from Antiquity to Modern Times.* With particular reference to The Development of Bar Associations in the United States. St. Paul: West Publishing Co., 1953 ----------9

"The Prisoners' Counsel Bill." 15 *The Law Magazine* 394–402 (1836) ---48

"Prisoners Defence Bill—Report from the Select Committee." 68 *Journals of the House of Lords,* Session 1836 [q. v.], Appendix No. 4, pp. 50–61 --48

Privileges and Responsibilities of Lawyers in Arizona. Phoenix: Arizona Weekly Gazette, 1958 ----------------------------180

"Privileges of the Bar . . ." 22 *The Law Magazine,* No. XLVI, Art. I, pp. 259–272. London: Saunders & Benning, 1839 ----227

Proceedings, Alabama State Bar Assn. (1887) [microfilm, The Cromwell Library, American Bar Foundation, Chicago] ------177

Proceedings of the 18th Annual Meeting of the Alabama State Bar Association. Held at Montgomery, Ala., July 10th and 11th, 1895. Montgomery, Ala.: The Brown Printing Co., 1895 ----------177

Professional Ethics. See: Sharswood, George. *A Compend of Lectures . . .*

The Publications of the Selden Society. 87 vols. London: Quaritch, 1888–1970 ---------------------------------------,--------------2, 52

The Queen v. Palmer. Verbatim Report of the Trial of William Palmer at the Central Criminal Court, Old Bailey, London, May 14, and the following Days, 1856, Before Lord Campbell, Mr. Justice Cresswell, and Mr. Baron Alderson. Transcribed from the Short-hand notes of Mr. Angelo Bennett, of Rolls Chambers, Chancery Lane. Copyright ed. London: J. Allen, 1856 --62, 332–336

Radin, Max. "The Ancient Grudge: A Study in the Public Relations of the Legal Profession." 32 *Virginia Law Review* 734 (1946) --13

Réau, Louis. *Iconographie de L'Art Chrétien.* 3 vols. Paris: Presses Universitaires de France, 1959 ----------------------------13

The Record of Old Westminsters. A Biographical List of all those who are known to have been educated at Westminster School from the earliest times to 1927. Compiled by G. F. Russell Barker and Alan H. Stenning. 2 vols. London: Printed at the Chiswick Press, 1928 --VI

The Records of the Honorable Society of Lincoln's Inn, Admission
 . . . [1420–1893]. 2 vols. London: Lincoln's Inn, 1896 __VI

Redelius, Augustinus Casimirus. *Annus coronatus hymnis sanctorum omnium.* Lovanii: Joannis Jacobs, 1761 [1696?] ----------13

Report of the Alabama State Bar Association. vol. 35. [Birmingham, Alabama?]: The Alabama State Bar Association, 1912 ------177

Report of the Trial of Courvoisier for the murder of Lord William Russell June 1840. Intro., Sir Harry Poland, K.C. App. and notes, J. E. Latton Pickering. London: Printed for Private Circulation at the Chiswick Press, 1918 --------------------132, 135, 136

Reports of the American Bar Association. 95 vols. Chicago: American Bar Association, 1878–1971 -----------------177–179

Robertson, A. J. ed. and tr. *The Laws of the Kings of England from Edmund to Henry I.* Cambridge: University Press, 1925 ----41

Robin Conscience; or Conscionable Robin. [1683]. In 1 *The Harleian Miscellany* 63. [q. v.] ----------------------------10

Robinson [Mr. Serjeant]. *Bench and Bar, Reminiscences of One of the Last of an Ancient Race.* 2d ed. London: Hurst and Blackett, Limited, 1889 --------43, 44, 86–87, 93, 94, 131, 132, 136, 215, 224

Rodell, Fred. *Woe Unto You, Lawyers!.* New York: Reynal & Hitchcock, 1939 --2

Rogers, Showell. "The Ethics of Advocacy." 15 *The Law Quarterly Review,* No. 59, pp. 259–280. London: Stevens & Sons, Limited, 1899 --------------------------149, 189, 215, 229, 241, 264

Romilly, Samuel. *Memoirs of the Life of Sir Samuel Romilly.* Written by Himself; with a Selection from His Correspondence. Ed. by his sons. 3 vols. London: John Murray, 1840 --------24, 149

Ropartz, M. S. [Sigismund]. *Histoire de Saint Yves,* patron des gens de justice (1253–1303). Saint-Brieuc: L. Prud'homme, 1856 __13

Rubin, Jerry. *Do It!.* Scenarios of the Revolution. New York: Simon and Schuster, 1970 -------------------244–245, 267

Rules and Canons of Ethics. Austin: State Bar of Texas, 1958, and *Supplement* . . ., 1961 ------------------------------180

Russell of Liverpool [Lord]. *Though the Heavens Fall.* London: Cassell, 1956 --VI

St. Germain, Christopher, *Doctor and Student.* William Muchall, ed. Cincinnati: Robert Clarke & Co., 1874. [1st dialogue publ. in Latin, 1523; next in English, 1530; both in English, 1532] __49, 145–146, 155–156

St. Thomas Aquinas. *Summa Theologica.* 1st Complete Am. ed. 3 vols. Tr. by fathers of Eng. Dominican Province. New York: Benziger Brothers, Inc., 1947. [written 1265–1274] __145, 147, 208

Sanderson, Robert. *XXXVI Sermons.* 8th Ed. London: B. Tooke, T. Passenger, & T. Sawbridge, 1686 --------------------------147

——. *The Works of Robert Sanderson, D.D. Sometime Bishop of Lincoln.* Collected by William Jacobson. 6 vols. Oxford: University Press, 1854 --147

The Scofield Reference Bible: The Holy Bible Containing the Old and New Testaments Authorized Version. C. I. Scofield, ed. New York: Oxford University Press, [1945] -------------2, 3, 6, 212

Selden, John. "Table Talk." [1689]. *Table Talk of John Selden.* Frederick Pollock, ed., for the Selden Society. London: Quaritch, 1927 --2

Selden Society. See: *The Publications of the Selden Society.*

Selected Opinions of the Committee on Professional Ethics of the Florida Bar. The Florida Bar, 1969 -------------------180

Shakespeare, William. *The Second Part of King Henry VI.* Arden Edition. Andrew S. Cairncross, ed. 3d ed., 1957. London: Methuen & Co., Ltd., 1965 printing --------------------------2

Shakespeare's Holinshed, An Edition of Holinshed's Chronicles (1587). Richard Hosley, ed. New York: G. P. Putnam's Sons, 1968 ----2

Sharswood, George. *A Compend of Lectures on the Aims and Duties of the Profession of the Law.* Philadelphia: T. & J. W. Johnson, 1854 ------------------------------11, 173–175, 204, 258–259

——. *An Essay on Professional Ethics.* 5th ed. Philadelphia: T. & J. W. Johnson & Co., 1884 ------------------------------149

Shaw, Bernard. *Selected Plays.* 3 unnumbered vols., with general Preface to Ayot St. Lawrence Ed. preceding Preface to "Mrs. Warren's Profession." New York: Dodd, Mead & Company, 1948–1949 --12

Shawcross [Baron]. *The Functions and Responsibilities of an Advocate.* Intro., Ernest A. Gross. 17th Annual Benjamin N. Cardozo Lecture delivered before Association of the Bar of City of New York, May 25, 1958. New York: Association of the Bar of the City of New York, 1958 --------------------165, 264

Shower, Sir Bartholomew. "Reasons for a new Bill of Rights: Humbly submitted to the Consideration of the ensuing Session of Parliament." (1692). In 10 *The Somers Collection of Tracts* 568–579. [q.v.] --55

Smith, Reginald Heber. "Foreword." In Blaustein and Porter, *The American Lawyer* vi. [q. v.] ----------------------------9

——. "Survey of the Legal Profession Its Scope, Methods and Objectives." In Pound, *The Lawyer from Antiquity to Modern Times* vii. [q.v.] ------------------------------------9

Smith, Sydney. "Counsel for Prisoners." (1826). In 2 *Works* 200–226. [q.v.] --57

——. *The Works of the Rev. Sydney Smith.* 2d ed. 3 vols. London: Longman, Orme, Brown, Green, & Longmans, 1840 -----------57

Some Advertisements for the new Election of Burgesses for the House of Commons. Anon. [1645]. Follows "To the Reader" in Cooke, John, *The Vindication of the Professors* . . . .. [q.v.] ------12

States of America. 7 vols. Washington, D.C.: Government Printing Office, 1909 [known as "American Charters"] _____166

The Times. London, 1840, 1849 __16, 19, 26, 27, 30, 32, 35–36, 57–58, 62, 64, 69, 132, 142, 188, 194–198, 199–203, 213–216, 222, 228–229, 252

Townsend, William C. *Modern State Trials.* 2 vols. London: Longman, Brown, Green and Longmans, 1850 _____161, 189, 190

Trial of Queen Caroline. Report of the Proceedings Before the House of Lords, on a Bill of Pains and Penalties against Her Majesty, Caroline Amelia Elizabeth, Queen of Great Britain, and Consort of King George the Fourth. Collated with the Journals of the House of Lords. J. Nightingale, ed. 3 vols. London: J. Robins & Co. Albion Press, 1820–1821 _____188, 189, 237–240

United States Constitution. See: *Constitution of the United States.*

Vies Des Saints. ed. Les Petits Bollandistes. 17 vols. Paris: Bloud et Barral, 1878 _____13

Les Vies des Saints de Bretagne. See: Lobineau, Gui-Alexis.

Walbrook, H. M. [Henry MacKinnon]. *Murders and Murder Trials 1812–1912.* London: Constable & Co. Ltd., 1932 _____26
129

Walford, Edward. See: Thornbury, Walter and Edward Walford.

Walpole, Spencer. *A History of England from the Conclusion of the Great War in 1815.* 6 vols. London: Longmans, Green, And Co., 1912–1913.

Warren, Samuel. See: *Correspondence Between Samuel Warren, Esq., Barrister-at-Law, and Charles Phillips, Esq.* . . .

——. *Miscellanies Critical, Imaginative, and Juridical Contributed to Blackwood's Magazine.* 2 vols. Edinburgh and London: William Blackwood and Sons, 1855.

——. "The Mystery of Murder, and its Defence." 2 *Miscellanies* . . . 1. [q. v.] _____135, 190, 194, 206, 221, 224, 225–226, 227

[Warren, Samuel]. "The Practice of Advocacy.—Mr. Charles Phillips, And His Defence of Courvoisier." *The Law Review*, vol. 11, No. XXII, Art. X, pp. 376–436. London: 1849. [in bound vol. for 1849, but written Jan. 26, 1850].

Warvelle, George W. *Essays in Legal Ethics.* Chicago: Callaghan & Company, 1902 _____9, 149, 175–176, 259

Webster's New International Dictionary of the English Language. 2d ed. Unabridged. Springfield: G. & C. Merriam Company, 1934 __4

Weeks, Edward P. *A Treatise on Attorneys and Counsellors at Law.* San Francisco: Sumner Whitney & Co., 1878.

Whately, Richard. *Bacon's Essays: With Annotations.* 2d ed. rev. London: John W. Parker & Sons, 1857.

Whewell, William. *The Elements of Morality, including Polity.* 2 vols. London: John W. Parker, 1845 _____255–256

——. *Two Introductory Lectures to Two Courses of Lectures on Moral Philosophy, Delivered in 1839 and 1841.* Cambridge: John W. Parker, 1841 --12

White, Edward M. "Thackeray's Contributions to *Fraser's Magazine.*" 19 *Studies in Bibliography.* Papers of the Bibliographical Society of the University of Virginia. Fredson Bowers, ed. p. 67. Charlottesville: The Bibliographical Society of the University of Virginia, 1966.

Wigmore, John Henry. *A Treatise on the Anglo-American System of Evidence in Trials at Common Law.* 10 vols. rev. by John T. McNaughton, and others. Boston: Little, Brown and Company, 1961. With Pocket Parts, 1970 ----------------------------137, 138

Williams, Henry. *Legal Ethics and Suggestions for Young Counsel.* Carlyle H. Ross, ed. Philadelphia: George T. Bisel Company, 1906 --9

Williams, Joshua. *Letters to John Bull, Esq., on Lawyers and Law Reform.* London: Henry Sweet, 1857.

Wolverton, Charles E. "The Ethics of Advocacy." 8 *The American Lawyer* 62 (1900) --------------------------------------9, 265

Wordsworth, William. *The Complete Poetical Works of William Wordsworth.* 10 vols. Boston: Houghton Mifflin Company, 1919 --3

York, John. "ABA President-Elect Jaworski—Defender of Unpopular Causes." 51 *Harvard Law Record*, No. 4, p. 6 (1970) --------270

Yunck, John A. "The Venal Tongue: Lawyers and the Medieval Satirists." 46 *American Bar Association Journal* 267 (1960) --11, 12

*

TABLE OF CASES

References are to Pages

INDEX